To Dave & Kim,

I hope you enjoy ~ read where all is revealed, Not quite!

It's great meeting up after all these years — what a coincidence that was.

Best wishes
Bob
October 2020

# THE

# COMMON

# TOUCH

## MY AUTOBIOGRAPHY

Written by

Bob Mynett

First published in Great Britain in 2010
By
Bob Mynett

Copyright © 2010 Bob Mynett

1st Edition Printed 2010

The right of Bob Mynett to be identified as the Author of the Work has been asserted by him in accordance with the Copyright, Designs and Patent Act 1988

All rights reserved. No part of this publication may be reproduced, stored in a retrieval system, or transmitted, in any form or by any means without the prior written permission of the publisher, nor be otherwise circulated in any form of binding or cover other than that in which it is published and without a similar condition being imposed on the subsequent purchaser.

A CIP catalogue record for this title is available from the British Library

Hardback ISBN 978-0-9565977-0-0

Printed and bound in Great Britain
by the MPG Books Group
Bodmin and King's Lynn

# Contents

| | |
|---|---|
| Acknowledgements | ix |
| Synopsis | 1 |
| Rudyard Kipling's 'IF' | 2 |
| 1  Formative Years | 3 |
| 2  Lancashire Constabulary – Dog Section | 20 |
| 3  Seaforth Division | 31 |
| 4  Sudden Deaths | 54 |
| 5  Love at First Sight | 59 |
| 6  Telehire Limited | 67 |
| 7  Ind Coope Northern | 75 |
| 8  Den of Iniquity | 79 |
| 9  Deputy Area Manager | 92 |
| 10  Tenancy Area Manager | 100 |
| 11  Suicide | 104 |
| 12  Garstang | 113 |
| 13  Managed House Area Manager | 131 |

| | | |
|---|---|---|
| 14 | Actons of Lymm | 163 |
| 15 | Bereavement – A Service of Hope | 183 |
| 16 | The Barley Mow | 189 |
| 17 | Armed Robbery | 201 |
| 18 | High Legh  Knutsford | 207 |
| 19 | You are Never Too Old | 210 |
| 20 | Sandbach, Cheshire | 217 |
| 21 | The Paradox of Our Time | 212 |

*This book celebrates
The relationships of my life
The love of Lynn,
The blessing of our three children
Karen, Mark and Alison
And the joy of our grandchildren*

# Acknowledgements

My special thanks for my lovely wife Lynn for coping with my many hours of absence over the past seven years whilst writing the book, locked away with my computer. For my son Mark, in producing the first hardback copy and his enthusiastic support, also for my daughters, Karen and Alison's advice. For Bal Unnithan, my friend and Rotary colleague and his valuable time and patience in formatting the book and conversion to PDF. For Jean Williams (Author of the Gentle Ribbon) for her encouragement and support, also to Jim Moorby for his invaluable advice and recommendations re: certain omissions which were required, also to my sisters Anne and Linda, for confirmation and reminiscing of my earlier life as a boy.

Warm thanks to Nigel Mitchell of MPG Biddles and John Chandler of Chandler Book Design for their patience and guidance in the final formatting and production of the book and cover design.

Finally, a word of gratitude, recognition and appreciation for all those mentors referred to in the book with 'The Common Touch' who have influenced me and impacted on my life story.

# The Common Touch

## Synopsis

Throughout his life the author; Bob Mynett has been influenced by people with 'The Common Touch' i.e. the ability to communicate effectively, with leadership, man management and motivational skills and the ability to talk to persons from all walks of life on their own level. Many of these people have reached the pinnacle of their careers and display no signs whatever of one-upmanship, snobbery or the dreadful habit of talking down to people in a superior manner. They have the ability to immediately put one at ease and to talk with them in such a way as to put one on an equal footing, with no airs or graces. Bob's experiences as a police cadet with the dog section of Lancashire Constabulary at the age of 17 and 18; when his police dog attacked the Deputy Chief Constable and other interesting and hilarious stories make for a fascinating read. At the age of 19 becoming a policeman on Merseyside dealing with sudden deaths, domestic disputes, drunks and accidents; give an interesting insight into his experiences as a young policeman on the beat and driving the section police car. On leaving the police force, Bob became a brewery area manager with the then biggest drinks combine in Europe, covering all aspects of the licensed trade i.e. free trade, tenancy and managed houses. During his 18 years in the brewery business he was to deal with many bizarre situations, some tragic, but never losing sight that laughter is the best medicine. At the age of 45, suffering from depression and close to an emotional break-down, Bob gave notice to leave the brewery; having reached the cross roads in his life. This remarkable experience was to mark a totally different direction for the rest of his life. He eventually achieved his lifelong ambition, becoming the owner of his own up market furniture business in Cheshire, bringing him into contact with a variety of different and interesting people. Rudyard Kipling's poem 'IF' has had a great influence on Bob. 'If you can walk with Kings nor lose 'The Common Touch' you'll be a man my son.' It is the reason for the title of the book.

# IF

If you can keep your head when all about you
are loosing theirs and blaming it on you;
You can trust yourself when all men doubt you,
But make allowance for their doubting too;
You can wait and not be tired of waiting,
Or being lied about, don't deal in lies,
Or being hated, don't give way to hating,
And yet don't look too good, nor talk too wise:-
If you can dream – and not make dreams your master;
You can think – and not make thoughts your aim;
You can meet with Triumph and Disaster
And treat these two imposters just the same;
You can bear to hear the truth you've spoken
Twisted by knaves to make a trap for fools;
Or watch the things you gave your life to, broken,
And stoop and build 'em up with worn-out tools;-
**If** you can make one heap of all your winnings
And risk it on one turn of pitch-and-toss,
And lose, and start again at your beginnings
And never breathe a word about your loss;
You can force your heart and nerve and sinew
To serve your turn long after they are gone,
And so hold on when there is nothing in you
Except the Will which says to them: 'Hold on!'
**If** you can talk with crowds and keep your virtue,
Or walk with Kings – nor loose the common touch,
Neither foes nor loving friends can hurt you,
All men count with you, but none too much;
You can fill the unforgiving minute
With sixty seconds' worth of distance run,
Yours is the earth and everything that's in it,
And - which is more – you'll be a man my son.
RUDYARD KIPLING

# 1

## Formative years

Florence Mynett, nee Rigby, was admitted to Bairstow Street maternity hospital in Preston, Lancashire on the 6$^{th}$ April 1940 where she gave birth to a 'fine bouncing baby boy' who weighed in at over 10 pounds and was carried around the ward being shown off to other mothers to be. I was the baby referred to and having been born shortly after the start of the Second World War, would ensure that I would be known henceforth as a 'war baby.'

I was christened as an infant into the Anglican Church and given the name Robert Anthony Mynett - My parents chose the initials RAM, probably due to the fact that I was an Aries. I was to discover that in spite of the fact that my mother was a highly intelligent and academically gifted person, who achieved a distinction in the sixth form at Balshaw's Grammar School, Leyland, going on to Teachers Training College at Cheadle, Manchester, (no mean feat in those days) she was nevertheless highly superstitious. (it would appear to be a Lancashire trait in those days.) Mother would never look at a new moon through glass or her spectacles because it was allegedly bad luck. At New Year, as a young boy at our house in Preston, 'Grey Gables', I was required to go out of the back door with a piece of coal and bring it in through the front door. This was supposed to bring good luck for the New Year. Quite preposterous stuff!

Growing up as a child in Hartington Road, Preston during the war was certainly an interesting experience. Memories of American soldiers come flooding back. They couldn't resist children asking the question "give us some gum chum." They would always respond by giving you some chewing gum.

At 5 years of age I followed a brass band from the family home in Hartington Road to Avenham Park, a distance of some 2 miles. I was intrigued at that age with the music, particularly the kettle drums, marching along in step. My parents were worried sick wondering where I had disappeared to, only to arrive home with a police escort - they had found me in Avenham Park and brought me home. That was clearly the first indication that I was to enjoy a lifetime of the love of music.

A very vivid earlier memory when I was 4 yrs of age was Granddad Bob keeping hens at his large house on Woodlands Avenue, Preston. One of the hens was past its best and Bob took hold of the hen in my presence, stroking it under its neck saying 'come on my little chuck, I'm not going to hurt you.' The next minute he was wringing its neck but the poor little blighter simply wouldn't die. Not to be outdone, he went into the garage and came out wielding an axe and promptly chopped its head off. I was quite horrified but also fascinated when the headless hen ran around the garden before finally expiring. I can't have been all that upset because while it was still warm, I plucked out all the large feathers which Bob and I made into a Red Indian head dress.

At the age of five the family, i.e. Mother Florence, Father Arthur, my eldest sister Anne (two years older than me) and my younger sister Linda (4 years younger than me) moved to Grey Gables in Ribbleton, Preston, just round the corner from my grandparents (my mother's parents) Robert James Rigby and Mary Ellen Rigby. My first memories of Grey Gables were a beautiful garden and red lights in practically every room which lit up when the front doorbell was pushed. The elderly lady who lived there previously had been stone deaf.

The front room at Grey Gables was only used on Sunday's and for when visitors arrived. On the mantelpiece was a hideous bronze figure of the devil, about 12" in height. Whilst I had my own bedroom, on occasions I was required to sleep in the front room whilst a visitor used my room. As a child I was terrified sleeping in the room. I imagined that I could see the devil walking up and down the mantelpiece and was scared out of my wits!

I discovered a trap door in the floor underneath the stairs and was curious as to what I would find. Squeezing through the door led me to a depth of about 12" beneath the flooring of the house. I was able to crawl with difficulty to a brick air vent at the rear of the house, shouting to my sister Anne on one occasion who was by the back door. Anne was quite startled, wondering where my shouting was coming from. By the time I returned to the trap door I was filthy. My mother was not at all amused at the state of my clothes, notwithstanding her concern over the fact that I could well have become stuck under the flooring.

I was very fond of my Granddad. He was a real character and I have early memories of sitting on his knee with him holding his

Waltham pocket watch to my ear - which I now own and treasure. There was a grandfather clock, usually referred to as a long case clock, with a Westminster chime situated in the hallway. I can remember clearly, how at the age of 5 standing by this clock and watching for the minute hand coming up to the hour, so that I could listen to the magical Westminster chime followed by striking on the hour. Granddad Bob was a real raconteur, a born story teller; telling fantastic stories about how he kept lions under the table, Spring Heel Jack and Mary Anne Dick and the intriguing magical world of Alice in Wonderland. He kept a huge leather strap in the garage with nails protruding from the end with the ultimate threat that if our behavior was unsatisfactory, then it was 'the strap.' My Granddad preferred to be called Bob by all of his Grandchildren rather than Granddad.

One of my Granddad's more hilarious stories (which he swore was true) was the young inexperienced policeman walking the beat in Preston during the early hours of the morning. In those days the night duty copper would 'shake hands ' with the door knobs of business premises to make sure that they were secure. This young policeman came across a property with the sash window ajar, so, sliding the window up further, he pushed his head through shining his torch into the room.

He was horrified to see an open coffin with a body in it, on trestles immediately beneath the window. His reaction was to pull back, crashing his head on the sash window, knocking his helmet off which rolled into the room. He had no alternative but to climb into the room very gingerly to retrieve his helmet. By this time the poor lad was so nervous, in his panic to get out of the room as quickly as possible, he stumbled into the coffin, knocked it off the trestles causing an almighty crash. He threw himself out of the window as quickly as possible and legged it down the road. The mind boggles at the thought of the bereaved person being wakened by the commotion, coming down and finding the coffin on the floor.

There were other stories of which one was the policeman who found a dead horse in Tithebarn Street. He couldn't spell Tithebarn Street so he dragged the horse into Church Street. I then seriously began to wonder whether the previous story of the policeman and the body was simply make belief!

My Granddad Bob's sister Lilly, known to us as Aunt Lilly, married a Roman Catholic, much to the disgust of her mother and even though she lived in the same street in Preston, would never see or speak to her daughter Lilly again. When Lilly's husband died at an early age, his body was brought into the house and the local priest made her swear over his coffin that she would bring her two children up in the catholic faith. Granddad Bob arrived at the house to console his sister and upon hearing what the priest had said to Lilly, was so incensed and angry, throwing the priest out into the street.

I must have been about nine or ten years of age when the family had a holiday by the seaside at Morecambe. My great aunt and uncle on my grandparent's side (Edith & Billy Elkin) lived in Morecambe off Skipton Street, which was parallel and very close to the promenade. They were always fondly known to me as Aunt Edith and Uncle Billy. I spent a couple of very happy holidays staying with them in their tiny house. The radio would be on from morning, noon till night. My Aunt Edith had a knack of foretelling the future but I can clearly remember her saying never to get involved with the Ouija board, that it was evil and was 'getting in touch with the dark side' My Aunt Edith advised her daughter, also Edith, that it was a waste of time going to Southampton to join a cruise ship for a holiday in the Caribbean. She was adamant that the cruise would be cancelled. Lo and behold, when Edith got to Southampton the cruise was cancelled. The cruise ship had been commandeered as a troop ship at the start of the Second World War. Aunt Edith was also to predict the death of my father quite some time before he died. She was too sensitive to actually state that my father was to die but did refer to a death in the family.

My sister Anne would spend much of her time whilst on holiday in Morecambe in the many fruit machine arcades. Her strategy was quite simple; she would watch the punters putting their pennies into the one armed bandits, having remembered when the jackpot was due to drop and when they gave up, Anne would go onto the machine and invariably win the jackpot.

The owners of these arcades soon got wise to Anne's tactics and barred her from the arcades! Not to be deterred, Anne would then disguise herself in my mother's clothing but the ruse was soon spotted. I remember Anne returning to Aunt Edith's house one year with bags full of coppers she had won, with the fingers of both hands quite green from the coins. The proceeds of these winnings were used to buy Enid Blyton Famous Five books, which I would also enjoy reading.

My Grandparents had worked day and night building up a very successful baking, confectionary and news agency business in Preston. Granddad Bob would go down to the railway station in Preston with a handcart to pick up the newspapers. Grandma worked in the bake house of the business and they regularly worked until the early hours of the morning baking. People would beat a path to their shop to buy their really tasty meat and potato pie's. This was at a time when the Lancashire Cotton Industry was thriving. The ultimate threat of being unemployed in those days was to end up in 'the dreaded workhouse'

Granddad Bob had been a worker in the cotton industry and eventually became an overseer/foreman in the mill. As a direct result of their hard work they were able to invest in several properties in the Preston area, retiring from business when Granddad Bob was in his mid forties, no mean feat in those days. They were able to enjoy the fruits of their labour in retirement, buying a huge detached house with a tennis court and going on cruises each year. My mother and her brother Harold would accompany them on these cruise holidays. My grandparents were quite wealthy compared to the average wage earner who would typically work in the cotton mills.

Over the years I was to start progressively spending more and more time with my Grandparents, especially at weekends. This was as a direct result of the most dreadful atmosphere developing at home due to my father's regular shouting, ranting and raving. As young children we simply couldn't understand why. Father worked at Courtaulds some 2 miles away in Grimsargh in the acid recovery department and would invariably walk to work.

I can remember one day his shouting and bawling at mother because he didn't have chops for dinner, throwing his dinner onto the open coal fire which was burning in the dining room and storming out to go to work. Mother would never retaliate and just cringed and cowered at the verbal onslaught. The whole circumstances were very sad. Fortunately, our father didn't drink alcohol and to the best of my knowledge never struck mother during his violent outbursts. I was to later plead with my mother to divorce him but in those days it was simply not the thing to do. The stigma attached to divorce was unacceptable. I started to carry out odd jobs for Granddad Bob whose eyesight was becoming progressively worse.

When I was a little older my regular routine on Saturdays was to cut the lawns for Bob. Afterwards he would get the woods out and we would play bowls on the lawn. Grandma at that time was president of Preston Ladies' Bowling Club. Following these routine jobs my Granddad and I would sit and chat and his stories were intriguing. His brother had married a very beautiful woman who eventually ran off with another man and as a result of this Bob said "Beauty is only skin deep and some of the buggers want skinning!"

The sad thing about my father was his split personality. He was an attractive, good looking man who could be quite charming on the one hand, but then totally unreasonable, storming out of the house cursing and swearing for what appeared to be no apparent reason. He was also an inveterate liar, but would be caught out because clearly to be a good liar you have to have a very good memory. When we were out socially as a family and someone mentioned some foreign holiday they had been on, then father would say he had also been there and we knew full well that he was lying. My sisters Anne, Linda and I will never know the reason for this unreasonable behavior.

I was to learn from a very close lifelong friend of mothers - Lola Williams-Bailey, that mother had met my father on the re-bound of a previous very close relationship which had almost resulted in marriage. Lola told me some eighteen months before she died that in her opinion mother had 'married beneath her.' It would appear that my parents marriage was doomed from the word go.

Preston, like Liverpool had a very large proportion of Roman Catholics. The town used to be called 'Priest town.' The most awful thing in those days was that if you were an Anglican you were called a 'Prodydog' and if you were a Roman Catholic you were known as a 'Redneck.' This resulted in an 'Us and Them' culture. I would hear my grandparents referring to their next door neighbours as 'rednecks' and yet they were the loveliest Christian couple you could wish to meet. During Preston Guild the competition to outdo 'the opposition' in the big parades was quite laughable. The Catholics always put on a far better show than the enemy; the costumes they wore were quite magnificent and they always seemed to have bigger and better bands and banners. This was probably due to the funds which were raised from the Catholic social clubs and licensed premises in Preston.

Preston Guild is a historic event celebrated every 20 years. A well known saying in Lancashire is 'once every Preston Guild.' The Guild dates back to the granting of Preston's first Charter by King Henry in 1179; which recognizes Preston as an important settlement in England giving the town a number of rights and privileges and to hold markets in the town. The town are preparing for the next Guild in 2012 when the whole community come together to celebrate many attractions i.e. Church, trade and torchlight processions, fireworks, sporting events and open air concerts in Avenham Park. People travel from all over the world to Preston to join in the celebrations.

Sadly, a similar situation was also the case in Liverpool regarding the antagonism between Protestants and Catholics. However, when David Shepherd, the then Bishop of Liverpool Anglican Cathedral met with Derek Warlock, the Bishop of the Roman Catholic Cathedral, nicknamed to this day as 'Paddy's Wigwam' they became firm friends and thereafter attitudes changed and Catholics and Protestants lived together more peacefully. The two Bishops became known as 'Fish and Chips' by virtue of the fact that they always appeared in the newspaper together!

Grey Gables was opposite St Mary Magdeline's church in Ribbleton and whilst the name suggests that this was a Roman Catholic Church, it was in fact an Anglican church. There was no chance of a lie in until late on Sunday's, due to the ringing of the church bells which the verger used to carry out with great gusto. He was a big, hearty fellow who would swing on the bell ropes with great enthusiasm. It was quite comical the way he would stand in the vestry during services, with the church door wide open singing along with the hymns at the top of his voice. I was convinced that the whole of Ribbleton could hear him.

The first time I ever kissed a girl was in the porch of St Mary Magdeline's church as a dare during the 'very scary' game in those days of 'truth, dare, force or promise.' I can remember very well at the age of ten 'falling in love' for the very first time with Jennifer Brown who attended my primary school – Greenlands. The trouble was my good pal David Williamson was also in love with Jennifer.

It was quite comical the way we would follow Jennifer home from school each day to Woodlands Avenue, until her father put a stop to that!

The Roman Catholics had planning permission approved to build a new church a hop skip and a jump from our St Mary Magdeline's and that's when the fun and games started! When the footings were dug out and completed by Irish navies, my mates Jackie Wharton, Joe Stott, Pete Larraway and I would go on maneuvers in the trenches. Our weapons were grenades made from the wonderfully pliable clay which was dug out of the ground and we went to war against our enemy the 'rednecks.' We would arrive home absolutely exhausted and full of mud - but what a great time we had.

We established an 'Enid Blyton' type gang and spent some of this time at 'headquarters' which was a shed in Joe's back garden. We managed to obtain a couple of 'Hank Jansen' books which were probably the randiest books around at that time. The four of us once dissected a frog in Joe's shed (ugh). One day the three of us were larking around in the field at the back of Joe Stott's house when Joe and I had a big argument. Joe stormed off into the house and a short while after, Pete, Jackie and I started to make our way through Joe's back garden when a voice bellowed out of the upstairs window "you're not coming through my back garden Mynett." When I looked up, there was Joe in his bedroom pointing an air rifle at me. I told him not to be so stupid and carried on walking. The next minute Joe pulled the trigger and shot me in my left thigh. I was livid, charged into the house (fortunately his parents were out at the time) ran upstairs, thumped Joe - took the air rifle off him and took it home. Fortunately, the injury to my leg was only slight. For the next couple of months I had great fun with Joe's air rifle at Grey Gables, shooting at targets from my bedroom window.

Pete and I attended St Mary Magdeline's each Sunday and sat with the lads in the back pews whilst Linda and Anne sat with their friends. We found the sermons so boring that to pass the time we would tell jokes. Quite unexpectedly one Sunday morning during jokes, not realising the boring sermon had finished, the Vicar, a man called Driscall, came up behind me and boxed me across both ears. I simply didn't dare to tell my parents what had happened because there is no doubt that I would have been punished once again. During one sermon, I can clearly remember that awful vicar Driscall, referring to the Roman Catholics as "that lot up the road."

We had a piano in the front room at Grey Gables and I would spend hours playing around on it. I was very proud when I learnt to play the tune 'chopsticks' I must have been only 5 or 6 yrs of age then. My eldest sister Anne was very fortunate to be able to go to piano lessons for which I was really envious. Sadly, I never had the opportunity of learning that wonderful gift of being able to play the piano. Mother would play the piano very occasionally and I would sit there enthralled, watching her beautiful hands moving over the ivory keys. Strangely enough, my favourite tune mother would play was 'policeman's holiday'; little realising that one day I was to become a policeman. Anne was to progress to a quite reasonable level of playing and achieved reasonable grades, but eventually lost interest and gave up playing altogether.

My mother had the most amazing memory and could quote the whole of the Pied Piper of Hamelin and Hiawatha. Rudyard Kipling's 'If' was one of her favourites and has also become one of my best loved verses; particularly the reference to 'If you can walk with kings, nor lose 'the common touch', you'll be a man my son.' A verse which mother would also regularly quote was 'Times Paces' a poem by Henry Twells (1823-1900) which is attached to a clock in Chester Cathedral, located behind the organ :-

When as a child I laughed and wept, Time Crept.
When as a youth I waxed more bold, Time strolled.
When I became a full grown man, Time ran.
When older still I daily grew, Time flew.
Soon I shall find, in passing on, Time gone.
O Christ! Wilt Thou have saved me then?
Amen.

On reflection, referring to the above verse, for some reason I could never understand why mother would never recite the last line. Maybe it was her concern over the last line of the verse which begs the question 'is my faith sufficient to be saved by then?'

As a young boy at Grey Gables I would spend some time kicking a football against the gable end of the house. One day whilst kicking the ball against the wall underneath the dining room window, I smashed the window and I now find it quite hilarious that I ran into the house claiming that some boys running up the road had caused the damage. On another occasion I was throwing stones over the poplar trees in the side garden when one of the stones hit a neighbour, a bus inspector, breaking his spectacles. He was very lucky not to loose an eye.

On both of these occasions my father took me upstairs, took my trousers down and walloped me on the backside with a leather strap! Another pastime of mine was throwing a huge throwing knife from a distance of some 8ft into a poplar tree. With a hedge behind the tree and the pavement behind the hedge, I dread to think of the consequences should that knife had missed the tree and hit someone walking past.

As a young boy I am embarrassed when I recall a scam which I got involved in with other boys whilst attending Greenland's Primary School. The trick was to stuff paper into the return section of the public telephone box i.e. when the caller didn't get through and pressed button 'B' the money should have been returned but didn't. After several days we would take out the paper rammed up into the return section and hey presto, all the pennies would come tumbling down. Additional pocket money for halfpenny sticks of Spanish liquorice and the like.

My sisters Anne and Linda shared a bedroom at Grey Gables. Linda was in the habit of banging her head against the pillow to get to sleep. Head Banging wasn't yet the rage in those days regarding heavy metal music! In preparation to stop this irritation, Anne would surround her bed with objects to throw at Linda i.e. slippers shoe's etc. and would throw them at Linda together with some rather crude expletives to stop the irritating habit of 'head banging' which clearly kept Anne awake. However, Anne would hang out of the bedroom window smoking cigarettes which were made from the dog ends left in ashtrays by our parents. Linda was threatened with pain of death not to disclose the fact that Anne was smoking.

My sister Anne and I were very close as we grew up in the family. However, unfortunately for Linda who is 4 years younger than me, Anne and I would tease her quite often, our perception being that Linda was the favourite, undoubtedly as is often the case in families. Mum would say to Linda 'Don't take any notice of them.' and an oft repeated statement to Anne and me from Linda would be 'Take no notice of you.'

Anne had saved up for a brand new bike, a sports bike with drop handlebars and three speed gears. Anne threatened me on pain of death never to ride her bike which was her pride and joy. I was 14 at the time. I had never had a bike and the temptation was simply too great not to have a ride on the bike. Whilst Anne was out of the house I took her bike out for a ride. Big mistake! Anne arrived home as I was returning with the bike and blew her top. She was so angry that she picked up a tin of Heinz baked beans and threw it at me with some force. The tin hit the back of my right leg and made quite a nasty gash. This was the only time in which Anne and I had fallen out.

I went through a phase of building model aircraft which I would fly in nearby fields. I had a 6ft glider suspended from my bedroom ceiling which I was very proud of; I would be about 13 or 14 years of age at the time. There was a picture of Tonia Bern in a bikini, my favorite pin up girl on my bedroom wall. She was stunning. Tonia Bern was to marry Donald Campbell who was sadly killed on Lake Coniston whilst attempting the break the world speed record on water in Bluebird. He was killed at the age of 46, a split second before breaking his own water speed record in his jet powered Bluebird, travelling at more than 300 MPH. It was quite bizarre when Donald Campbell's body was recovered from Lake Coniston in 2001, 34 years after his death. His widow, Tonia Bern-Campbell travelled from her home in America to attend his funeral service at the parish church in Coniston. She would be in her sixties at the time and appeared on national television. Seeing her at the time took me straight back to her picture adorning my bedroom wall all those years ago! The Ruskin Museum at Coniston has video footage and photographs of Bluebirds demise on Coniston.

My sister Anne was quite a character as a teenager. I suppose it would be correct to say that Anne in those days as a teenager was a 'Teddy Girl' with her hair in a D.A. (ducks arse!) She would constantly listen to Radio Luxemburg whilst jiving with the door! Mother was one day summoned by the headmistress of the Park School, the girls' grammar school in Preston. She was worried sick about what Anne had been up to. She tried not to burst out laughing when the headmistress complained that Anne was seen regularly smoking on the school bus and wearing the wrong coloured socks! My younger sister Linda, will often remind me of the time when Anne and myself had tied her up to a bench in the garden at Grey

Gables and ran off! Poor Linda had to remain tied to the bench until my mother returned from school. In relating to that story, Linda refers to me in a jocular fashion as 'Bob the bastard!'

Mother was a schoolteacher, her commitment and love of the job was very evident. A teacher of maths and English she specialized in teaching backward children to read and write. Mother's view was that virtually every child in mainstream schooling could and should be taught to read and write. To be given the opportunity of achieving literacy and numeracy is the essential aim of attending school in the first place. She taught in some very tough secondary modern schools in Preston and took a pride in her successes. Mother would come alongside children from deprived backgrounds, latchkey children who were dragged up, not brought up. The thing that never ceased to amaze me was that this 7 - 8 stone woman ruled with a rod of iron. At school she was a feared and extremely strict disciplinarian and the strap wasn't simply the ultimate threat - it was used regularly. The system adopted was quite brilliant! Inevitably, the child would pull their hand away as the instrument of punishment was bearing down on the child's hand - so mother would hold the wrist of whichever hand was to be strapped and wallop - no escape. For the really persistent offenders it would be the strap on both hands.

The most feared bully at Fishwick Secondary modern was a big strapping lad by the name of Kenneth Hornby. He was the product of a broken home and the only teacher who could make any sense out of him was my mother. He had no chance of learning with any other teacher because they simply banned him from their classes. He inevitably ended up in mother's class.

One day he arrived at mothers classroom door in tears, stating that his history teacher, a despised man by the name of Tragan, had called him 'a big fat slug.' throwing him out of the classroom. The headmaster of the school at the time - another feared and strict disciplinarian by the name of Dr Pickard, knew that the only way of giving Kenneth Hornby a chance at the school was to regularly point him in the direction of mother's classroom. A real bond developed between Kenneth Hornby and my mother and even after leaving school at the age of 14, he would visit her at school just to let her know how he was going on. Tragan was taken to Court for indecently assaulting girls in the classroom - convicted and was never to teach again.

At the age of fourteen, my mate Pete Larraway and I were playing on the park at Ribbleton, when I decided to do some forward rolls on a parallel bar. I was upside down and staring at the tarmacadam floor beneath me when I became dizzy, let go and smashed my face on the ground. That is when I lost my three front teeth. Pete took me home and my Mother was horrified at the state of my face. She said "Oh Bobby – those beautiful teeth." She rang my Uncle Harold who took me to his dentist in his car in the middle of Preston, who extracted what was left of my three front teeth. It was a quite horrible experience having those teeth extracted. The dentist used gas and I vomited quite profusely.

Several quite comical situations arose with my three false front teeth. They once fell out in the deep end of a school visit to the swimming baths. Half the class were diving down and they were eventually rescued. On another occasion they fell out whilst I was queuing for school dinner, they were trodden on by the children behind and I ended up picking up the pieces!

By the time I became a teenager, Preston North End was really on the map and my hero was Tom Finney. As a boy I was privileged to see that great sportsman Sir Tom Finney, playing in his prime. His partnership with Nat Lofthouse for England provided some of the finest ever performances of any England player. He could kick the ball with both feet and play on either wing or as centre forward. He possessed amazing poise and balance. Throughout his long career he was never cautioned or even spoken to by a referee and his sportsmanship was admired by thousands of Preston North End and England's supporters alike. Comparing the hero worshiping, overpaid and overrated players of today, it is a great pity that the likes of Sir Tom Finney will never be seen again. I very rarely missed a home match and the delight of watching the likes of Docherty, Waynman, Baxter and of course Tom Finney was brilliant. The local Derby between Blackpool and Preston was always guaranteed to provide entertainment. There was many a punch up resulting from arguments as to whether Tom Finney was better than Stanley Matthews. It went something like this 'of course Tom Finney is better than Matthews, he can play in any position on the field - Matthews can only play on the right wing.' Etc - etc.

My two sisters Anne, Linda and myself would do the washing up on a weekly Rota basis but when Anne started courting and spent evenings out with her current boyfriend, she would pay me sixpence to wash up for her! A regular job for me was to chop firewood for lighting the coal fire we had in the dining room. Following being a Cub at Mary Magdeline's church, I joined the 3$^{rd}$ Ribbleton Boy Scouts. This scout troop was pretty boring. Unlike other scouts in Preston we never went abroad on holidays or even in this country. The most exiting thing we ever did was to camp for one night in Moor Park, Preston when the Head Scout, visited Preston.

I was very envious of the Catholic Scout Troop whose scoutmaster was a lovely man by the name of Tom Tootle. Tom was a distant relative of my Grandma Rigby. He was headmaster of a catholic school in Preston and would take his boy scouts on annual holidays to Austria, Switzerland and Germany. I couldn't understand why my parents didn't have the foresight to let me join Tom's scout troop, undoubtedly it would be something to do with the fact that they were 'Catholics' and never the twain should meet.

Apart from my weekend visits to Preston North End when the team were playing an away game, I would go to Preston Railway station with my mates train spotting and recording their names and numbers. We would all take sandwiches and sometimes spend a whole day there. There was great excitement when a 'Winnie' came steaming through on the London to Scotland run. The Sir Winston Churchill was without doubt the most memorable experience, passing through Preston Railway station en route to London. What a fantastic sight. Unfortunately, we were eventually to be barred from those visits. The reason given was that it was unacceptable for the dangerous practice of putting pennies on the line for the trains to flatten. Thereafter, my mate Dave Williamson and I would go to Brock, near Garstang and sit by a bridge to watch those magnificent steam engines passing by.

As children we were very fortunate to go on holiday each year to the Isle of Man. We would sail from Fleetwood on board the Mona's Isle or The Manxman, arriving at Douglas Harbour. We stayed at the Balqueen Hydro in Port St Mary, a large and pretty up market hotel on the front overlooking the bay of Port St Mary. The hotel had their own raft, which at high tide would be some 25 yards from the shore. It was great to swim out to the raft, climb onto it and dive back into the water. Doug Hoyle, an elderly man of over eighty was the entertainments manager of the Balqueen, he would go for an early morning swim every day. What a character he was. He organized all the entertainment for the hotel which would consist of walks, hiring bicycles for rides around the island, talent contests for the evening and dances in the ballroom One year my sister Anne fancied the lift boy, a good looking lad from Liverpool. My Grandma Rigby was not amused when she found out and slapped Anne on the legs!

At the age of fourteen, I became very friendly with the Fitton family who owned a beautiful yacht which was moored in the harbour at Port St Mary. Their son was the same age as myself and was really keen for me to sail back with them to Glasson Dock, near Lancaster. My mother forbade me to sail back with them and no amount of pleading would change her mind. She was clearly over anxious for my safety! That was very much one of my great disappointments in life. I have always been fascinated with sailing ships and the sea. I would spend hours as a boy carving out boats from a solid piece of wood dreaming of going to sea. The closest I came to sailing as a boy was at Morecambe, when I boarded a small sailing boat with an outboard motor from a wooden pier. It was a fishing trip in Morecambe Bay and I was delighted to catch several fish which we called 'flatties' a type of plaice.

All the teenagers staying at the Balqueen would gather in the evening at 'Smokey Joe's, a café with a juke box. Ken Leigh and I became very friendly and would regularly visit Smokey Joe's weighing up the 'talent' but were too scared at the age of thirteen/fourteen to ask for a date. Ken was a very talented pianist and would play at the evening concerts. His style was very much along the lines of Winifred Atwell, or 'Winny' Atwell as she was to become known. Her unique style of playing was to put drawing pins on the hammers of the piano, producing a honky tonk sound which I thought was terrific.

Those holidays in the Isle of Man were very much an extended family affair. My Uncle Harold, Aunt Annis, their two son's Peter and Stewart, my grandparents Grandma and Bob and my family would stay for two weeks each year. My father chose not to accompany the family on these holidays. We would spend countless hours on the beach, walking to The Sound and generally exploring the island. The first pint of beer I ever had was at the age of fourteen in a pub between Port St Mary and Port Erin. Ken

Leigh and I were cheeky enough to walk into the tap room and ask for pints of bitter and surprisingly the landlord actually served us!

My grandparents were probably one of the first people in Preston to have a black and white television installed. I loved to watch the football finals at Wembley and variety shows. It now seems so strange thinking of my grandparents singing along to Songs of Praise in those days. Unlike today there were no words on the screen. I now regularly watch Songs of Praise and sing along with the benefit of the words on the screen.

On leaving secondary modern school at the age of 15 with no academic qualifications, I started work at Goss Fosters in Preston (now Meihle Goss Dexter) Printing Press Manufacturers. My mother attended my initial interview rather than my father and I started work in the drawing office as an office boy. One day as I was operating the blue print machine, an original drawing jammed so I very foolishly opened the end of the machine with the arc light still moving backwards and forwards, I was shading my eyes from the brightness of the lights with my left hand when the arc caught my left hand between the thumb and forefinger. The electric shock threw me across the room, crashing into the wall some seven feet away. I was taken to the first aid room and given a hot sweet cup of tea. That accident could well have been fatal. With today's health and safety regulations it simply would not be possible to open a machine of that nature whilst in operation. I have since always had a healthy respect for electricity.

At Christmas, it was the custom for the office boy to stand on top of the filing cabinets and sing. I chose to sing 'The River of No Return' from the film with Marylyn Monroe and Robert Mitcham. I got quite a reasonable amount of money for the enthusiastic way in which I delivered the song. I have been known since to sing that particular song and others at various brewery functions, much to the cringing reaction of my better half Lynn! Mr Wallbank was the boss of the drawing office and I shall never forget his blonde bombshell secretary. What a page three girl she would have made! The rumour going around the office was that Mr Wallbank was having an affair with her.

After 2 years at Goss's, the grass on the other side looked decidedly greener and my eldest sister Anne, constantly said that I should consider becoming a police cadet. Anne at the time was working for Lancashire Constabulary at Headquarters, Hutton,

Preston in the wages and salary department. I decided to check it out and struck up a friendship with Vinnie Whittle. Vinnie lived close by in Ribbleton. He was an adopted child, a Roman Catholic and a police cadet at Hutton. Fortunately our differences in religion made no difference to our friendship. Vinnie at one time was the most feared boy in Ribbleton, he was a very powerfully built lad with broad shoulders. When Vinnie was 13/14 years of age he had fought and beaten the local and most feared bully at the time. As a direct result of this vicious fight, Vinnie was barred from the local catholic school but this only added to his street cred. His parents lived in a council house close to the Greenlands estate and simply idolized him. Vinny didn't have to lift a finger at home - everything was done for him from the daily cleaning of shoes, to the more mundane tasks which would normally be carried out by a lad of his age. No-one was more surprised than me when Vinnie became a police cadet. He would ride to work in his police cadet's uniform on his Lambretta scooter and we often went out for jaunts together on his scooter. Vinnie convinced me to leave Goss's and join Lancashire Police as a police cadet, but it was my sister Anne who deserved the credit for constantly recommending me to join the Lancashire Force.

## 2

## Lancashire Constabulary – Dog Section

I took my sister's advice and applied to Lancashire Police to become a police cadet. Following an interview at police headquarters, I was selected from over 100 applicants for one of 5 positions, to be based at H.Q. I simply could not believe my luck when I was offered the opportunity of choosing whether to be based at Head Office doing a clerical job, or joining the police dog section at Moor Farm. I jumped at the opportunity of working at dog section and so my career with Lancashire police was to begin, thanks to my sister Anne.

I was to attend Vinnie's wedding shortly after becoming a policeman - sadly, his marriage ended in divorce and the last I heard of Vinnie was during the period that I was a brewery area manager with Tetley Walker. His ex wife was running a tenanted pub for Tetley's close to Ormskirk. Nobody was more surprised than me to find her behind the bar with her new partner during one of my visits to the tenanted estate.

As a police cadet it was a requirement to go to night school to learn shorthand and typing. That was really good because I was the only male there amongst some eighteen or so females. I had no problem getting the odd date here and there! I found later that it wasn't necessary to use Pitman's shorthand but learning the skill of touch typing was to become invaluable. When I became a policeman I was to be complemented quite frequently as being probably the fastest typist in the division, although most policemen amazingly could almost keep up with me using just one finger on each hand. Because my handwriting is so dreadful, I am fortunately able to type far more quickly than writing and furthermore it is legible!

One very memorable evening when we were police cadets, Vinnie invited me to Saul Street baths in Preston to watch the Lancashire Police water polo team playing Liverpool City. Both teams comprised serving policemen from both forces. There were gasps of surprise when both teams emerged at the poolside. The Liverpool team towered over the Lancashire lads. They were all over 6' - Vinnie was 5' 9" and it appeared that our team was going to get a thorough thrashing. Halfway through it became apparent that our team was putting up a very good performance and the Liverpool lads decided to start playing dirty. This was right up Vinnie's street. He could mix it with the best of them and retaliated with some remarkable underwater punches, thumping and generally playing the Liverpool lads at their own game. They didn't know what had hit them and ended up being thoroughly thrashed.

Becoming a police cadet with the dog section of Lancashire Constabulary was to completely alter my life. The next eighteen months were to become probably the most exiting period of my life. The sergeant in charge of dog section was Harold Herdman, a Cumbrian who lived in a police house opposite to Moor Farm on Lindle Lane. The police motor school was based at Moor Farm, the mounted section and the photography department (for scenes of crimes). The outdoor life was fantastic and the summer of 1957 was glorious.

My role on dog section was the cleaning out of kennels, feeding the dogs, exercising them along with my cadet colleague's Brian Eland, Joe Rimmer and Digger Rigby. We cadets were each allocated an Alsatian puppy to train in obedience, tracking and at a later stage man work. I was thrilled when Harold Herdman allowed me the choice of litter of 5 pups from the bitch Dawn. All the pups had to be named with a 'D' and I was to call mine Duke. A real bond was to develop between me and Duke. He became a brilliant tracker, excellent at obedience and very good at man work. It was so sad when I had to hand him over to a police dog handler when his training was complete.

During the summer of '57 we cadets were assisting with 'laying' Hawthorne hedges. Bill Brightmore, another Cumbrian and police dog handler was supervising. Bill was a huge fellow and a Cumberland and Westmorland wrestling champion He was stationed at Lancaster and Morecambe division. We had some hilarious times with Bill, especially when he invited us to have a 'Hod'. This meant wrestling with him and he would take us on two and three at a time. Clearly, we didn't stand a chance with this mountain of a man.

One of my many roles was to wear a padded arm and run for the police dogs in what was referred to as 'man work' the dog handler would give you a running start and shout the command 'assault', the dog would chase after you and the idea was for the dog to detain you by biting into the padded arm. This was the only protection we wore and was often supplemented by old wellington tops put under the padded arm for extra protection. If you were lucky the dog would go for the right arm, however, there were many occasions when other parts of the anatomy proved to be far more enticing for the dog and I've still got the scars to prove it !

There were two police constables attached to the dog section, Their role along with Harold Herman was to train new police dog handlers on the courses which were held at Moor Farm. Vince Rowland's was a good man; but a detestable vicious man by the name of Bateson was unfortunately also a police dog handler. Bateson had a Doberman police dog and it was a regular occurrence for him to beat, kick and thrash that poor dog if it deviated at all in the manner he wanted it to behave. Vince Rowland's hated Bateson for his disgraceful demeanor. One day following a heated argument in my presence, they started a fight in the kennels. I've seen a few fights but never one as nasty and viscous as this one. Both their faces were quite bloody and it was only by the intervention of Bill Brightmore and Alan Donalon that they were separated. Had this incident got back to headquarters they would certainly have been on form 14. (a disciplinary procedure). Eventually Bateson was transferred away from dog section much to the relief of us all.

One of the funniest things I've ever witnessed was one day when we were training the police dogs in man work on a field known as four acres. I had been running for the dogs for some time when Bill Brightmore offered to do the running to give me a rest. Alan Donalon, a good mate of Bill had quite a nasty and very unpredictable Alsatian bitch called Dina. Unfortunately for Bill it was Dina's turn to have a go. Bill set off up four acres with Alan giving the command 'assault' to Dina - she went straight in like a rocket and nailed Bill right on the backside, totally ignoring the padded right arm. Alan called Dina off with Bill cursing and swearing and that's when the fun started. Bill was taking his trousers down to examine the damage to his rear end and as his trousers were at half mast, Alan gave the command to Dina once more to 'assault'. Poor old Bill simply didn't know what to do for the best so he started pulling his trousers up and running at the same time. Everybody was falling about laughing; it was such a comical sight. Fortunately for Bill, Alan was able to call the dog off before she could do any more damage.

Many police dogs were bred at Moor Farm. Special secure quarantine kennels were built to house Alsatian dogs and bitches for breeding purposes which had been purchased as pups from Germany. This was a first for the Lancashire force to import dogs from abroad. However, many dogs were brought in for training, having been accepted from members of the public. It was necessary to establish whether these dogs would ultimately be suitable as police dogs. One of these dogs had been selected by Harold Herdman, but unfortunately, whilst this was a magnificent Alsatian, he was totally out of control and had killed several of Harold Herdman's hens. The sergeant set me a challenge with this dog. He told me that if within a period of some three months I was unable to train the dog to a satisfactory standard, he would be shot. The dog had been named 'Jet' by his previous owners. Jet was a big, black very powerful dog with a mind of his own.

I set to with obedience in the training compound and this was certainly a battle of wills. It would have been useless progressing on to tracking and man work without the basic training in obedience. I had to be very tough with Jet and was determined he wouldn't get the better of me. Initially, I simply didn't dare to let him off the lead but after about ten days, thankfully, Jet started to come under control which led on to training in tracking and man work. I was so pleased when the dog was able to be handed over to a policeman based in a tough area of East Lancashire. Jet was not a dog to be messed with and I've no doubt that he earned his keep, purely from his visual appearance. The Deputy Chief Constable, Bill Palfrey was soon to learn to his discomfort that Jet didn't take prisoners. (See later.)

The Chief Constable of Lancashire Constabulary at the time was Colonel T E St Johnson. He would arrange regular shoots on an estate at Longridge, near Preston and would arrange for me to go beating for him on these shoots. I would receive a telephone call from Chief Inspector Parrott who made the arrangements for the shoots. The comical thing which was quite a joke amongst the police cadets was that the Chief Inspector insisted on being called Mr Parrow - not Parrott! The Chief was a very good shot. His daughter who was probably about 12 at the time would accompany him on his shoots and tag along with me when I wasn't in the front line beating. I think she took a shine to me! On one occasion I was quite shocked when the chief shot a hare but didn't kill it. The poor thing was screaming and the chief's daughter ran up to it, picked it up by its back legs and took it to daddy, who gave it a rabbit punch in the back of the neck killing it immediately. The Chief's daughter didn't flinch in the slightest. A standing joke in Lancashire Police at that time was that there were only two guaranteed means of promotion - one was to become a Freemason and the other was to marry the chief's daughter. Little was I to know at the time that I was to become a Freemason.

Bill Palfrey was the Deputy Chief Constable and he loved his police dogs. He was quite a character. Following a visit to the States to study their method of working with police patrol cars, he adopted many of their systems and procedures. He even acquired a sort of American twang and became known by the nickname of G I Joe. One weekend when I was out exercising my dog Jet, I was returning across fields towards the motor school when I saw Bill Palfrey showing a party of friends around 'his motor school' He spotted me and called me over. I will never forget the incident as long as I live.

The deputy Chief was wearing plus fours, a deerstalker hat and was carrying a walking stick. He said to me "Is that dog any good?" to which I replied "He's a good un sir." Fortunately for me, suspecting that Bill Palfrey was going to do something rather stupid; I put Jet on the shortest lead possible. The next thing, the Deputy Chief raised his walking stick in the air and crashed it down on the dogs back. Jet went absolutely berserk, attacking the chief and it took all my strength holding him back. Bill Palfrey went white, I backed him up against the motor school wall, he dropped his stick and his deerstalker hat fell off. I allowed the dog to get within six inches of the chief. The sight of a powerful dog with huge fangs barking and snarling within inches must have been quite a shock to Bill Palfrey and certainly his cronies. When I called the dog off and calmed him down the deputy chief congratulated me on what a fine police dog Jet was. Bill Palfrey was a showman and that demonstration to his cronies suited him down to the ground.

One of my roles on dog section was to accompany my sergeant, Harold Herdman, to various exhibitions when I would put on the padded arm and run for various police dogs, demonstrating their ability to apprehend criminals. The biggest and most prestigious of these events was undoubtedly the Royal Lancashire Show and it was at this particular show in the summer of 1958 that the Deputy Chief, Bill Palfrey set me a challenge. I was to run for perhaps the fiercest and biggest Alsatian dog in Lancashire police by the name of 'Simba.' His handler 'Nodder' Brown was very proud of Simba. The dog's reputation for apprehending hardened criminals was well known throughout the Lancashire force. Bill Palfrey bet me half a crown that I couldn't shake Simba off, once he had got hold of (hopefully!) the padded arm. I rose to the challenge replying "you're on sir."

The large enclosed arena at the Royal Lancs Show was surrounded by hundreds of people. Harold Herdman announced over the loud speaker system that I was a dangerous and armed criminal who had escaped from prison. I entered the arena in scruffy attire with my right arm protected by the usual pad, but knowing that I was running for Simba, I put extra protection underneath by way of a couple of old wellington tops. I was carrying a revolver loaded with blanks in my left hand.

The routine on these occasions was for the dog handler to be patrolling the perimeter of the arena in his dog van, on spotting me skulking around with a revolver, would stop on the far side with me in the middle of the arena. On this occasion 'Nodder' got out of the van taking Simba out of the back and shouted for me to remain where I was, I hurled some abuse at him and started to run away. The response to this from 'Nodder' was "If you don't stop - I'll set the dog on you."

Imagine running away from a huge Alsatian with a reputation like Simba - he was like a lion. When feeling more disposed to being friendly towards me he would put his paws on my shoulders and lick my face, no mean feat with me standing at 6' 2". When Simba was some 15 yards away I would turn, whilst still running and fire all six blanks directly at him, the noise was deafening with flames coming out of the barrel of the revolver. This didn't put Simba off in the slightest and he came in like a rocket, fortunately going for the arm. He dragged me to the ground but I was determined to win my half a crown from the deputy chief. I managed to get up, dropped the revolver from my left hand which I used to lever my right arm up, lifting Simba slightly off the ground and putting him off balance, I then kicked him with my left foot as hard as I could in his soft underbelly, temporarily knocking the wind out of him and making him release my arm.

In my jubilation at having won the bet, I turned to Bill Palfrey in the crowd with a big grin on my face, waving my arms in the air and running away from Simba as fast as I could. It was a big mistake taking on that bet. Simba came back in at me with a vengeance and bit so hard on the padded arm; his huge fangs went right through all the protection and made a dreadful mess of my right forearm. It took Nodder Brown all his efforts to call Simba off. Bill Palfrey was so concerned for me that after the demonstrations were over he came over to where we were all lined up to look at my arm. He was horrified to see the mauling I had received and the amount of blood and insisted I went straight to hospital for an anti tetanus jab. I advised him that this wasn't necessary as I had had an anti tetanus jab a few weeks previously from a not dissimilar experience I had had, whilst demonstrating at Cumbria Police Headquarters in Penrith. The irony over that bet with Bill Palfrey was that I never got my half a crown from him!

A tragic set of circumstances occurred whilst I was a cadet at Moor Farm. There were two police cadets of a similar age to myself stationed at the mounted section, whilst I knew them, we tended to carry out our respective duties with the dog section and mounted section and didn't socialize out of hours. One of these cadets had acquired a Triumph Bonneville 650 twin motor cycle which was his pride and joy; I was quite envious having just purchased an old Royal Enfield 250 c.c. motor bike which I claimed at the time would only do 40 M.P.H. downhill with a wind behind you. The two mounted cadets were returning to Moor Farm one day, along Lindle Lane on the Triumph Bonneville, lost control of the bike on a bad bend and smashed into an oak tree. Both of the poor lads were killed instantly and the whole of Moor Farm was in mourning.

After the funerals; Inspector Spence who was in charge of the mounted section at the time sent for me and asked if I would consider transferring to the mounted section. I was in a real dilemma and felt I was being put on the spot. I have always loved horses and this was a real opportunity. However, I was so happy and thoroughly enjoyed the work with police dogs that I declined the offer of the transfer. It was one of those decisions which I shall never really know was the right one. I was advised at some later date that following the deaths of those two young police cadets, that cadets were never to be used again in the mounted section.

We cadets had lots of fun on dog section. A favourite pastime was to go over to the mounted section when there was no one about. Several police horses were put into a large enclosure and we would call them over to the fencing, jump onto one of these 16/17 hand magnificent horses and ride them bareback around the enclosure. Had Inspector Spence caught us we'd have been in trouble.

The nature of our work with the police dogs didn't require us to wear our cadet's uniforms, other than for formal occasions. This was really great. When it was necessary to go to Headquarters we would ride over on bikes in all our scruff. This was good fun which involved cycling through woods to get there. Some of the more snootier pen pushing cadets at H.Q. would look down their noses at us because of our attire, but we couldn't care less.

An incident which I shall never forget really upset me at the time. A goat belonging to Harold Herdman was due to give birth to two kids. The Herdman family drank nothing but goat's milk. I accompanied Sergeant Herdman as the goat gave birth to two kids. It was very moving to see those two little kids being born, the mother licking them as they struggled to stand up. I was really shocked when Harold Herdman picked up the newly born kids one at a time by their back legs and smashed their little heads on a large rock, killing them instantly. The awful thing was that this was done in front of the mother. It would have been far kinder to remove them out of sight before carrying out such a barbaric act. The goats milk was required by the Herdman family, hence the reason for getting rid of those two little kids.

Any police dog which didn't reach the required standard would be shot by Harold Herdman and buried in a field. We cadets would dig the grave and the dog would be shot in the head at the graveside. On one occasion the sergeant shot a dog in the head and the breach of the rifle jammed. Fortunately, the first shot killed the dog. This was one of the more unpleasant tasks we had to carry out. I can only recall about 4 dogs being shot during those eighteen months on dog section. It would have been unacceptable to hand these unsatisfactory dogs over as pets because of the nature of their training. In today's world, risk assessments and health and safety regulations would certainly apply.

Two of the most powerful police dogs, Simba and Kim hated each other. Unfortunately they were off their leads in the training compound with their handlers during a training session when they attacked each other. The most terrible fight ensued. It was clearly going to be a fight to the death until Bill Brightmore picked up a 5 foot length of 3x2 timber and smashed it down on Simba's head. It was such a blow that we all thought he'd killed the dog – but Simba shook it off and recovered after a while. Goodness knows which of those two dogs would have survived had Bill not intervened.

Another decision which I had to make was about the time of my eighteenth birthday. National service had come to an end just before my eighteenth and I was seriously considering signing on for two years. However, after much consideration I chose not to go into the armed forces having been advised by colleagues that I would get all the self discipline necessary in Lancashire Police.

Joe Rimmer, a cadet on dog section at that time and the same age as me had decided that he would sign on for two years. The purpose was to get abroad and see a bit of the world. Joe joined the military police and ended up pen pushing in an admin job for the whole of his two years, never achieving his ambition of getting abroad. By the time Joe came out of the forces I had completed my two years probationary period and was a fully fledged policeman on quite a reasonable salary. Joe was really frustrated that he had made the wrong decision and joined the Southport Borough Force two years later than he otherwise would have done.

Upon reaching the age of seventeen I acquired my first motor cycle – a Royal Enfield 250cc mentioned in an earlier chapter. It used to break down regularly, but probably the worst experience was returning from a jaunt to Blackpool one evening with my mate Brian Eland on the pillion. It decided to conk out just outside Preston in the pouring rain and pushing the thing home wasn't much fun! I got rid of the Royal Enfield and purchased a BSA Shooting Star 500 twin on credit whilst still a cadet on dog section. This bike was a different ball game altogether and it frightened me to death on my first trip out. I rode onto the M6 motorway (Preston by-pass as it was then known – the first motorway to be built in this country) the acceleration was quite frightening. I kept this BSA twin for nine months after becoming a policeman on the beat in Seaforth Division. Having attended fatal accidents involving motor cyclists, I realized just how dangerous motor cycles were, sold the

B.S.A. and purchased my first car at the age of 21; my pride and joy! A Wolseley 6/80.

There wasn't a lot of love lost between Lancashire Police and Preston Borough Police in those days and unfortunately I was to learn the hard way just how true this was. I very foolishly overlooked renewing the road fund license on my Royal Enfield Motor cycle and was stopped by a Preston Borough Policeman in Walker Street, Preston, close to the Masonic hall. On seeing my expired license and having established that it had not been renewed he took out his pocket book and was clearly intent on booking me. I explained that it was an oversight and apologized to him, explaining that I was a police cadet with Lancashire Police based at headquarters. He wasn't the slightest bit interested and clearly took great satisfaction in booking someone from the opposition, in spite of the fact that I also told him of my concern that the booking would result in my being put on a discipline charge.

Form 14 was the dreaded disciplinary procedure in Lancashire Police at the time and I was required to report to the Chief Constable, Colonel T. E. St Johnson. I shall never forget being kept waiting outside his office, in uniform and then being taken in by his Secretary. There sat the Chief behind his huge desk in shirtsleeves, wearing red braces. I stood to attention in front of his desk, a mere 18 years of age thinking that I was going to be dismissed from the force. The chief was very understanding when I explained the circumstances to him, but went on to advise me that unfortunately the disciplinary matter would remain on my file. I was more embarrassed in that meeting by the fact that I had personally worked for the Chief on many weekends, assisting on his shoot, cleaning the guns and beating etc. Understandably, no mention was made of this by the chief; so much for the relationship with Preston Borough Police. I was not to know at the time that I was once again to cross swords with the Preston Borough Force, but through totally different circumstances.

At the age of eighteen and three quarters I left the dog section to commence thirteen weeks of basic training to become a policeman. The course took place at Bruche, Warrington and I was given the No P.C. 2907. The irony was that I remained on a police cadet's salary for those three months whilst my colleagues who were over the age of nineteen were on a full policeman's salary. I shared accommodation with a Manchester City Trainee and during the evenings we would sit on our beds bulling up our boots with spit and polish, learning legal definitions.

One which comes to mind is 'Evidence' In law the term evidence is used to indicate any fact or point in issue or question which may be proved or disproved in a manner complying with the legal rules governing the subject.' We would meet on the parade ground in the mornings and with my height (I was the tallest on the course) would be the right hand marker. Sergeant Halpin, an ex Guardsman was the drill instructor and it was quite comical the way he would shout and scream at us when marching on the drill square.

I remember clearly celebrating towards the end of the course with a visit with my mates to the Barley Mow, a Tetley pub in the centre of Warrington. It was then a typical tired old boozer but with excellent hand pulled Tetley ales. I never imagined at the time that I would become a Brewery Area Manager with Tetley's, with the Barley Mow as one of my best managed houses, following major structural alterations. (See Managed Houses.)

# 3
## Seaforth Division - Merseyside

My posting was to be to the Seaforth Division, Waterloo Section on Merseyside and within days of my nineteenth birthday I travelled from Preston to Lime Street Station, Liverpool and from there by train to Waterloo. The train stopped at Seaforth Railway Station before arriving at Waterloo. I recall thinking 'what a dump this place is that I've been transferred to!' The view of Seaforth from the railway station looked dreadful. The next stop was Waterloo where I was to spend the next two years as a young policeman on probation.

I made my way to Waterloo Police Station with my uniform in my suitcase where I was met by Chief Inspector Bird who was in charge of the Crosby and Waterloo sections. He went through the basics with me in his office as to what was expected of me as a P.C. in his section. Bill Eccles, John McCrone and Sergeant Dixon were the three Sergeants in the section. They reminded me very much of Dixon of Dock Green. Bill Eccles had the most beautiful copperplate handwriting and used to make fun of my dreadful unreadable writing which looked like a drunken spider had crawled out of the inkwell all over the paper, and still does!

P.C. 542 Eric Brownlow at Waterloo Section became a firm friend and was to teach me to drive at the age of nineteen, prior to my taking the Police Driving Course at Hutton H.Q. His car was an old Ford eight manufactured in 1937 and Eric would boast that the car was older than his wife! There was no starter motor which meant that the only way of starting the car was to put a handle into the crank shaft at the front of the car and turn it until the engine started. The only way of changing gear was to double de clutch and the hilarious thing was that there was only one door handle to open both drivers' and passenger doors.

Whilst living in digs at Waterloo with Mr. & Mrs. Rimmer, I decided to become a member of the Crosby Barbell Club. The club was essentially a weightlifting club. There was a full size wrestling ring where members of the club were taught. Crosby Barbell Club was owned by Tony Buck, a very well known body builder and wrestler on Merseyside. He was a huge fellow who had developed a very muscular physique following years of lifting weights. Tony was a gentle giant and a very popular guy.

My first day at the club came as quite a shock. Tony knew that I was a policeman and with several members training at the time, Tony advised me that all new members were required to step into the wrestling ring with him. Club members gathered around the ring as I climbed in to face Tony. He said I was to imagine I had a knife and was to attack him. I rushed at him with this imaginary knife but simply didn't stand a chance. For such a huge chap he was remarkably agile and had me on the floor in no time. It was all good fun and there was no way in which Tony, a professional wrestler, was attempting to embarrass me.

I started to work out with a very pleasant chap who worked for British Rail. With us both working shifts, it was quite convenient to meet at the club at different times of the day and evening. Weight lifting is very hard and strenuous. I positively hated doing the squats. This involved holding a bar with weights on each end, placed on your shoulders and squatting down and standing up again. Apparently, this exercise was necessary, prior to working out on a bench. After some six months as a member of the club, I found it too difficult to fit in with shift work and ceased attending.

Whilst living in Waterloo, I started making a scale model of HMS Bounty. Mr. Rimmer and his wife ran a business from their home from a workshop opposite the house and I was able to use the woodworking workshop for making the model. There were many intricate details on the model, particularly the rigging. It took 2 hours to make one section measuring some 4". On completion of the Bounty, I entered it into the Lancashire Constabulary Horticultural Show and Arts and Crafts Exhibition on the 21st August, 1962 and was delighted to win first prize.

My mother had moved into a bungalow in Preston with my youngest sister Linda and her son Anthony. I decided to leave HMS Bounty at my mother's house, displaying it in a very prominent position. On arrival home one weekend, I was horrified to see the model quite badly damaged. The main mast had collapsed and the rigging was quite badly damaged. My mother had let Anthony 'sail' my treasured Bounty in the bath! I was not at all amused. If you're reading this Tony – you owe me a couple of pints!

A very embarrassing moment occurred at the Pier Head in Liverpool whilst Eric was teaching me to drive. There was a policeman on point duty in a raised box directing traffic and on our approach he gave the number one stop signal. I stopped with a number of cars behind me and when the policeman signalled me to proceed I stalled the engine. Eric said "you berk! You know what you've got to do." So I got out with the starting handle to wind up the crank shaft to start the engine with that policeman glaring at me as though I had committed a felony.

Eric was an excellent driving instructor and taught me not just how to double de clutch effectively but to change gear with 'sustained revs' ensuring a smooth gear change. Favourite expressions were "be careful on this bend, there could be a Centurian Tank round the corner." And "I want you to imagine there's a bucket of shit on the passenger seat and you mustn't spill any." That expression amuses me and remains with me until this day.

I took my test in Walton, Liverpool. The examiner was a huge fellow and after I read the number plate of a car at the required distance, he walked round to the passenger door looking rather perplexed that there was no door handle. Trying to keep my face straight I removed the handle from the drivers' door, walked round and opened the door for him explaining that the car only had the one handle. Fortunately I passed first time.

One evening during my early days as a policeman at Waterloo, I was present when Eric Brownlow brought a drunk into the police station. He had refused to go home, was shouting and swearing and Eric had had no alternative than to arrest him. He was taken into the charge office where he absolutely refused to give his name and address. Chief Inspector Bird was called into the charge office and asked him for his name to which he replied "Sam Plank from the wood yard." The Chief Inspector smacked him with the flat of his hand across his face, sending him sprawling across the charge office. The comical thing was that at the same time the Chief Inspector's watch flew off his wrist landing on the floor next to the drunk. The drunk gave his name very quickly after this incident!

Another hilarious incident was to occur when I arrested a man for being drunk in charge of a vehicle. He was alone driving down South Road, Waterloo, stalled the car having mounted the pavement and slumped over the wheel. The procedure in those days was to call the police doctor to examine the drunk driver. This was during the early hours of the morning.

The Police Doctor arrived in his car clearly the worse for drink and started his examination of the drunk. This involved the drunk walking down a straight line and a general examination. Both the police doctor and the drunk were very much the worse for drink and started an argument as to who had drunk the most that night. It was quite unbelievable to witness the hilarious exchange of drunken banter. Clearly, we couldn't get the doctor to certify the drunk to enable us to take him to court; so the drunk was kept in the cells overnight and thrown out the next morning. That was the last time that police doctor was used to certify any drunk.

At the age of 19 I was to experience a very sad situation resulting from a fatal accident at Ince Woods, Crosby. A young man of nineteen was riding his scooter along a notoriously dangerous stretch of road in Ince Woods when the engine of his scooter suddenly and without warning seized up. A double decker bus travelling behind ran right over the poor lad killing him outright. The driver of the bus blacked out temporarily and the passengers on the bus were screaming. I was left alone in Waterloo Police Station whilst all other available officers went to the scene. By the time they got to Ince Woods the ambulance had already collected the body which they brought to Waterloo Police Station.

The ambulance driver came into the station asking for the key to the mortuary. The mortuary was situated just behind the station. I had to lock up the station and accompany the ambulance men, open up the mortuary and help them to place the body on a mortuary slab. Shortly after the ambulance men had left a colleague joined me, we took our tunics off and removed all the clothing off the poor lad. His back was broken and when I removed his damaged crash helmet my fingers sank into his broken skull. The parents were notified and Sergeant Dixon and I accompanied them to the mortuary to identify the body. Clearly, they were absolutely distraught.

On the way back to the police station, the mother of the deceased told me that their son was their only child, asked me how old I was and when I said I was nineteen, she told me that her son was also nineteen. What really shocked me was when the mother told me her son was a Crosby Herald newspaper reporter; his office was next door to Waterloo Police Station. Not only did I know him well, but when I was on the beat he would regularly stop and have a chat with me. Due to the awful mutilation of his body I could not possibly have recognized him on the mortuary slab. As was the custom with any sudden death, it was the responsibility of the officer in the Seaforth Division to attend with the death and be present at the post mortem. Colleagues in other areas told me that they were not involved at all. A coroner's police officer dealt with all sudden deaths. It would have been emotionally very difficult for me to attend the post mortem of a person I knew, however vaguely.

By that stage I had already dealt with a couple of sudden deaths and witnessed the procedure of a post mortem.

Early one evening, Eric Brownlow and I were patrolling the Waterloo area in the section car, when we received a call that a man had climbed onto the roof of a house and was behaving in a very unreasonable manner. On arrival we saw a young man perched on the edge of the roof. When he spotted us he threatened to jump off the roof. It took quite a while to coax him down, but he became violent and there was no way in which we could make him see sense. After quite a struggle we managed to put handcuffs on the lad. It became clear that he had some sort of mental illness. We therefore made the decision to take him to the mental hospital in Ormskirk.

When we arrived at the hospital the lad was taken to a padded cell by the hospital staff. I shall never forget what happened in that mental hospital. Eric and I took off the handcuffs and as soon as we did the lad became very violent. It took the member of staff at the hospital, Eric and me to restrain him whilst a straight jacket was fitted on him. The method of fitting a straight jacket is to put the arms through (like putting a jacket on back to front), which is then tied at the back. As soon as the lad was released, he started screaming and throwing himself around the cell. We left the cell, locking the door and I was shocked when I looked through the small viewing panel to see the lad behaving like a wild animal. He was throwing himself onto the padded walls and frothing at the mouth. It was a terrible thing to see a human being behaving in such a way. It turned out that the poor lad was suffering from schizophrenia.

Adjusting to shift work as a policeman took quite some time. The regular shifts were 6am to 2pm, 2pm to 10pm and 10pm to 6am. The night shift of 10 to 6 was the one which played havoc with sleep patterns. During evenings and up until midnight, one of the main incidents to deal with was domestic disputes. The main cause would generally be as a result of alcohol where the husband would come home the worse for drink, an argument would occur between husband and wife and very often this would result in the wife being assaulted. Sadly, the only course of action you could take as a policeman in those days would be to advise the wife that if she wished to take legal action for the assault, would be to consult a solicitor or contact the magistrates' clerk. Where there was serious injury then the perpetrator would be arrested and charged with wounding.

I discovered very quickly in those domestic dispute situations never to take sides. A colleague of mine was smacked on the back of his head with a frying pan by an irate wife who did not like the fact that her husband was given the benefit of the doubt. A sergeant at Kirkby Division was seriously injured by a nasty and very violent individual following a domestic dispute. He rammed a poker straight through the poor sergeant's upper arm. On one of the very first domestics I attended I was greeted at the front door by the man shouting back into the house "Look what they've sent – they've only sent us a lad!" I told this guy in no uncertain terms that if they behaved like adults then the likes of me as a lad wouldn't need to become involved.

Perhaps one of the saddest domestics I attended was a call to a house where the electricity had been turned off for non payment of the electricity account. I arrived about 11pm and was invited into the house by the wife. As I entered the dark hallway I could feel crunching under my feet and on shining my torch onto the floor found that I was treading on large beetles which were crawling all over the hall. When I had read the riot act out to this argumentative couple and calmed them down, knowing that there were young children in the family, I insisted on going up to the bedroom to establish that the children were safe.

It brings tears to my eyes even now to recall the shock of what I saw. There were three very young children sharing a double bed, huddled up sideways in the bed which had the filthiest blankets covering them. They were wide awake and quite startled with their little eyes staring at me. The shouting and screaming of their parents had clearly upset them but they assured me that they were alright. I wondered what sort of future would face those little children who were being brought up in a household where both parents were unemployed and hated the police. A copy of my report went to social services.

A series of smash and grabs were taking place in Waterloo by a gang who used the most unusual modus operandi. They would smear a blanket with treacle, press it firmly against a shop window and throw a brick at the blanket smashing the glass. This was to deaden the noise of breaking glass. These raids took place in the early hours of the morning and a period of surveillance was set up. I was involved in this exercise, spending countless hours hiding in shop doorways often in atrocious weather conditions. Retail shops with displays of expensive items were the ones to suffer from these attacks.

Bill Winnard was one of the older constables at Waterloo; he witnessed the gang smashing the window of a jewellers shop in South Road, the main shopping area in Waterloo during the early hours of the morning. Bill was either very brave or very foolish because he tackled the three men. He was beaten dreadfully; punched, kicked in the head and ribs and left bleeding on the pavement. Bill was to spend a week in hospital recovering from his injuries. Surprisingly, he went on to complete thirty years of service before retiring. To the best of my knowledge the gang was never caught.

Chief Inspector Bird retired some twelve months after my posting to Waterloo Section. His replacement was a very unpleasant man by the name of Chief Inspector Ferrington who transferred from Widness Division. Even before he arrived his reputation preceded him. He had a very superior attitude and simply would not tolerate any constable doing a 'one line entry' in relation to traffic accidents; i.e. where an accident occurred and both drivers' exchanged names and addresses and insurance if necessary, then no further action would be taken. This had always been the procedure with Mr. Bird.

Ferrington simply insisted that where a traffic accident occurred someone was to blame and therefore a court case had to take place. This was ridiculous taking into account the amount of time required to take statements and prepare all the necessary paperwork for court. As a mere P.C. I was to cross swords with Ferrington over this issue, arguing that with an overstretched workload it was a waste of valuable time. This exchange took place in the charge office when he found me typing the paperwork for three ongoing accidents I was dealing with, which meant spending my day off at the police station instead of catching up on some much needed sleep.

This was to be my first experience in life of working for a totally unreasonable boss with a complete lack of leadership and motivational skills. Because I tended to be rather outspoken about unfair issues of this nature, the relationship between myself and Ferrington hit rock bottom. In his view it was clearly a case of 'how dare this young P.C. on probation question my judgment.' A P.C. colleague also at Waterloo would not tolerate Ferrington's nasty attitude and resigned but not before telling the Chief Inspector his fortune! He went back to his home town of Lancaster to take up a career in selling.

Whilst still a young P.C. at Waterloo at the age of nineteen, I met a very attractive tall, blue eyed blonde German girl by the name of Bridget. We met at a dance at the Floral Hall in Southport. Bridget was working at a residential hotel in Southport, essentially to improve her English. Her parents were quite wealthy farmers near Dusseldorf, West Germany and very staunch Roman Catholics. Bridget regularly attended a Catholic Church in Southport and I declined to attend those services with her. As a committed Christian now, how churlish I think when I reflect on that situation, that I refused to enter a Catholic church. I blame my upbringing and the 'us and them' attitude between Catholics and Protestants when I was a boy in Preston.

Chief Inspector Ferrington discovered that I was friendly with 'a German girl' and was absolutely furious. So much so that he made every effort to get rid of me from his section at Waterloo. I can only think that this reaction was probably because he had fought against the Germans in the Second World War. My position became intolerable and I made a request in writing to meet with Chief Superintendent Jackson, the head of Seaforth Division.

I stood to attention in front of the Chief Supers desk and explained to him that I considered Ferrington's attitude to be totally unreasonable, that I worked extremely hard and was very conscientious. Mr. Jackson was very fair and said that as long as my relationship with 'this German girl' was honourable then he didn't have a problem with it at all. I was very pleased when he told me that he knew of my endeavours and commitment to the job and that he would give me a fair crack of the whip. He arranged for an immediate transfer to the Seaforth Section and I was delighted with the move. Shortly after my move to Seaforth division, Bridget returned home to her parent's farm in West Germany. I have no doubt that our differences in religion had influenced her parents that Bridget should end the relationship.

I was twenty one years of age on my transfer from Waterloo to Seaforth Section. Just before the move occurred and whilst I was still in 'digs' with Mr. and Mrs. Rimmer in Picton Road, Waterloo, I received a telephone call on the 16$^{th}$ June, 1961 which happened to be my day off and also my Mother's birthday. Bill Winnard, a P.C. 'phoned me from Waterloo police station and I shall never forget the conversation. Bill said "Hi Bob, I'm ringing about your Dad." When I asked what it was about he simply said "He isn't any more, he's dead." He went on to tell me that his body was in the mortuary at Preston Police Station and that I was required to identify the body. The news was bad enough but to be told in such an uncaring way over the telephone was unbelievable. It's normal practice to advise anyone of a sudden death in person, not over the telephone.

I arrived at Preston Borough Police Station and was taken into the mortuary by a constable who dealt with all the sudden deaths in the area. My father was lying on a mortuary slab covered with the usual white sheet, when his face was uncovered his eyes were closed, he had no teeth in and had an awful pallor. I identified the body and was told that a post mortem had already been carried out. The constable told me that the post mortem had revealed from the contents of the stomach, that my father had taken at least a handful of sleeping tablets. I was absolutely furious and so angry that my father had chosen to commit suicide on my Mother's birthday.

I went straight from the mortuary to Grey Gables to console my mother who told me that she had found my father in bed late that morning apparently unconscious. An ambulance was called by the verger of St. Mary Magdeline's but on arrival they had found my father to be dead. The funeral could not go ahead until an inquest had been held. At that time my eldest sister Anne and her husband Johnny had just returned from a posting in Germany. Johnny had been posted there with the R.A.F. and Anne was pregnant with her second child.

I attended the inquest with my mother who explained to the coroner that my father had been so looking forward to Anne's return from Germany and particularly to seeing his new Grandchild. In view of this evidence the coroner surprisingly decided on an 'open verdict.' rather than suicide. I could simply not accept this decision in view of the fact that he had taken a 'handful' of sleeping tablets. I shall never know the truth, but I do suspect that my mother's brother Harold Rigby, a very prominent and well known person in Preston had persuaded the Coroner to go down the route of an open verdict. The stigma of a member of the family committing suicide was unacceptable.

Shortly after my twenty first birthday I purchased my first car, a 680 Wolseley in British Racing Green. It was my pride and joy and quite luxurious compared to my BSA 500 twin. A very amusing incident was to occur one weekend when I took my Mother and Grandparents, Grandma and Bob for a drive out to Southport. Travelling along Lord Street we approached a young policeman on point duty standing in a raised wooden platform. He gave me the No.1 stop signal and I stopped some fifteen feet from him.

Not realising that the traffic behind him was straddled across the road he waved me on. I remained stationary expecting him to look behind and see that the road was blocked but he didn't. I shall never forget how that young policeman got down from his box, striding towards me full of importance and preparing to give me a rollicking. As he was doing so I was winding my window down and taking my warrant card out of my pocket. As he came alongside his exact words were "If you had been to No. 1 District Police Training Centre you would know how to do point duty." I showed him my warrant card and replied "It just so happens that I have been to No. One District Police Training Centre at Bruche and the way you're going on you could do with going back for a refresher course." I then pointed to the traffic still blocking Lord Street. He blushed and skulked back into his box in the middle of the road. By this time my mother, grandparents and myself were roaring with laughter. I certainly spoilt that poor lad's day for him.

I sold my 680 Wolseley after doing quite a lot of body repairs, buying another 680 which was in far better condition. I rented a garage and stripped down the engine of the car, putting new big ends and new pistons into the six cylinder engine. I was thrilled when I started the engine, following the quite lengthy work to hear the reconditioned engine running so smoothly. At the age of twenty two, I sold the 680 and purchased a Wolseley 690. This was my ultimate dream car with leather seats. I have to laugh when I remember the way I would drive around in the car with my string back gloves on! What a poser!

During the first two years as a policeman you were on a probationary period. Sergeants' and Inspectors' would forward reports regularly as to your suitability. During this time a period of two weeks were spent with C.I.D. and motor patrol duties. The divisional motor patrol H.Q. was based in Maghull. The two weeks I spent as a passenger with motor patrol were fantastic. Being driven round in high powered police cars was a terrific experience. The first time I ever travelled at over 100 mph was on the way to a serious accident on the notorious A580 Liverpool to Manchester road. We were in a white soft top M.G.B. When the speedometer nudged over 100, the whole car felt as if it was about to take off. Sadly, that accident turned out to be a fatal. We were first on the scene and had to block off the entire road. The fire brigade had to cut the deceased out of the car and the ambulance drivers' removed the body from the scene. There was a very competitive spirit at H.Q.T.P. (Head Quarters Traffic Patrol) in Maghull. On the wall in a prominent position was a league table indicating the number of motorists each motor patrol constable had booked. Woe betide any constable whose name was at the bottom of the league table!

Aintree Race Course was owned at the time by Mirabelle Topping and the Deputy Chief, Bill Palfrey loved nothing more during Aintree races than driving around the track in a white open topped MGB police car with Mirabelle Topping seated in the passenger seat, for ever the showman. I was to spend a twelve hour night shift during the famous annual Aintree races looking after Lord Derby's race horses. It was the accepted thing for the constable carrying out this duty to accept a gift of £5.00 at the end of the races; this was placed in a white envelope and handed over by one of Lord Derby's staff. On another occasion I was on duty on the course itself standing by Beechers Brook as the race took place. It was quite scary watching the horses jumping over the huge fence with the large brook on the far side. I saw many riders fall at that notorious evil jump.

Chief Inspector Ted Bentham was in charge of the uniform division of Seaforth Section. He was totally dedicated and committed to the job. He would be on duty for all three shifts and would very rarely get home before midnight. He was a stickler for attention to detail and one of his favourite expressions was "Are you in a state of awareness – P.C. whoever!" The night shift dreaded being on duty with Ted Bentham at weekends, particularly Saturday. He insisted on a team of uniformed officers visiting the Caradoc Pub at closing time. The Caradoc was situated very close to Seaforth Docks.

When the punters left the pub they would congregate on the pavement outside the Caradoc causing an obstruction. With the backing of two or three constables he would demand that they dispersed and when things got a bit ugly he would start prodding difficult individuals with his stick. I arrested many a drunk outside the Caradoc pub for 'drunk and disorderly' behaviour. However, my view was such that if these customers had been left alone, they would have dispersed of their own free will. All they wanted to do was have a friendly chat before going home. Can you imagine the scene, you're having a pleasant chat after a few drinks and this irate Chief Inspector arrives on the scene shouting about 'The Riot Act' prodding and poking people with his stick!

Inspector George Ekins was the finest Police Inspector one could ever wish to serve with. He was without doubt the smartest and most imposing man I have ever seen in uniform. He commanded great respect from all the constables in Seaforth Section. George Ekins was a rear gunner in a Lancaster bomber during the Second World War but never spoke of his experiences during the war. He most certainly had 'The Common Touch'. One evening we were on the beat together and I was saying what scum some of the 'scousers' were that we had to deal with, particularly the drunken dockers we regularly had to arrest. I was quite surprised when Inspector Ekins gave me a gentle lecture in response to my comments. He told me that many of those so called 'scum' to whom I referred were the backbone of the army during the war, that they were on the front line and went into battle without fear and had laid down their lives for their country. That advice has remained with me to this day and drove home to me the fact that there is good in most people.

There were many occasions where George Ekins would give you his full support when the going got tough. He wasn't afraid to get stuck in and I saw him break more than one stick assisting me with a particularly difficult arrest. His leadership, communication and motivational skills were second to none. I shall never forget his support over a particularly difficult incident which occurred when I was home at Grey Gables one weekend. I heard shouting and screaming outside the house and ran out to find a boy of some thirteen years of age on the floor being kicked unmercifully by a boy of a similar age. His glasses were broken and I was just in time to drag the boy off as he started to kick the lad on the ground in the head. I took the lad into the kitchen, showed him my warrant card and told him that I was going to call the police and report the vicious assault. He couldn't care less and told me to 'fuck off' several times. I smacked him across the face with the flat of my hand and he skulked off shouting and swearing abuse at me.

Later that afternoon the mother of the foul mouthed youth came to the house accompanied by her son, demanding an explanation as to why I had struck him. When I explained the manner of the assault that I had witnessed and his abuse towards me, the boy denied everything and the mother started swearing and calling me a liar. The most ridiculous statement she made was in relation to my 680 Wolseley which was parked outside the house. It went something like this "You people who drive around in cars think you can get away with anything."

About 8.30pm that evening a police sergeant from Preston Borough arrived at the house stating that they had received a complaint that I had assaulted a boy. This sergeant's attitude and body language told me immediately that I was in the wrong, in spite of explaining all the circumstances to him and asking him if he would have stood by and done nothing and been spoken to in the manner which I had, would he not have reacted in the same manner. Once again it was obvious to me that Preston Borough Police had absolutely no time at all for Lancashire Police. The sergeant told me that he would be sending a report through to Seaforth Division.

About ten days following the above incident, George Ekins called me into his office. He showed me a report from Preston Borough which had been sent to Chief Superintendent Jackson. Inspector Ekins said that he had been asked by the Chief Super to deal with the matter. I explained all the circumstances to him and true to form the Inspector's reaction was very supportive, stating that he would have done exactly as I had. He then asked if there had been any witnesses to my slapping the boy across the face. I told him that there weren't. Imagine my surprise when George Ekins said "Bob, the biggest mistake you made was admitting to hitting the lad. You should have denied it." The response was typical of George Ekins and he sent his report back to the Chief Super stating that no further action should be taken.

I discovered that working with older men enabled me to mature far more quickly than I otherwise would have done. This was particularly applicable with my first posting to Waterloo where many of my colleague's were old enough to be my father. The move to Seaforth Section therefore seemed in some ways a reversal of this situation. Most of the constables at Seaforth were either a similar age or even younger than me. By the time I had reached the age of twenty three, I had taken the advanced police driving course and was regularly driving the section police car in Seaforth. Chief Inspector Bentham had the confidence in me to regularly ask me to take on the role of Acting Sergeant. This entailed parading the men on, asking them to 'produce appointments' i.e. showing their truncheon's and handcuffs and allocating them to the various beats. One and two beats combined and three and four beats were the toughest area's to patrol with five and six the cushiest, being the more outlying area's of Seaforth section in Litherland.

Whilst Chief Inspector Bentham was a pretty tough disciplinarian, I was to discover another side to him. When he found that I was a lover of classical music, on more than one occasion whilst on nights he would typically say to me "Meet me at 11.20pm P.C. Mynett at the sausage works – there's a Beethoven concert on the radio and we can listen to it together." At the appointed time he would arrive in his Rover saloon car which he was so proud of. I would jump into the passenger seat and we would park within sight of the police box at the sausage works. In those days there were no mobile phones or modern systems of communication as there are today. If the light on those boxes started to flash on and off then the beat constable would open the box with his key and pick up the phone to receive the message.

Ted Bentham loved his car. He claimed that the engine was so quiet that you could hear the clock ticking over the sound of the engine. Furthermore, the only way to close the drivers door on entering the car was to open the window slightly, the seals were so effective that it was not possible to close the door whilst the windows were up. On reflection, it was quite a privilege for me as a constable to sit listening to those concerts with the Chief Inspector. I became quite fond of the man in spite of his many quirky ways. Unfortunately, Ted Bentham had a massive heart attack one night when assisting to restrain a prisoner in the cells. Surprisingly, when he recovered he returned back on duty but clearly was no longer able to participate in more strenuous activities.

Bootle Borough had their own police force which operated completely separately from the Liverpool City force. Their boundary was adjacent to the Seaforth Section of Lancashire Police. The Chief Constable of Bootle Borough was a man by the name of Legg. The ridiculous situation with this Chief Constable was that he insisted that all reports started with the words 'I respectfully beg to report.' We would occasionally meet up with Bootle Borough police car drivers whilst on nights. The force used Humber Hawks, very much more prestigious cars compared to those used by Lancashire Police.

One evening whilst speaking to one of their police car drivers, I was told that the Bootle Chief Constable had asked one of the drivers to take him to a road on some obscure new housing estate which the constable had never heard of. Because this unfortunate policeman had no idea where this new address was, Legg took him off duties with motor patrol section and put him back on the beat. It goes without saying that morale in the Bootle force was rock bottom as a direct result of this Chief Constable.

Terry Woods was my Sergeant on many occasions. A very amusing situation arose when Ted Bentham pinned a handwritten note on the charge office door which said 'This door must be kept closed at all times.' I was following Terry one evening into the charge office when he stopped abruptly in front of the door saying to me "How on earth am I supposed to get through this door if it's got to be closed at all times?" Ted Bentham was within earshot and bellowed out at the top of his voice "You fool sergeant – you open the damned thing." Having entered the charge office and closed the door we just burst out laughing! I'm sure that Ted Bentham also saw the funny side of the situation!

Sergeant Ike Whittaker was one of the senior sergeants at Seaforth and a real stickler for action. Many of the constables found it difficult to work with him. I liked Ike a great deal in spite of his apparent dislike of motorists. I had many a conversation with him during which he told me of his great disappointment that he had been overlooked for promotion to Inspector. When parading the men on for the morning or afternoon shifts, he would state that not one of the constables would be allowed back into the office, even for their refreshments (food and drink' popularly known as refs.) until they had booked a minimum of three motorists. His policy certainly didn't endear him to the motoring public in Seaforth Section! Paddy, a big strapping Irish lad would hide behind a big oak tree by a 'T' junction in Litherland on five and six beats. He would stop and book every motorist who failed to stop at the 'T' junction. This was good enough for Ike Whittaker but Paddy got some stick from me and colleagues for booking motorists for such a paltry offence.

I acquired an uncanny knack of being able to stop motorists and particularly motorbikes where there was no current insurance policy in place. There was no question of a caution and I would throw the book at them. Often, it also transpired that there was no road fund license in place and on the odd occasion no current driving license. Therefore, when Ike Whittaker was on duty I had no problem in booking three motorists/motor cyclists. However, I did have the advantage when I moved from patrol duties on the beat to driving the section police car.

The only time I ever booked a motorist for speeding was as a direct result of the nasty attitude of that particular motorist. My policy was to stop the car or motorbike, give them a rollicking stating that if I caught them speeding once more then they would be booked. The motorist I booked had a really bad attitude problem. He was doing forty five in a thirty mile an hour area. When I pointed out the offence to him his reply was "I'm a personal friend of Chief Superintendent Jackson constable." Up and till that point my pocket book had remained in my tunic, without hesitation I took it out and booked him for speeding. When I submitted the report, the Chief Super wrote across it in red ink 'PROSECUTE.' The man pleaded guilty and the magistrates' fined him a hefty fee.

My two weeks of C.I.D. training were a fascinating experience. Norman Taylor was the D.S. (Detective Sergeant) and Jack Watson the Detective Inspector. When there was not a lot of crime to attend to, Norman Taylor would love to have a bit of fun. A popular game on the streets for the unemployed on Merseyside was 'pitch & toss' I never really understood the rules but a group of men would throw coins into the air, the 'belt man' would whiz his belt in the air until the coins had settled on the ground.

To me this was a harmless pastime, but Norman Taylor took great delight in disturbing these games. Because this activity was illegal; the gang playing the game would have young boys watching on street corners for the police. We were in plain clothes and an unmarked C.I.D. car which enabled us to get close up to these games before the gang realized we were police. It was hilarious to watch these scousers picking up their coins off the floor, running off in all directions. It was a harmless bit of fun disturbing these games and such a paltry offence that no one was ever arrested. Whilst Norman Taylor was a D.S. at Seaforth, he would spend every opportunity studying for his exams for promotion to Inspector. A lot of this study was spent in a C.I.D. car parked up on the foreshore at Waterloo.

Adrian Mott was a D.C. at Seaforth whilst I was doing my fortnight of training with the department. He was a big strapping lad of some 16 stone. One day whilst I was in the C.I.D. office, Adrian was sat down with his feet up on a desk reading a newspaper when the D.I. Jack Watson walked in. He was furious to see Adrian reading with his feet up and asked him what on earth he thought he was doing. Without hesitation Adrian replied that he was scouring the paper for any possible advertisements that may be for property that was stolen! Clearly it was a porky pie but the Inspector accepted the explanation. The Inspector would never know the truth but maybe thought it to be quite an innovative line of enquiry. It was very quick witted of Adrian, but you had to hand it to him for such a prompt response!

Norman Taylor was promoted through the ranks to Chief Superintendent and his final days were spent in charge of the Southport Division. Sadly, when leaving his office one day on Lord Street, Norman had a massive heart attack and died. Jack Watson became Detective Chief Superintendent in charge of all C.I.D. departments for Lancashire Constabulary. An interesting story was to circulate throughout the force about Jack Watson. He was interviewing for promotion at Headquarters for the position of D.S. at Seaforth. The detective constable was asked 'Do you get round the pubs in Seaforth?' The reply to this was that he did. Jack Watson then said 'Then you will know Joe Delaney.' The

Detective Sergeant hadn't a clue who Joe Delaney was and didn't get the job.

Joe Delaney was the licensee of the Caradoc Pub, situated close to the docks in Seaforth. The Caradoc was a very busy pub frequented by dockers and all sorts of drop outs/thieves and the like. It was a favourite haunt for most conscientious C.I.D. officers who were not only provided with free pints, but advised of all the criminal activities that were going on in the area. The uniform branch was also encouraged to call in at the Caradoc after closing time. Terry Woods and I would often pop in for a couple of pints after the pubs in the area had closed. For the C.I.D. there is no doubt that pub landlords were an excellent source of information. It was also a good pastime for those C.I.D. officers who enjoyed a pint or two. It was almost a requirement if one wanted to get into C.I.D. to enjoy a drink.

A certain sergeant at Seaforth Division was very fond of a drink and would often arrive on duty the worse for drink. I shall refer to this sergeant as 'sergeant x.' for reasons which are self evident. The arrangement with his wife was that if he got home after midnight, he would be locked out! I was driving the police car on the night shift when Terry Woods told me in confidence that Sergeant x was very much the worse for drink and with the night watchman at the Sausage Works. Terry was most concerned that Inspector George Ekins was out looking for the sergeant who he had suspected for some time was often on duty the worse for drink, but had never been able to catch him. It was obvious that the sergeant would be dismissed from the force if ever caught drunk on duty. I was to go to the Sausage Works and ensure that the sergeant remained there until he had sobered up.

When I arrived at the Sausage Works I hid the police car round the back, knowing that George Ekins was on the beat looking for the sergeant. I was shocked to see the sergeant. He reeked of alcohol, his eyes were glazed, his speech slurred and he was slumped in a chair rambling on incoherently. The night watchman was worried sick. I asked him to put the kettle on and make a very strong black coffee to sober him up. About 2.30am the fun started. The sergeant staggered to his feet and told me he was going to ring in from the police box by the sausage works. This was situated in the middle of a very busy junction. The thought of a police sergeant, in uniform, the worse for drink staggering across to the police box horrified me, particularly bearing in mind that George Ekins was on the prowl looking for him. I explained to the sergeant the serious nature of what he was attempting to do and that he would be dismissed from the force if George Ekins caught him in that state. However, he was determined to have his own way and attempted to leave.

I took him by the shoulders and sat him back down on the chair; he promptly staggered back up and started fighting with me, attempting to punch me, yelling incoherently to get out of his way. It can be quite comical fighting with a drunk, ducking and weaving to avoid the attempted punches. Fortunately for me, I had the advantage and was eventually able to restrain the sergeant and keep him under control until 6am; when I ran him home and dumped him off with a not very amused wife!

Terry Woods was a very likable character and certainly not your usual run of the mill police sergeant. A most memorable incident occurred when we were on night duty together on New Years Eve 1963. I was driving the section police car accompanied by Terry when we were invited to a New Years Eve party in Litherland; after all the pubs had turned out and things had settled down, we arrived at the party about 12.30am which was in full swing. I parked the police car outside the house, ensuring the car was locked and secure and rang headquarters with the message '394 - 394 - off watch Litherland, enquiries.' To which the response were guffaws of laughter from H.Q! It was pretty obvious that we were off somewhere celebrating.

We remained at this party drinking, dancing and thoroughly enjoying ourselves when Terry said it was time to leave. It was 5am and time to get back to the police station to hand over to the morning shift. We put our tunics back on, left by the front door with our arms around each others shoulders saying what a great way it had been to see the New Year in. To our horror, the police car had gone. It was nowhere in sight and we sobered up immediately. We made the decision to walk to the Green Lane sub police station, a distance of one mile to report the police car having been stolen.

The conversation on the way went along the lines of "we're going to get the sack for this. You simply don't get a police car stolen and get away with it." Terry was more concerned than me, stating that he would lose everything, his career in the police, his police house plus the fact that he was married with four children. I was still single at that time and had far less to lose than Terry. On arrival at Green Lane sub station, Terry rang Seaforth Police Station to report the car as having been stolen. 'Spider' Williams, as he was known, the duty officer answering the 'phone clearly knew what was going on and told us that he would immediately circulate to the division and surrounding forces that the police car had been stolen, advising us to start walking back to the police station and that he would arrange for the crime patrol boys to pick us up en route.

About 5.30am, walking along the main road to Seaforth; feeling dreadful about the whole situation, we heard the sound of a car horn behind us and our 'stolen' police car pulled up alongside being driven by sergeant 'x', grinning all over his face. Sat in the passenger seat was Ma Pickering, a lady who cleaned at the police station and cooked breakfast for the early morning shift. We very gratefully jumped into the back of the car and sergeant 'x' told us what had happened.

Sergeant 'x' had arrived home after midnight; having celebrated new year's eve in Southport and of course had been locked out by his wife! He decided to go straight to Seaforth Police Station and get his head down until he was on duty the following morning at 6am. The crime patrol boys (which became known as Z cars) had called in at the station to find the sergeant asleep, had woken him and suggested he accompany them in the back of their police car until he was due on duty at 6am. They had spotted our police car outside the house of the party, parked around the corner out of sight and all three had stealthily crept up to the house, peering through a gap in the curtains, watching Terry and myself enjoying ourselves dancing and drinking.

What happened next can only be described as hilarious. With a spare car key the two crime patrol lads unlocked our police car and pushed it around the corner well out of sight. All three then hid behind a hedge directly over the road from where we were enjoying ourselves. Watching us exit the house and seeing the alarm on our faces when we saw the car had gone; they were falling about laughing (as quietly as possible) at our reaction. They saw us start walking to the sub station and drove off with our police car. The tale was told around the division to hoots of laughter for some time after the event.

Chief Superintendent Jackson, the head of Seaforth Division was very aloof to the uniform policemen on the beat and it was paramount that when he drove past with his chauffer that you saluted him. He once called me up to his office and gave me a rollicking for not immediately picking up the phone when he called the switchboard whilst I was on station duty. I explained to him that I was dealing with a '999' call at the time and felt it was more important than to answer this call. He was outraged at my explanation and clearly couldn't care less about the emergency call!

It was common knowledge that the Chief Superintendent was a Freemason. He would regularly drive home from Masonic meetings under the influence of drink. On one such evening two crime patrol officers were parked on Crosby Road North about 11.30pm when the Chief Super drove past them on his way home. He was clearly under the influence of drink and hadn't even seen them (an unmarked Ford Zephyr) the two officers followed him at a safe distance and as the Chief Supers car approached the traffic lights at Cambridge Road, the traffic lights changed to red. The chief's car careered onto the offside of the road and went straight through the lights on red without stopping. Fortunately, there were no vehicles facing him at the lights on the opposite side of the road.

Unbelievably, the crime patrol lads didn't stop him but followed the car home to his house in Blundellsands. Quite remarkably the chief was able to 'aim' his car through the large stone pillars of the driveway, stop and stagger into the house. This incident became common knowledge throughout the division. I was to later speak to the driver of the crime patrol car, asking him why on earth they didn't stop the chief from driving. His answer was that they dare not stop him because of the repercussions. The chief was such a nasty individual that he would have given the two of them a dog's life and most probably have put them back on the beat.

A fatal road accident occurred in Litherland which was attended by my good friend Bob Bateson who was acting sergeant at the time. The driver of the car who was charged with causing death by dangerous driving turned out to be a personal friend of Chief Superintendent Jackson. Bob prepared a very detailed and lengthy report submitting it to Jackson with the clear recommendation that the driver be charged and taken to court. The Chief Super called Bob into his office, ripped up the file in front of Bob, throwing it into a wastepaper bin saying that the case would not go to court and that his decision was to be kept confidential.

Bob was naturally absolutely furious at this dreadful situation and went to speak with Superintendent 'Jock' Little (second in command of the division) about it. The Superintendent thought the whole affair was outrageous and told Bob to prepare the file once again, wait a couple of weeks until Jackson went on holiday and he would authorize prosecution. The case did go to court; the offender was banned from driving and given a hefty fine to pay. Bob was absolutely elated at the result. It never became known what that situation did to the relationship between Jock Little and Jackson, but one can only imagine! There was a rumour going around the division that the driver belonged to the same Masonic lodge as Jackson! This set of circumstances certainly didn't have a long term adverse effect on Bob. He went on to become a Chief Inspector at Runcorn, Cheshire, but sadly died of a massive heart attack whilst playing cricket for the Cheshire cricket team. He was bowling at the time. The sad thing was that Bob chose not to increase his police pension to cover him for up to 30 years service. As a result of this his widow received a much smaller pension than she otherwise would have done.

Bob Bateson was a unique, genuine and totally dedicated policeman. His number was 179 and it is amazing the number of times since Bob's death that the No. 179 has cropped up; each time reminding me of what a good man Bob was. He most certainly possessed 'The Common Touch.' Having served with George Eakins, there is no doubt in my mind that a lot of the Inspector's leadership and communication skills had rubbed off on Bob. As he rose through the ranks and attended social functions, before making his way to the privileged V.I.P. bar to be with the upper ranks, he would spend time with his men. Bob was a coppers copper and was never afraid to get stuck in, no matter how dangerous the situation. I was very saddened to hear of Bob's death.

Night duty could be very tedious after all the pubs had turned out and domestic disputes dealt with. The worst times were between 3am to 5am when boredom and tiredness would set in. This was where one used ones initiative i.e. because we were limited to a certain mileage on the police car; the drivers' in the section discovered a means of disconnecting the Speedo. This was great and enabled us to drive out of the Seaforth section as far as

Southport, which was a borough force in those days. How on earth this dodge was not discovered I will never know. The mileage returns must never have been checked!

The oddest thing was that Seaforth section was responsible for all crime that was committed in the Albert Dock, in spite of the fact that Liverpool City Police controlled the whole of the seven miles of docks. During the early hours of one morning (about 2.45am) three of us drove into the Albert Dock when the 'Windsor Castle' was in the dry dock, booking off watch with the usual corny excuse of enquiries. We were given the most glorious guided tour around this wonderful ocean going liner by one of the night security men. The highlight of the tour was standing on the captain's bridge looking down to the bottom of the Albert Dock. The height was unimaginable.

Keith Hulme was a fellow P.C. at Seaforth and an absolute nut case! But nevertheless good fun. He owned a 2.2 air rifle and when on nights together we would occasionally go down to the local tip in the police car with his rifle, shooting rats. Imagine the scene with Keith driving with the headlights on full beam picking out these huge rats, me standing up with the passenger door open shooting them. We'd then swop over and it would be Keith's turn.

Two other fun things on nights with the police car were to drive down Hatton Hill Road in Litherland, towards the town hall. The road sloped downwards in that direction. The trick was to hold your speed about 45m.p.h. turn the ignition off momentarily and switch it back on. The result was an almighty, really loud bang from the exhaust pipe. It must have frightened the residents to death. When the roads were wet, another great pass time was to deliberately throw the police car into a skid and to control it around traffic islands. The best policeman ever for skid control was Jack Wareing. He frightened the living daylights out of me one early morning, literally throwing the police car around an island at an unbelievable speed. Jack was one of the original crime patrol 'Z' car drivers, eventually transferring to H.Q. Hutton as a police driving instructor.

# 4

## Sudden Deaths

One of the more unpleasant duties at Seaforth Division was dealing with sudden deaths. I've lost count of the number which I dealt with. Many of them were very upsetting and quite emotional to deal with. Probably the saddest was a little girl by the name of Paula Stirk who was 3 years of age and was killed in a road accident. Paula's mother was walking along Linacre Road, Seaforth, holding her 18 month child with her left hand. Paula was holding onto a shopping basket in her mother's right hand. Mrs. Stirk stopped at a junction when she saw a Trinidad Lake Asphalt lorry coming towards her with it's indicator on to turn right in front of her. Without warning, little Paula suddenly let go of the shopping basket and ran right into the path of the lorry as it was entering the junction. The lorry ran right over Paula killing her outright. I accompanied the ambulance with Paula's body to the mortuary and was to later attend the post mortem and the inquest. Whilst this sudden death was very traumatic, it was the only sudden death involving a child which I had to deal with as a single man. Whilst this was emotionally very difficult to handle; later, as a married man with three young children, it's now unimaginable what the impact would have been on me.

An elderly man had died of emphysema which had been caused by heavy smoking. When the pathologist had taken out the lungs from the body on the mortuary slab, they were black and quite disgusting. The pathologist said to me "This is what heavy smokers can look forward to." I've often quoted that experience to heavy smokers, but of course they just bury their heads in the sand. A fortnight after this experience a very attractive 19 year old girl committed suicide by drowning in the river Mersey. I dealt with this sudden death and the same pathologist said to me "remember the man's lungs a fortnight ago? the lungs of this young girl are healthy and pink just as they should be."

At the age of 24 years, I was carrying out the duties of Acting Sergeant, driving the section police car accompanied by a 20 year old probationer by the name of John. The time was 1.45pm on a Friday and I was looking forward to finishing at 2pm and a long weekend off i.e. Saturday and Sunday off, returning for my next tour of duty at 10pm on the Monday. I was not at all amused when H.Q. called "394,394 to Manor Road, Seaforth, man committed suicide." When we arrived at the house, an elderly woman was stood outside the front door, white as a sheet and trembling, pointing behind her with a look of horror on her face towards her husband who had hung himself over the stairwell. I arranged for the next door neighbour to come in and brew up for her whilst John and I dealt with the body.

It's not a pretty sight looking at someone who has been hung. Tongue black and sticking out, eyes wide open and staring. The man was clearly dead but still warm. John was very nervous indeed. He had never seen a body before let alone attend a sudden death. I said to John "As I lift the body up, remove the noose from his neck and keep it intact for the coroner." As I lifted the body, the head of the man landed on my shoulder, with the ghastly sight of his face next to mine. I laid him down on the landing on his back and by this time poor young John was terrified. I decided to have a bit of fun and lighten up the situation saying to John "Quick John, no time to waste – mouth to mouth respiration." Poor John didn't know what to do and had turned green, shaking like crazy. When I started to laugh he realized that I was winding him up and called me all the names under the sun. Obviously, this was said quietly so that the bereaved lady couldn't hear.

Whilst it may sound callous and uncaring to joke in such circumstances, the very nature of dealing with that type of sudden death could seriously affect your mental stability and confidence. Many young policemen attending their first post mortem have been known to faint or throw up. It's not a pretty sight to see a body being cut up. Fortunately for me, I was introduced to my first post mortem where a very elderly lady had died in a nursing home in Waterloo. She had had a good and long life but it seemed so sad that a P.M. had been necessary in that instance.

The boundary with Bootle Borough Police on Linacre Road cut right though the houses i.e. dividing the front lounge from the back kitchens. The kitchens were in Bootle Borough and the lounges Lancs/Seaforth Section. I was called to a sudden death by Bootle Borough Police in that street where a man had died in the lounge. It was my responsibility to deal with the sudden death. On another occasion, a further sudden death in the same street occurred whilst I was on duty. When I arrived I found the body of a man to be in the kitchen and it gave me great pleasure to hand it back to Bootle Police to deal with. I quoted my Granddad to colleague's about the Preston Borough Policeman and the horse, joking that Bootle Borough had dragged the body from the kitchen into the lounge in order that Lancs County should deal with the sudden death!

It's never pleasant having to deal with sudden death. A young housewife was preparing breakfast for her two young children one morning, had put her hand up to her head and fallen down onto the kitchen floor to die of cerebral hemorrage. This was one of many sudden deaths I dealt with which involves taking statements off witnesses, family re: past health etc. I was told by Ike Whittaker, an experienced long serving sergeant, not to use the phrase in my statements that 'he/she enjoyed good health.' The reason being logically that the person may have had good health but had not necessarily 'enjoyed' it!

A lady came into the police station late one evening, very concerned that she had called at her father's house on her weekly visit. She had a front door key but couldn't open the door. Looking through the letter box she could see what appeared to be her father's jacket behind the door and feared the worst. I accompanied her to the house and found the situation just as she had explained. I asked the lady for approval to break into the house; went round the back and smashed the rear kitchen window with my truncheon. I climbed through the window and on going into the hall saw the ladies father slumped against the back of the front door looking up. The most amazing thing was to see him with his eyes wide open with a big smile on his face! He'd been out drinking with his pals, managed to open the door with his key and died as soon as he had entered the house. I didn't disturb the body, went round to the front and invited the daughter in; telling her that sadly her father had died, but that she must see him where he lay. The daughter was very distraught and in tears when she saw her father, but fortunately I was able console her saying what a wonderful way it was for him to die with a smile on his face. I quoted to her an oft used statement of mine that "I'm not afraid of dying; I just don't want to be there when it happens"!

Sergeant Albert Cunliffe was an old timer and approaching retirement with thirty years of service under his belt. He was my duty sergeant one day when I was driving the section police car.

We received a call from H.Q. that a body had been seen floating in the canal in Litherland. On arrival at the scene we found a middle aged female floating face down in the canal, close to a small bridge. There were several young boys on the bridge watching us deal with the body. Albert Cunliffe yelled at them to disperse but one cocky young lad insisted on staying to watch. We dragged the body out of the canal with great difficulty, turning it onto its back; it was a pretty gruesome sight. Bodies which have been immersed in water for some time become very bloated, but fortunately this body had not yet started to decompose. We heard a thud from the direction of the bridge to see that cocky young lad had fainted at the sight of the body. Serve him right!

The body was taken by the local undertaker to the mortuary, situated close to the lift bridge and adjacent to the canal. The post mortem had been arranged for that evening. I arrived at the mortuary some quarter of an hour before the pathologist was due. It was dark at the time and having attended previous post mortems at this mortuary, knew that the light switch oddly enough was situated at the far end of the mortuary. I therefore had to shine my torch to locate the switch, passing the body on the mortuary slab which was covered in the usual white sheet. This was quite a scary experience, to be in the pitch black with my torch illuminating this rather morbid scene. Having put the light on, I removed the sheet covering the body and got quite a shock. The body which had been very bloated; had reduced considerably in size to a point that it looked like a completely different person. The pathologist carried out the post mortem in my presence. The result was drowning through suicide.

There is no doubt that the most frightening experience I ever had as a policeman on Merseyside was during the early hours of the morning. I was on my own driving the section police car around 2.30am, when a call came through to attend a domestic dispute in Seaforth. Incredibly, I was the only policeman available to attend to the call with no one at all to call for assistance. A very violent man lived at the house with his mother. He had convictions for assault on police, drunk and disorderly and had served time for these offences. I had no choice but to attend on my own.

On arrival at the house I knocked on the door and it was opened by the man's mother. She was terrified and invited me in. Her son, a big powerfully built docker was in the kitchen at the far end of a long narrow corridor. As soon as he saw me he went berserk, picked up a large carving knife, charging at me shouting and screaming abuse, telling me to get out of the house. I asked him to calm down as I was sure that he was going to stab me with the carving knife. However, as he reached me he threw the knife past me towards the closed front door, opened the front door, came back to me grabbing hold of either side of the collar of my tunic, lifted me off my feet, carrying me to the front door where he threw me out onto the path, slamming the door behind me. I fell over the front gate, completely out of breath.

This incident occurred at a time when I was seriously considering leaving the force for reasons which I shall explain later. I knew that I was not able to arrest the man on my own, so decided to carry out a course of action of which I am not particularly proud. We're talking here of a despicable 'scouser' with a criminal record who was detested by all the neighbours'. Many of these neighbours' had been disturbed by the commotion and were watching from their front windows.

When eventually I got my breath back, I drew my truncheon and hammered on the front door, hoping that the man who had attacked me would open it. Fortunately, he did open the door but I was too quick for him. I drove my truncheon as hard as I could into his stomach, he doubled up and as he did so I grabbed both of his ears and hair and smashed his head down onto my knee, breaking his nose. He fell on the floor where I kicked him unmercifully in the ribs. Not surprisingly, his mother applauded me for what I had done and said it was about time someone stood up to him. As I opened the door of the police car to drive away from the house, several neighbours' that had seen it all were clapping and applauding me for dealing with this despicable neighbour.

The man ended up in hospital. I knew that even if I had been able to arrest this man, the particular Inspector who would have been called out was not only afraid of his own shadow, but would simply not have approved of the way I had dealt with this situation. He would certainly not have allowed the case to go to court. Can you imagine me in the witness box saying to the magistrates' "your worships – this man kept beating his head on my fists"! Not surprisingly this nasty individual made no complaint as to my treatment of him.

# 5

## Love at First Sight

The second of January, 1962 will forever be indelibly imprinted on my mind. This was the date I met my lovely wife Lynn. For the past few weeks I had seen Lynn walking home from Seaforth Railway Station towards Litherland about 5.50pm. I was determined to meet this gorgeous very attractive girl, a tall blonde with blue/green eyes. It was love at first sight. I parked the police car at the end of a row of army houses off Hawthorne Road, Litherland, facing the direction in which Lynn would be walking towards, little realising that Lynn would have to pass me to get to her home, No 6, M.Q. (married quarters.)

It was quite cold that early evening of January and snowing lightly. Lynn was walking straight towards me wearing a green coat with a cream woolly hat. I couldn't believe my luck. I wound down the window of the police car and simply sat there grinning like a Cheshire cat as Lynn approached. Amazingly, Lynn was the first to speak saying "Are you parked here for the night?" Before I could reply Lynn carried on walking to No. 6. Wow! That really made my day and I was determined to be there at the same time the following evening.

The following evening, Lynn arrived home about the same time, with me sitting in the police car once again. Lynn stopped and spoke with me, telling me that she was going to a dance at Litherland Town Hall that evening. I invited her to get into the passenger seat of the police car but she declined! We arranged to meet at the town hall following my refreshment break back at the police station.

I arrived at the town hall parking the police car by the entrance, booking off with H.Q. with the usual message "394/394 off watch, Litherland Town Hall – enquiries"! The dancing was in full swing when Lynn spotted me in the entrance and came out to speak with me. I stood there in uniform having taken off my flat cap. Lynn was clearly a little embarrassed and was actually blushing slightly. We chatted for a while and arranged to meet the following evening which was my day off. Lynn said she would like to go to the local cinema to watch Elvis Presley in the film Kid Galahad. We sat on the back row of the cinema holding hands.

Lynn was seventeen years of age when we met, I was 22. (My colleague's said it was cradle snatching!) Her family had moved from Hong Kong to Liverpool, an army posting. Lynn's father 'Pat' was a Battery Sergeant Major in the Royal Artillery based at the time at Seaforth Barracks. Lynn's mother and her two brothers also lived at the army house in Litherland. It was quite bizarre to learn that after proposing to Lynn, her very good friend Anne Hiatt had said to Lynn "You'll marry Bob." That was whilst they were working together at a shipping agency in Liverpool; the day after we had met!

Twenty months after meeting, Lynn and I were married at St Philips Church, Litherland; on the 22$^{nd}$ August, 1964. The most bizarre situation arose before the wedding when my future father-in-law somehow managed to get hold of my new black pair of shoe's to be worn for the wedding. He bulled up by spit and polishing the right shoe, handing them back to me with the left shoe unpolished! I considered this to be some form of control. I was quite capable of putting as good a shine on the left shoe and made the mistake of doing so. I should have handed the other shoe back to him to also bull up! We spent our two weeks honeymoon at a hotel in Jersey, close to Mont Orgueil Castle, Gorey. My eldest sister Anne and brother-in-law Johnney were posted abroad at the time with the RAF and planned to move to Jersey on Johnny's retirement after 22 years service with the RAF.

We were shortly to be allocated accommodation in the police house 13 Brookfield Avenue, Waterloo, Liverpool. This was to be our first house following a short period in a first floor flat in Walmer Road, Waterloo. Whilst on honeymoon, I made enquiries about the Jersey police force and arranged to meet with the Chief Constable. Lynn and I met with the chief and after lengthy discussions I decided to transfer to the Jersey force. All that was required was for me to provide a satisfactory medical report from my doctor. This clearly would not have been a problem. We even went to look at the block of flats where we would be accommodated following the transfer to the Jersey police force. However, after much consideration, we eventually decided not to go ahead with the move to Jersey; in order to be more supportive of my mother and in particular in view of the following situation:

Six months after Lynn and I were married; Lynn received a telephone call at work from her eldest brother Patrick. He was very nervous about the call, telling Lynn that my younger sister Linda was pregnant and that he was to be the father of the child. He wanted Lynn to break the news to me before meeting up with me at our police house in Waterloo and was naturally very concerned about how I would react. Both Lynn and I were clearly shocked at receiving the news, realising the implications of the way both families were to be affected.

By the time Patrick called to meet with Lynn and myself, I had come to terms with the news and discussed the situation with Patrick, asking for his views as to his responsibilities should Linda go ahead with the pregnancy, giving birth to the child. Both Linda and Patrick had made the decision not to marry. Friends of Linda had suggested a possible abortion, but that situation was to be totally unacceptable to both Linda and my mother who was very supportive indeed and encouraged Linda to go full term and give birth to the child. Anthony was born on the 23rd September, 1965 and was to be brought up jointly by Linda and my mother in his formative years at her home in Preston.

It proved to be very difficult bringing Anthony up in mother's small bungalow, particularly as my Grandma Rigby was to stay with mother for a period of six months every year. There were four generations under one roof. However, it was to be a joy for Linda and mother, in spite of the difficulties. We lived just around the corner from mother's bungalow and Lynn would regularly assist by taking Anthony out for long walks with our own children.

Tony went on to gain a degree at Cambridge University. Linda later met and married John who made an excellent father for Tony and has always considered him equal to their two further children. Tony is now a big strapping lad, married with two children of his own and living in Wanaka, South Island, New Zealand. He is self employed as a computer programmer, living in his own beautiful detached house overlooking the lake in Wanaka.

A certain Inspector at Seaforth, to whom I shall refer to as Inspector 'x', was not only frightened of his own shadow but was also a coward. My colleague's simply couldn't stand the man and hated being on duty with him on the same shift. He wasn't prepared to back up any of us when a particularly difficult situation arose. I crossed swords with him on two occasions with particularly difficult arrests. The first of these situations was a call to a house in Seaforth where a violent man was terrorizing his wife and children. Fortunately for me, I was accompanied at the time by Paddy, a big strapping Irish lad. (Halt sign Paddy)! As I drove up to the house and before we could get out of the police car, the front lounge window was smashed by a pram being thrown at it from the inside of the house. The front door was open and we could hear the man inside shouting all sorts of threats and abuse at his wife. The children in the house were terrified and screaming.

Without any hesitation I went straight into the house with Paddy following. The man was in the kitchen with his wife who was cowering against the wall, He was totally out of control throwing whatever he could get hold of around the kitchen. He calmed down a little when he saw us. I told him I was very concerned for the safety of his wife and children and that he was being arrested for his own safety and that of his family. At this point he became very violent attacking Paddy and myself. We had a dreadful struggle getting the handcuffs on him but eventually handcuffed him with his hands behind his back.

The police car was directly outside the front door. As we got the man to the front gate, he momentarily broke free from us and kicked as hard as he could at the rear nearside of the police car, denting the door quite badly. By this time neighbours and passers by had congregated by the front door and were booing and jeering us, with one of them spitting at us. We bungled the man into the back seat with Paddy sitting on him. On arrival at the police station we took him straight to the cells. Terry Woods was the duty Sergeant and came into the cell with Paddy and myself. As soon as I removed the man's handcuffs, he turned around quickly and punched me in the stomach. I fell to the floor winded. Terry shouted for assistance and two more of my colleague's came into the cell and gave the man a thorough hiding before searching him, removing the usual items like his belt and other possessions.

Inspector 'x' sat in his office during all the commotion, even though it was within earshot of the cells. The Inspector called me into his office saying "What are the circumstances of this arrest P.C. Mynett?" I explained to him in detail what had happened, then the next question was "Did you ask the man you arrested for permission to go into the house?" I considered this to be a stupid question from a senior officer and when I said "No" I was absolutely flabbergasted when he said that I had had no power of arrest in the circumstances. He then went on to tell me that he would be prosecuting in court the next day and that he would not mention in his evidence that I had been assaulted in the cells.

I was furious with the Inspector and said that had I not intervened, it was quite possible that a serious injury or even a fatality could have occurred, thereby leaving myself open to disciplinary action for neglect of duty. The man pleaded guilty in court the next day and of course Inspector 'x' didn't mention my being punched in the stomach in the cell. The defendant got off with a pathetic judgment from the Magistrates'. I was not particularly surprised to hear during the court proceedings, that the defendant had been a soldier in the British Army and had boxed for the army! No wonder we'd had difficulty in arresting the man.

The second incident involving this Inspector occurred when I was driving the police car on nights (10pm – 6am) He decided to accompany me after parading on at 10pm. What happened next can only be described as 'pathetic' and typical of the man. As he got into the passenger seat he deliberately didn't close the door properly, clearly trying to catch me out. I asked him to close the door before we set off. About 10.45pm a call came through that a drunk was in the middle of Linacre Road holding up all the traffic. I acknowledged that we would attend and on arrival, a large group of people were gathered around this drunk who was in the middle of the road, waving his arms about and entertaining quite a large crowd.

Traffic had stopped in both directions unable to get through. I parked in a side street and incredibly the Inspector said to me "Go and see what that man's doing P.C. Mynett.'" My reply was to the effect that it was pretty obvious what he was doing, getting out of the car to deal with the situation. The Inspector clearly had no intention of getting out of the car. When I asked him to assist he replied "I'll stay in the car and listen to the radio." (Meaning H.Q.) I was disgusted with the Inspector's attitude but had no option but to deal with the situation on my own.

I had to push my way through the crowd to get to the man. He was quite drunk, facing away from me. My thoughts were, 'crikey! Here's a guy as tall as me but twice as broad, here goes.' I tapped the man on the shoulder and as he turned round and saw the uniform, he went absolutely berserk; lashing out at me. After a bit of ducking and weaving I managed to trip him up, turn him onto his stomach and with great difficulty get my handcuffs onto his left wrist.

On reflection, I have to smile at the circumstances. The crowd was cheering the drunk wanting him to get the better of me and that's exactly what happened. I was so exhausted that the drunk managed to get to his feet and was swinging at me with both fists with the handcuffs flying through the air. He caught me a couple of times on my body, by which time I was getting very worried. Without warning, two big blokes pushed through the crowd and I thought 'oh no - this is it'! However, the two of them pulled the drunk off me, secured the loose handcuff on his free wrist and frog marched him to the police car where the Inspector was still sitting in the passenger seat. I staggered along behind them to see them throw the drunk into the back of the police car, thumping him at the same time. I wasn't close enough to hear what these two guys said to the Inspector, but it was clearly verbal abuse at their disgust, seeing him simply sitting there.

The two men took me to one side and told me that they were off duty Liverpool City Policemen. They had been playing water polo for the police and were on their way home when they had come across the crowd. They told me in no uncertain terms of their disgust seeing the Inspector sitting there not coming to my assistance. They said I should report the man for neglect of duty and would be more than happy to back me up and provide the necessary statements. I thanked them most profusely for their assistance, but foolishly didn't take up their offer to take proceedings against this cowardly Inspector, telling them that I was very dissatisfied with the job and had already considered resigning.

As I sit at my computer putting this on record, I simply cannot believe that I didn't go ahead with an official complaint. This was the second occasion I had crossed swords with this pathetic Inspector. Back in 1964, it would not have been the thing to do i.e. making a complaint of this nature regarding a senior officer. Had I known then what know now, I should have taken the matter further, but hey ho, you can't put an old head on young shoulders! Both Ted Bentham and George Ekins would have come to my assistance in a situation of that nature. They would have been horrified to hear of the cowardly way the Inspector had sat in the car watching all that was happening. There is no doubt at all that had those two off duty Liverpool policemen not come to my assistance, I would have ended up in hospital with serious injuries, not one of the bystanders would have intervened.

Sylvia was a young lady who operated the switchboard at Seaforth Police Station. She had a very good sense of humour and told me one day how she hated mice. One early evening, it was my responsibility to take the prisoners out of their cells individually, for exercise in a long, quite narrow purpose built very high walled yard at the back of the cells. This particular prisoner having walked about for some five minutes; suddenly ran the full length of the yard and stamped on something by the end wall. I wondered what on earth he was doing. It turned out that he had seen a mouse and stamped on it, killing it. I took the prisoner back to his cell, locked him up and had a bright idea. I went back into the exercise yard and picked up the dead mouse by its tale. It was quite a large mouse.

Putting the mouse behind my back I went into the office where Sylvia was sat at the switchboard. As I approached her, she could tell from the expression on my face that I was up to something. I slowly brought the mouse round to show Sylvia. It was a pretty gruesome sight hanging there by it's tale between my thumb and forefinger, with one of its eyes hanging out of its head. I'll never forget the look of absolute horror on Sylvia's face. She started to scream in terror. I didn't quite expect such a reaction. In no time at all there were policemen running into the office from all directions to see what was going on. George Ekins was one of the first to arrive, his office being very close by. The Inspector saw the funny side but had no alternative than to give me a warning not to frighten anyone again to that extent whilst on duty at the station. Sylvia eventually forgave me telling me it was such a rotten trick knowing how afraid she was of mice.

In 1965 at the age of twenty five, I finally made the decision to resign from the force after eight years of service, which included eighteen months as a cadet on dog section. Had I continued, I could have retired at the age of forty four with a pension. I had reached a stage where I considered that there were far better prospects ahead for me. Furthermore, at that time it wasn't possible to purchase one's own house and that was to be a further deciding factor. On receipt of my resignation, the then Chief Superintendent, Ronny Booth, called me into his office and spent an hour trying his best to dissuade me from resigning. I remained adamant that I would leave. The Chief Super finally gave up and told me I would be back in no time at all to continue my career with the force. This was not to be the case. It was many years later that I was to meet up with Ronny Booth once again. I met with him in his office at divisional H.Q. at Preston as a brewery area manager with Tetley's.

# 6

## Telehire Limited

Lynn and I decided to return to my home town of Preston; following my resignation from Lancashire Constabulary. We were very fortunate to be able to buy a new house in Arnold Close, Ribbleton, close to my mother Florence, who had moved to a bungalow in Arnold Close from Grey Gables. The Halifax Building Society provided a mortgage, but with the proviso that we had a guarantor. The semi detached house was £3,800, whereas the average semi in those days was in the region of £2,800. My mother stood as guarantor to enable us to purchase the property. We were clearly very grateful for the support.

The properties in Arnold Close had been built on the site of a former convent. The close had been named after Arnold R Duckett who had purchased the convent building as head office for his company Telehire Ltd. Bernard Watson, the builder had purchased the remainder of the land to build houses. As a boy I can remember sitting on the top of a double decker bus en route to work at Goss Foster's, looking at the convent through a mass of tree's which always seemed to have rooks making a dreadful racket. They had built their nests in the top of the trees.

Lynn had obtained a full time job as secretary to the sales director of Telehire, Brian Crabtree and was conveniently able to simply cross over from our home to head office. I had also successfully applied for employment with Telehire, a T.V. rental company and retailer of white goods (washing machines/Hoovers etc.) and was initially based at their Preston retail outlet as a trainee branch manager. During this training period a meeting was called at the Lamb Hotel on Church Street, Preston. It was at this meeting that I first had an encounter with Arnold Duckett, Chairman and Managing Director of Telehire. On arrival at the pub I saw the Chairman's car parked outside, a Rolls Royce with the registration No. ARD 1. Wow! was I impressed! Arnold Duckett addressed the meeting and I shall never forget his words. In a broad Lancashire accent he introduced himself and said 'When I was fourteen I started sellin pullets on Blackburn Market.' He then went on to tell us how he had formed the company with his first branch in Blackburn.

Whilst living in Arnold Close and some 2 years following our marriage, Lynn announced in sheer delight that she was pregnant; she was still working at Telehire at the time. Lynn's pregnancy had the oddest effect on me; I would wake up in the early hours of the morning absolutely ravenous, go into the kitchen and prepare two boiled eggs, accompanied by two slices of brown bread and butter with a cup of tea which I would really enjoy. I was able therefore to go back to bed and sleep. This strange effect on me was to occur with Lynn's two further pregnancies! So, strangely, it was me who had the funnies rather than Lynn. Apparently this is not unusual!

We had no idea at the time as to whether the baby would be a boy or a girl. Lynn was admitted to Preston Royal Infirmary and I accompanied her to the hospital, to be told that I would not be allowed into the delivery room to support Lynn during the birth. I was flabbergasted, but that was the procedure at the time. Lynn gave birth to our first child, a beautiful baby girl who was baptised Karen Louise.

We were so fortunate to have two further children whilst living in Arnold Close. Lynn gave birth to Mark Jeffrey in the downstairs bedroom with a Quaker midwife in attendance during the long 17 hours of labour. During much of the time I was at the bedside holding Lynn's hand. As the head was delivered I exclaimed "it's a boy" and sure enough it was! Alison Dawn was also born in Preston Royal Infirmary whilst I was present at the bedside supporting Lynn. I will never live down the fact that I was sat at the bedside eating two boiled eggs with bread and butter immediately prior to the birth! I blame myself that Alison has never enjoyed or eaten eggs in any shape or form since then! Talk about the power of transference! Lynn would have loved to have two further children, but the thought of having 5 children to bring up was simply not on as far as I was concerned. We agreed to settle on 3!

Arnold Duckett was a brilliant communicator and most certainly blessed with 'The Common Touch.' He was a down to earth man and encouraged all employees from the top down to the caretaker and cleaners. On arrival at Head Office he would acknowledge all employees, speaking with them on their own level. I had a great deal of respect for Arnold Duckett. George Gallon, a director with the company, had been a director of Hoover and was in overall charge of training, assisted by Keith Austin who ran the training from an upper room at head office.

George Gallon had been brought into the company, essentially to work alongside and train Arnold Duckett's son Keith; to eventually take over the running of the business. The head office building, formerly a convent was reputed to be haunted. A former nun, who had been named Rebecca, had been seen by several employees of Telehire, floating around the building in a long white dress. Whilst Lynn had never seen this apparition, she did comment that it seemed most odd when using the loo, imagining that nuns had formerly used the toilets when the building was a convent. The body of the ghost Rebecca was allegedly buried in the cemetery immediately behind Telehire head office, adding more street cred. to the story.

Following my basic training at the Church Street branch in Preston, I took over the Southport branch as Manager. I was provided with a Telehire van for travelling to work which I would use for occasionally delivering Hoover cleaners and televisions to households in the area. Following a period of some seven months at Southport and having achieved good sales figures, I was asked to transfer to the Morecambe branch. There were major problems with the Morecambe branch. I had been sent there by management to clear up a horrendous problem of debt. There were customers who owed considerably large amounts of rent on TV's and washing machines and had simply stopped paying anything whatsoever. In many cases as long as twelve months rent was due. The previous manager had only been interested in selling and renting products to increase his commission. He couldn't care less about the debts.

As an ex policeman I found my experience most helpful. On more than one occasion I had to put my foot in the door to stop debtors' slamming the door in my face. I would go out in the evenings collecting debts, on which I was able to claim seven and a half percent commission. It became obvious that I was totally unable to reduce the debts satisfactorily on my own and appointed two collectors' to assist. One of the most difficult experiences I had with overdue accounts was a family in Heysham. They had a large television on rental and hadn't paid any rent whatsoever for a period of eighteen months. I arrived early one evening to find all the family at home and had difficulty in gaining entrance to the house.

Once inside, I saw that the 26" television in the lounge was in use. The householder, an obnoxious man refused point blank to pay off the outstanding debt. I told him that I had therefore no alternative than to remove the set. As I walked towards the T.V. to disconnect it, the man struck me across the face with the flat of his hand. At this point, the wife and two sons' surrounded me to stop me retaliating. I had no alternative than to leave the house without the television, threatening to take court action for assault. One of the riggers at the Morecambe branch was known as little Jimmy. I spoke with him about the difficulty I had experienced and my unsuccessful attempt to remove the T.V. Jimmy went along to the house one evening when it was dark, and cut out one inch from the coax television lead situated outside the rear of the house. Sure enough, the following day, obnoxious man rang to say the T.V. was faulty. Jimmy went along and was able to disconnect the set without any problem, stating that it had to be taken in for repair. I didn't consider it to be worth the hassle taking this man to court for assault. I was quite happy that this disconnection resulted in a large percentage decrease in the branch's debts.

Another evening call to Heysham resulted in my removing a T.V. from a council house. This was just before Christmas and I felt so guilty over those circumstances. The lady at the house invited me in. Her two young daughters were watching the television which had Christmas cards and decorations on the top. I pointed out the fact that no rent had been paid for some ten months and that she had not responded to my many letters. The lady told me that she was in a desperate situation with finances and simply could not pay off anything whatever. I therefore had no alternative than to remove the T.V. The girls were in tears as I removed Christmas cards and decorations off the television, taking the set from the house. I felt really dreadful having to disconnect that set.

I shall never forget disconnecting a Hoover Keymatic washing machine from a house in Morecambe. The debt which had accumulated over a period of time was outrageous. Little Jimmy came along with me to assist lifting the washing machine into the Telehire van. From arriving at the house to leaving with the machine must have been at least two hours. The debtor was a woman of at least twenty stone in weight. She clearly couldn't care less about not having made a single payment in rent since delivery and her initial deposit. When I went to disconnect the washing machine from the mains, she pushed me on one side and sat on top of the washer, refusing to move. Jimmy and I tried not to laugh in that hilarious situation. So, plan 'B' went into operation. I said to Jimmy "Go round to the police station and tell D.C. Jones that as expected we're having difficulty with removing this Keymatic." (There was no such person as D.C. Jones!). Jimmy left the house and simply went round the corner, lit up a cigarette and waited some twenty minutes before returning. In his absence I told the woman that I would rather avoid taking her to debtor's court, avoiding the adverse publicity. Jimmy returned to the house stating that D.C. Jones was on his way to arrest the woman (as if!). Following further persuasion, the woman heaved herself off the machine and allowed us to remove it; yet another large amount of debt to be removed from the Morecambe Branch.

I gained quite a reputation in Telehire for my success in reducing debt. As a result, the Managing Director of the company Keith Duckett, took me out to lunch at the Bull and Royal Hotel in Preston in appreciation for all my hard work. I was asked to transfer from the Morecambe branch to take over the Blackburn branch. This was the very first retail outlet where Arnold Duckett had started the company, a far bigger branch than either Southport or Morecambe. Blackburn was far closer than the Morecambe branch and entailed far less travelling.

The very first colour televisions had been launched whilst I ran the Blackburn branch. I was asked by George Gallon and Keith Austin in the training department if I would consider undergoing training, to present and demonstrate on behalf of the company the principles of colour T.V. I jumped at the opportunity and following a training period became one of the first persons in the North West to organise and arrange demonstrations of this completely new era where black and white TV's were to become redundant. The very first event which I organised was at the Five Barred Gate Pub and Restaurant, a large venue on the outskirts of Preston. About 120 dignitaries and local business men attended, including the Mayor of Preston and the Chief Superintendent of police.

Telehire Ltd was probably one of the first companies in Preston to install a computer system. It goes without saying that there were initially major problems occurring on a regular basis. A very amusing situation arose following my signing up a lady for a colour T.V. for a twelve month period. Having paid an initial deposit, the agreement was sent off to Head Office for processing in the computer department. Some three weeks later a very irate lady came into the branch asking to see the manager. When this lady showed me an arrears letter amounting to several thousand pounds, I couldn't avoid bursting out laughing, explaining that there was clearly a mistake. It transpired that a girl in the computer department had misread the date of the agreement; instead of dating it for 1967 she had dated it for 1907! The computer had backdated the rent for 60 years. Fortunately, the complainant saw the funny side and accepted my apologies on behalf of the company. As an employee of Telehire Ltd, it was becoming progressively more apparent that I would not be satisfied with long term employment with the company. I desperately wanted to get into selling proper to further my experience. I had identified a national company whereby I could progress in a career of selling with better prospects of promotion. This would have the advantages of a company car, expense account etc. Following several interviews for sales representative positions, I was told in no uncertain terms that my experience as a branch manager in T.V. rental was not adequate for the positions available.

A tragic situation arose whilst I was working at Telehire. During the early hours of the morning Lynn's younger brother Paul had rung my mother saying that he needed to speak to me as a matter of urgency. He didn't want to ring us directly. On arrival at my mother's home I rang Paul who told me that his brother Patrick had been killed in a car crash. He gave me brief details of the circumstances and I returned home to break the dreadful news to Lynn. Lynn screamed and cried at the dreadful news that her elder brother had been killed. Patrick was 24 years of age and had qualified as a quantity surveyor. He was a single man; his younger brother Paul, 17 years of age was living with him at Dorincourt, a large detached property in London where six friends had shared rooms. Patrick had purchased a Volvo saloon car which unknown to him had a spare tyre which did not match those fitted to the car i.e. the four tyres fitted front and back were radial, the spare was a cross ply. A puncture occurred on the front offside tyre and Patrick not realising that the spare didn't match, replaced the front offside damaged tyre with the cross ply spare. He was driving along on his own in a derestricted area, about 65 miles per hour when a blow out occurred on the front offside tyre. Patrick lost control of the car, swerving to his offside and collided head on with a car travelling in the opposite direction. The male driver of the other car was alone; he and Patrick were killed outright. Patrick was a real entrepreneur and I have no doubt that had he lived, he would have gone on to become a very successful and wealthy businessman.

Lynn's parents were based at the rocket base in Woomera, Australia, an army posting at the time of Patrick's death. They were given compassionate leave to return home. Lynn and I met her parents at Heathrow Airport and together with Lynn's parents made the necessary arrangements for the funeral. Following an inquest into the circumstances of the accident a cremation was held at Mortlake Crematorium; situated in eight acres of beautifully landscaped gardens on the south bank of the river Thames. It goes without saying the devastating impact the sudden death of Lynn's parents eldest son had on all the family.

I was very fortunate indeed to see an advertisement by 'The National School of Salesmanship' based in St. Anne's Square, Manchester. (No longer in existence) This training company offered a most unique written guarantee to the effect that following successful completion of their course, they would arrange as many interviews as was necessary to secure a satisfactory selling job to their clients. I signed up for the course, much to the consternation of Lynn who said "We could afford to buy a new television with what this course is going to cost." However, it proved to be a brilliant investment with the resultant success for my long term career prospects. Following six months only with the course, I was advised that I had progressed satisfactorily and the training company were prepared to start arranging appointments for me.

The very first interview which the National School of Salesmanship arranged was most amazing and was to secure a long term 18 year career in the brewing industry. This appointment was surprisingly with the managing director of Ind Coope Northern, the parent company of the then Allied Breweries, the biggest drinks combine at the time; in Europe. I arrived at the head office of the company on Quay Street, Manchester, in my best suit with shoes bulled up and was shown into the office of Bernard Frost, the Managing Director fondly known as 'Jack Frost.' He was accompanied by Henry Stark the Sales Manager of Ind Coope. I was advised that I was being interviewed for the position of sales representative for Ind Coope Northern whose main product was

Draught Double Diamond. If successful, I would be based at the Blackpool Office. The job involved calling on all free trade outlets in Blackpool and surrounding areas. My interview was successful and clearly when asked if I would accept the position I jumped at the opportunity. Lucky old me! The oddest question on reflection was Bernard Frost asking me "Do you enjoy a drink?" I could hardly say no could I! Bernard Frost advised me that it was the very first time as M.D. that he had carried out an interview of this nature, also that I was the first person ever to be referred to him by the National School of Salesmanship. Normally, the personnel department carried out initial interviews. Arrangements were made for me to meet with Gordon Nelson, the free trade area manager for the Blackpool area who was to be my boss. The M.D. told me that Gordon was hardly likely to object with his decision to appoint me! I met with Gordon at a very pleasant tenanted pub on the outskirts of Blackpool where we had lunch and a couple of pints of Draught Double Diamond. We agreed on a suitable date for starting and termination of my employment with Telehire.

*My mum as a young lady on holiday in Madeira.*

*Grandfather Bob Rigby with Grandma Mary Ellen Rigby.*

*Left to right sister Anne, Mum, sister Linda, granddad Bob and me on holiday in the Isle of Man.*

*Me and Anne having fun on our Grandparents lawn.*

*I must be about three on this one!*

*Linda and me on the form at Grey Gables. The form Linda was later to be tied up to by Anne and me!*

*On board the Fitton's yacht at the I.O.M. The yacht I wasn't allowed to sail back on to Glasson Dock.*

*The Balqueen Hydro, Port St Mary, Isle of Man.
The family spent many happy holidays there.*

*Family with grandparents at dinner, dining room at the Balqueen.*

*Me and Anne in the Garden at Grey Gables.*

*B.S.A. 500cc. twin Shooting Star motorcycle. My last motor cycle before purchasing my first car.*

*My first car – a Wolseley 6/80 to celebrate my 21st birthday.*

*Mum and me at Grey Gables with St. Mary Magdeline's church in the background.*

*18 years of age with police dog 'Jet' - the dog who attacked the Deputy Chief Constable.*

*P.C. 2907 Mynett – 19 years of age at Bruche police training centre, Warrington, prior to being set loose on Merseyside!*

*Crazy carnival in Bolton with Tetley shire horses, licensee's in carnival gear, me on horseback with Tim Mostyn, his arm around Miss Press Gala and Tim Hill, director with Lyn Jenkins dressed as a nurse.*

*Tetley shires outside the Crofters Arms, Wigan. One of my managed houses.*

*Passing out parade at Bruche. I'm third from the left – middle row.*

*Me with Major E.I.L.(Tim) Mostyn, my brewery director at a tenancy presentation evening.*

# 7

## Ind Coope Northern – Free Trade

My first day of employment with Ind Coope Northern was quite a surprise. I reported to the Huntsman Hotel, a huge pub in a very prominent position on the Blackpool seafront at North Shore. (The Huntsman was sold by Allied Breweries many years ago and demolished) The free trade office was in a bedroom at the Huntsman as a temporary arrangement pending finding suitable office accommodation. My Area Manager, Gordon Nelson introduced me to Peter Walker. Peter had been covering Blackpool and surrounding areas for several months as the Double Diamond Rep. The growth for the company had been such that my role was to assist and expand trade for Ind Coope. This was to be the beginning of my eighteen years of employment in the brewing industry.

The area allocated to me was central Blackpool, the Fylde Coast, Lancaster and Morecambe. I was soon to discover what a den of iniquity Blackpool was. Having worked as a policeman on Merseyside, I was soon to have my eyes opened as to the fiddles and corruption in the licensed trade which I had not experienced before. Free Trade in the brewing industry refers to those outlets which do not have a tie with a brewer i.e. where a brewer owns a pub; the licensee is required to sell those breweries products. My role was to call on Working Men's Clubs, Pubs, Hotels, Restaurants, Social Clubs and Night Clubs etc. where these outlets were free to purchase their beers, soft drinks, wines and spirits from whoever they chose.

My first company car was a brand new Morris 1100. The amazing thing was the generosity of the company in that all private mileage was paid for. We would take the family to Cornwall on holiday and I was reimbursed with all the cost of petrol. What a perk! A generous expense account covered all expenses i.e. gratuities to proprietors, bar managers etc. meals and hotel accommodation when required to stay overnight. Following my first couple of weeks; Gordon Nelson called me into his office. He said that he was quite concerned about my weekly claims for expenses. Imagine my surprise when he told me that I was simply not claiming enough! Gordon told me the amount I should be claiming. Then a further surprise when he said "Go and buy yourself a couple of suits and claim the cost back through your expenses." This was considered an acceptable perk at the time. So, I went and purchased a couple of very nice new suits. It transpired that the Managing Director was very keen for his Free Trade Reps to be well dressed at all times and turned a blind eye re: paying for suits through expenses.

The hours worked were 9am to 5pm. As a Free Trade Salesman it was a requirement to also work three evenings a week. This was particularly necessary for meeting with Working Men's club committee's and visiting night clubs. Gordon Nelson was a night owl and would often accompany me on those evening visits. The problem was that he enjoyed visiting the Lemon Tree Club at North Shore, a very upmarket members only night club. Following these evening visits invariably meant my arriving home about midnight or 1am. Clearly this did not go down well with Lynn. I was expected to be back in the office the next day for 9am! Whilst the evening work was at times very inconvenient, at least I didn't have to visit working men's clubs on a Sunday to meet with the committee. In East Lancashire these club committee's only met on a Sunday which meant the poor rep for that area had to attend to keep the committee happy, buy them drinks and visit potential clubs in the area to promote their draught and bottled beers.

It was a good time to start work in the brewing industry. Draught Double Diamond was already very popular and sales were progressively improving in Blackpool and the Fylde Coast. The main competition was Watney's Red Barrel; but it was never going to be a serious competitor to D.D.D. This was also a time when the sale of traditional draught bitter was in the decline, keg beer had the advantage of having a longer life, it didn't need to go on stillage, therefore creating fewer problems for storage in the cellar. This was also a period when draught lager was becoming very popular. Ind Coope's lager was Skol, but it was never to become as popular as Carlsberg or other proprietary brands.

Monday mornings was quite frenetic. All the brewery reps in Blackpool would belt round their best accounts, mainly working men's clubs, to obtain orders for the next week's delivery. During the season the amount of beer consumed over the weekend in

Blackpool was phenomenal. Following closing time on a Monday, most of the reps would meet up about 3.30pm in the Queens Hotel on the promenade and spend the rest of the afternoon socialising and enjoying a relaxed drink. I enjoyed these occasions but now cringe at the thought of the amount of alcohol consumed. This was before the breathalyser was introduced when many people were prepared to take the risk of driving over the limit.

Following an initial period of being introduced to the licensed trade, I was very fortunate to be given responsibility for looking after all three piers in Blackpool. The North Pier was without doubt the biggest trading pier in Blackpool, followed by the central piers Dixieland bar. I was also to be given working men's clubs, hotels, night clubs, social clubs etc. In my earlier days with the brewery, it seemed quite unreal to be enjoying myself visiting all these social outlets and being paid to do so, notwithstanding that I was also provided with a company car and a generous expense account.

The very first account I opened was to be the 'Aristocat Club' (Correct spelling) in Blackpool. This was a popular night club run by two brothers. The doorman was a big strapping lad called Dick who also was responsible for the cellar work and ordering all the beers. This was an evening visit and I would arrive about 9.30pm. The club at the time took all their beers from Greenall's, unusually for a nightclub; the bitter was traditional which took quite some looking after. Following several conversations with Dick it became obvious that he knew I was an ex policeman but he didn't let on. As I was leaving the club late one evening Dick made me an offer which he thought I couldn't refuse. The offer was of a roll of 'knock off' carpet which I could have at a very good price.

A little while following this offer from Dick, I called at the club when Dick put his arm around me and said "You'll do for me Bob – there was no knock off carpet. I wanted to know if I could trust you." He thought that I would probably go straight to the Blackpool Borough Police with the information. The following week I was given a very substantial initial order for draught and bottled beers by Dick. When I asked how he had managed to convince the proprietors to change to Ind Coope beers, he told me that he had kicked the Greenall's barrels on the stillage to make the beers cloudy. Dick then went on to tell me that it had become common knowledge in Blackpool that I used to be a policeman, had gained his trust and bars managers in the area now knew that I was O.K.

The really nice thing following opening my first account; was receiving a memo from the Managing Director congratulating me for the very substantial initial order. This was to boost my morale considerably and there were many such memo's from the M.D. for my further successes.

Whilst working in Blackpool as a free trade rep, I became a member of the Guildhall Conservative Club in Preston. My Uncle, Harold Rigby was Chairman of the club and also a very prominent Freemason in Preston. He commented to me one evening at the club that he was disappointed that neither of his two sons had expressed interest in joining the craft and that he thought it would be good for me to become a Freemason. I was unable to join his particular club which consisted of ex Grammar School Boys, but was advised that arrangements could be made for me to join the Lodge of Endeavour No 7036. Gordon Nield; an optician, was a past master of the Lodge of Endeavour and a close friend of my uncle. They were both worshipful masters of their respective lodges in 1964. I met with Gordon and my uncle at the Conservative Club one evening, when Gordon said he was prepared to propose me and would also arrange for a member of the lodge to second me. At my initiation as an entered apprentice freemason, my uncle, Harold Rigby was present when Derek Fairclough, a barrister who was to become a circuit judge; conducted a little ceremony, presenting me with a pair of white gloves. I progressed from an Entered Apprentice Freemason to Junior Deacon. On moving from our home in Garstang to the Manchester office, my commitment to the brewery was more important than Masonry and I decided to resign from the lodge.

# 8

## Den of Iniquity

The Stork at Condor Green, near Lancaster, was a Draught Double Diamond account which I had opened. I arrived at the Stork at lunchtime to find a new Rolls Royce with a personalised registration number on the car park. On entering the pub the licensee Jock, introduced two of his customers to me. They turned out to be two brothers. One was very well dressed in a pin stripe suit, the other in very casual working clothes. The well dressed man spoke with a rather upmarket accent, the other with a broad Lancashire accent. I bought the two brothers a pint of D.D.D. and the licensee joined us with a drink. Following a very convivial 30 minutes of chat, the two brothers left. I asked who the owner of the Rolls Royce was and Jock told me that one of the brothers who had left owned the car and asked me to guess which of the brothers the car belonged to. Quite naturally I said that I thought the smarter of the two in the suit was the owner. I was rather surprised to discover that the man in casual working clothes was the owner of the R.R. He was a down to earth millionaire scrap metal dealer, his brother was an accountant. Of the two men the scrap metal dealer was the better communicator and was certainly blessed with 'The Common Touch.' In later life whilst living in Knutsford, Cheshire, I would occasionally visit the Bears Paw, a free house in High Legh. A wealthy businessman would arrive at the Bears Paw in his Rolls Royce in scruffy attire wearing wellies. Goodness knows how he drove his roller in wellies! This was referred to locally as inverted snobbery.

I have referred to Blackpool as a den of iniquity and fiddles. There was also a lot of corruption, not just in the licensed trade but also in the local Blackpool Borough Police force; there are many tales which I hope will be of interest to the reader. The Dixieland Bar on the Central Pier was owned by the then Trust House Forte. Following the dismissal of the bars manager, an ex Blackpool Borough detective was appointed bars manager. This man had responsibility for the satisfactory running of this huge operation. There were two very long bars on either side of the venue with two cellars serving them, one to the north and the other to the south of the pier. This was a fortnightly visit and it was part of my job to visit both cellars on a regular basis to establish standards of cleanliness and good cellar management. A well known saying in the trade is that the cellar is the engine room of any pub.

Over a short period of time this bars manager divorced his wife and one of his barmaids became his girlfriend. He acquired a new sports car and was certainly living the high life. I became very suspicious as to how he was able to achieve this standard of living and decided to look into it. The Dixieland bar took barrels (36 galls) of bitter and lager, these were in the form of keg beer, being dispensed via a very sophisticated system from the two cellars. As part of my line of investigation into this manager, I arrived one day to inspect the cellars armed with my extractor key, a devise which enables one to safely remove the spiel from the top of the metal barrel. I had ensured that the manager was on his day off. I had noticed that over a period of a couple of months that oddly, a number of barrels were stacked up at one end of the cellar, but appeared to be full. I suspected that these may have been filled with water. The racking label which indicated the date of the brew had always been of current dates. However, over this period of time referred to above, I had written down the barrel numbers in my notebook. These are stamped into the top of barrels and cannot be altered in any way. There were six barrels with numbers I had recorded previously, positioned at the end of the cellar on the day I arrived with my extractor key.

On removing all six spiels from these barrels, I found that they all contained water. My suspicions had been confirmed. Rather than informing the general manager of the North Pier, I went straight to the office of Vic Wardman, Director of the Trust House Forte operation in Blackpool and told him what I had found at the Dixieland Bar. He was horrified and asked me to explain how this could have happened without his knowledge. I told Mr Wardman that their stock taker would have taken at face value that the barrels contained beer. They had no means of checking that the barrels actually contained water. The method used was to physically pull the barrels to check the contents. The clever way the racking labels had been substituted would fool most stock takers. Vic Wardman was very grateful that I had uncovered this fiddle and told me that he would immediately dismiss the manager personally. He explained to me that he would not be prosecuting this man due to the adverse publicity it would create for Trust House Forte. The irony was that within no time at all, this bent ex detective was to secure a job as an area sales manager for a food company.

The question then arose as to how the dismissed manager had been able to take money out of the Dixieland bar. The way it worked was this. The manager purchased an identical till to those installed in the Dixieland Bar which was located at the end of the northern bar. The only person who was allowed to use that till was his girlfriend. The manager then converted the amount of money taken from the till (which was the whole amount) in relation to the amount of water placed in the barrels in the cellar. It's hard to believe that this ex detective didn't have the common sense to realise that by putting water into barrels not only constituted perhaps the most serious fiddle in the licensed trade, but that it would clearly eventually come to light.

Blackpool Pleasure Beach was an account on my patch which was owned by the Thompson family. Geoffrey Thompson had overall responsibility for the running of this huge operation. His father was alive at the time and had had a large sign positioned at the rear entrance to the Horseshoe Bar which read 'THE CUSTOMER IS KING.' with a picture of a lion alongside. All suppliers and reps were required to use this rear entrance. One lunchtime whilst speaking with the bars manager, he insisted in telling me of his very profitable fiddle. The man was clearly the worse for drink and I told him that I didn't want to know. It went something like this, he instructed his bar staff to put one penny on the price of all draught beers, including D.D.D. which went into his back pocket. The sum of money he was making was quite staggering. I told him that he was a fool and that eventually his fiddle would come to light. I sought the advice of a very experienced rep in Blackpool over this situation. He advised me that Geoffrey Thompson would eventually catch this bars manager at it and not to take any action. Eventually, Geoffrey Thompson discovered what was going on and sacked the man. He made sure that this bent bars manager would never again gain employment in the licensed trade in Blackpool. This particular fiddle of adding one (old) penny to a pint of beer was typical of many landlords and bar managers in Blackpool.

A joke circulating amongst the brewery reps in Blackpool related to Working Men's Club committee members. These clubs were non profit making and relied heavily on the income from fruit machines. It went something like this. A policeman on the beat during the early hours of the morning spotted a man carrying a colour television out of a working man's club. He asked the man what on earth was he was doing. The man replied to the effect that he had won the T.V. at the club in a raffle and that furthermore, it was second prize. The policeman asked what the first prize was and the reply was, 'A job on the committee and keys to the one armed bandits'!

It was common knowledge in the licensed trade in Blackpool, that certain club stewards were jointly involved with a huge fiddle regarding fruit machines. More often than not it was the Club Treasurer who held keys for the machines together with the club steward. It wouldn't be possible now to carry out this fiddle due to the sophisticated security systems which manufacturers incorporate into their equipment. However, it was quite easy for money to be extracted in those days and certain club officials could be seen driving around Blackpool in Mercedes and other upmarket cars. Profit and loss accounts for many clubs revealed huge amounts of income. No wonder certain club committee members were doing their jobs voluntarily.

Whilst the job of free trade rep. in Blackpool was most enjoyable, the most onerous and difficult responsibility was dealing with over due's. These were accounts where late payments had become the norm, clearly through cash flow problems or sheer laziness on the part of the person responsible for regular payments. Thirty days credit was the norm when payment was due, however, national accounts i.e. Trust House Forte were allowed three months credit, which had the effect of increasing substantially my percentage of over dues. None payment would result in my having to close an account or putting them on cash with order.

The Club Ascot, one of my nightclub accounts in Blackpool was one such outlet which was cash with order. The Club Ascot was a strip club situated at first floor level in the centre of Blackpool and the proprietor, Ken Reynolds was very unreliable when it came to payment of his invoices. I called weekly at the club and the arrangement was that Ken would give me an order for the following week; I would work out the value of the order and collect cash, then arrange the delivery date. I called every Thursday evening at the club and this was my last call following visits to other clubs and evening calls. I arrived at the club about 11.45pm and the arrangement was for me to meet with Ken Reynolds after the strippers had finished their performances! Usually about midnight.

It's been a joke within my family ever since I left the licensed trade that Lynn would never accompany me on those Thursday evenings to visit the Club Ascot. I would say that it was one of life's experiences that she would find it quite entertaining watching the strippers go through their act. The strippers surprisingly were very attractive girls. The most popular one was known as Randy Mandy. Mandy was very professional and had the biggest pair of knockers you've ever clapped eyes on! The funniest thing I ever saw one evening at the club were a group of Chinese businessmen sat on the front row. Mandy's routine was to complete her act completely naked with nothing on but a tiny G string. On this particular evening she went and sat on the knee of one of the Chinese guys on the front row, placing one of her boobs on his cheek. He broke out in a cold sweat and the expression on his face was a picture. His colleagues roared laughing and clapped furiously. All the club members thought it was outrageously funny. It was as entertaining watching the reaction of the audience as the strippers. As many women would visit the club as men and the expressions on their faces was a picture. Some were of complete disgust, others fascination and many 'I don't half fancy her!' I suggested closing the account. It was very restrictive having to call weekly and collect cash but the directors' of the company were having none of it. They enjoyed visiting the club on their outings to Blackpool!

I made many firm friends on my patch and the club steward of the Wainwright Conservative Club was one of them. There were three full size snooker tables in the club. One lunchtime there were about seven club members drinking and playing snooker. I was having a drink with the steward when he told me that every member in the club at the time had a criminal record, pointing out those who had also served a prison sentence. The steward went through the criminal activities of each individual member. These included stealing cars and shipping them abroad, various kinds of theft and protection rackets. It is self evident that I should not divulge this information. The local C.I.D. knew of these people's whereabouts and in particular that they used the club.

The chairman of Allied Breweries beer division was George Smedley, a very impressive looking man who was chauffeured around in a Bentley. The sales of Draught Double Diamond were going extremely well and at the annual conference in Leeds, stated that he had set a target of 1,000,000 barrels of D.D.D. for the following year. At the following years conference he was delighted to announce that the company had achieved those 1,000,000 barrels.

The Fernhill Hotel and Restaurant at Preesall on the Fylde coast was an account I opened for D.D.D. and bottled beers. The Fernhill was an upmarket establishment owned by Jimmy Clitheroe, the very small well known comedian and entertainer. I never met Jimmy but often saw him performing on T.V. His popular image was dressed in short trousers as a schoolboy with a cap to match. The manager was Tommy Trafford who played the dame in pantomime. One day Tommy gave me a guided tour around the hotel. Jimmy Clitheroe's huge bedroom on the first floor had a massive bed in the centre of the room. Imagine my surprise when Tommy pressed a button on the wall by the bed and the bed slowly moved up into the ceiling! When Jimmy held parties at the Fernhill, the bed remained in the ceiling and the party was held in the bedroom. There was a very large tropical fish tank in the restaurant full with priceless tropical fish. Unfortunately, one day the thermostat went on the blink and all the fish were boiled alive! I don't know whether the insurance covered the loss. Whilst on holiday recently in Coniston, Cumbria I was to learn that sadly! The Fernhill had closed due to lack of trade. Another victim of the recession.

Probably one of the most difficult situations I ever had to deal with was taking my Grandma Rigby (my mother's mother) into a care home in Lytham St. Anne's. My mother Florence was at her wits end caring for her. The arrangement was that grandma would stay with mother for a period of six months, spending the remaining six months of the year with Harold and Annis, my aunt and uncle who lived in Penwortham, Preston. It was an intolerable situation with four generations living in a relatively small bungalow. This consisted of grandma, mother, my sister Linda and her young child, my nephew Anthony. Whilst I got on very well with my grandma, she was a very difficult and domineering woman. It was such a stressful situation for mother and when things got really bad, she would go into the kitchen, light up a cigarette and drink a large glass of sherry, swearing, to get the awful circumstances out of her system. Undoubtedly my grandma's determination in no small measure resulted in a very successful business for her and my granddad Bob.

Mother had started drinking heavily as a result of the dreadful atmosphere and our family were very concerned for her health. I had made enquiries at a very pleasant care home in Lytham St Anne's and established that there was a vacancy. It took me some time to persuade mother that her situation was intolerable and that grandma simply had to go. Eventually mother agreed and the plan was for me to take grandma out for a run in the country in my car, having packed her bags but not telling her that she was moving into a care home. I pulled onto the drive of mother's bungalow on the appointed day, put grandma's case into the boot and told her that we were going to have a run out into the country. She was delighted at the opportunity, not realising what was in store for her.

En route to the care home, I stopped the car in a lay by and explained to grandma that mother could no longer cope with the situation and that I was taking her into a care home. She started to cry and pleaded with me not to take her there. It was impossible to console her and proved to be a very difficult and emotional experience for me. I felt awful that I had been the one to make the arrangements and dreadfully guilty. On arrival at the care home, I pulled onto the driveway up to the entrance and that's when the fun and games started. Grandma refused point blank to get out of the car. I went into the home and explained to the proprietor who came out and spoke to grandma, but she would not budge. Eventually, grandma needed to go to the toilet and that was the only way I could get her out of the car. When she had visited the loo, she made a beeline for the front door but the proprietor blocked her way. Grandma started throwing punches at him and he had to duck and weave to avoid being hit. Between the pair of us we eventually got her to calm down and showed her to her room.

Neither my Aunt Annis nor Uncle Harold contacted me following my involvement of moving grandma. It must have been some considerable relief for them to no longer have their six months responsibility of looking after her. Grandma eventually died in the home at the age of eighty seven. On reflection, the sad thing about the whole circumstances was that the last time I saw my granddad Bob was in hospital just before he died. He asked me to ensure that grandma would be looked after following his death. It was clearly a decision based on priorities for my mother's survival and the dreadful nature of living in that intolerable situation that there was no option other than to move her into a rest home.

The Palatine Hotel was situated on the central promenade in Blackpool and was one of my best accounts. (It was demolished many years ago) The pub had six bars and during the height of the season received deliveries of 100 barrels plus per week, notwithstanding further deliveries from other breweries. Gordon Nelson looked after this prestigious account but fell out with the manager Doug Smith. This conflict of personalities resulted in the managing director, Jack Frost visiting the Palatine to come to a satisfactory conclusion as to who should look after the account. I had met Doug Smith on many occasions in company with Gordon. I got on with him quite well in spite of him being a demanding and rather belligerent character. Following the meeting with the M.D I was told that I would look after the account and that Jack Frost had assured Doug Smith that I would call at the Palatine three times a week. Unfortunately, this was to curtail my activities in seeking out new business.

Doug Smith was a rogue but ran the Palatine with a rod of iron. The three joint proprietors of the pub were more than satisfied with the manner in which the pub was run and enjoyed the profits which were churned out every year. However, what they weren't aware of were the serious fiddles and downright thievery which was going on in their premises. Annually, the directors' would set a price structure in place with Doug Smith and the bars managers'. Immediately following this meeting, Doug Smith called his own meeting telling his staff to ignore the directors' price structure, implementing his own prices. This meant one pence extra on every pint sold in the pub plus increases on bottled beers, wines and spirits. The most serious offence he committed was in relation to Whitbread's draught mild. The mild was delivered into a ten barrel tank and dispensed as bitter. The pale mild was so good that none of the customers knew it was actually mild and not bitter. Whilst one (old) pence increase doesn't sound like a lot, due to the huge volume of sales, this resulted in a very large amount of cash going into Doug Smiths back pocket.

Doug Smith had a huge ego. He wore gold bracelets, a very expensive Rolex watch and would boast openly with all the reps who called at the Palatine of the properties he had acquired up and down the country. It was only going to be a matter of time before his criminal activities would catch up with him. One lunch time whilst visiting the gent's toilets, he stood alongside me at the urinal and told me that he was in trouble. He had very foolishly had an affair with Kathleen Duffy, one of his bar managers. He went on to tell me that he had sacked her and he was very concerned that out of revenge she would spill the beans to the directors' regarding all his fiddles. I was to learn that Kathleen Duffy was not just taking drugs, but also pushing them. Her husband had signed on sick in spite of being quite well and drawing benefits. She had shopped him to the authorities and as a result of this he had committed suicide by putting his head into a gas oven. This evil woman was then living with a young man, young enough to be her son who she had encouraged to use drugs. It became known that she was in receipt of stolen property, particularly a colour television. The local Blackpool C.I.D. knew of her drug pushing and stolen property in her possession but chose not to take action. The reason for this was that she was an informant and grassed on many villains who frequented the Palatine.

Twelve prostitutes plied their wares at the Palatine. The most popular one was a rather small woman who was not at all attractive; by the name of Pat. I could never understand what the attraction was for the punters! One lunch time I called into the lounge bar of the pub which overlooked the sea front of Blackpool. As I was standing at the bar the prostitute Pat approached me, she was very upset and practically in tears and asked if she could have a word with me in confidence. We went to sit in the bay window of the lounge. I was horrified at what she told me. A detective sergeant was calling into the Palatine weekly and taking £10 off each of the prostitutes with the threat that should they refuse, he would bring to an end their activities at the pub. Pat gave me the policeman's name and I told her to leave it with me. I went straight back to the office and rang Detective Chief Superintendent Jack

Watson at Police H.Q. Hutton. Lancashire Constabulary had taken over the Blackpool Borough force by that time and it was therefore the responsibility of Lancashire Police to deal with the situation.

I had worked with Jack Watson during my C.I.D. training at Seaforth when he was a Detective Inspector. Fortunately, I knew him sufficiently well to know that I could be trusted and relied upon with such sensitive information. Jack Watson told me that he would arrange for me to meet with two senior officers from the Lancaster Divisional H.Q. who covered the Blackpool area. Chief Superintendent Alf Collins and Detective Chief Inspector Bob Crompton met with me at Gynn Square, Blackpool. I sat in the back of their police car and was not at all impressed with their surly attitude. They told me that they knew all about me from my time in the Lancashire Force and what was this ridiculous allegation about one of their detective sergeants calling at the Palatine. I told them that I was not at all impressed with their attitude, told them the name of the bent C.I.D. officer, finally telling them that if they didn't believe me, they should get in touch with Pat at the Palatine. They didn't even have the courtesy to thank me for the information.

I continued calling at the Palatine, but not one of the prostitutes mentioned a word about any action that may have been ongoing, including Pat. Any enquiries were clearly being kept confidential and low key. Several months after meeting with the two senior officers at Gynn Square, I called in to the Blackpool Police Club where I had opened an account for Ind Coope beers some months previous, to be met at the bar by Dick Smith, a detective based in Blackpool. Dick and I had worked together in Seaforth and had become firm friends. I bought Dick a pint of D.D.D. and whilst reminiscing he told me in strict confidence that I had really opened a can of worms regarding the Palatine Hotel. He told me that following my notification regarding the bent detective sergeant, observations had been carried out over a period of time where the detective had been followed. It had become clear that he was receiving money from the prostitutes at the Palatine. The man realised he was being followed and before he could be arrested he skipped the country, leaving behind a wife and children. This D.S. was formerly with the Blackpool Borough Police force, yet another bent officer making money in connection with the licensed trade. I was never to receive any thanks from Lancashire Police for providing this information and I really did wonder whether it was worth while bothering to become involved in a situation of this nature. Perhaps Alf Collins and Bob Crompton were too embarrassed to have the decency to thank me!

Kathleen Duffy did in fact mix a bottle for Dog Smith by telling the directors' of the Palatine of all the fiddles which were going on. Doug Smith was arrested; charged and went down for three years, serving his sentence at Kirkham Open Prison. Prior to the court case I was socialising at the Guild Hall Conservative Club in Preston, where I was a member and my Uncle, Harold Rigby was Chairman. Derek Fairclough, a friend of my uncle; the barrister I had met at the Masonic lodge; called me over to the bar. He told me that he had been appointed by the police to prosecute Doug Smith in Crown Court and what did I know about the fiddles at the Palatine and particularly in Blackpool. I was able to tell Derek Fairclough that the fiddles which Doug Smith had carried out were typical of many licensees' in Blackpool, but that unfortunately for Doug Smith, he had been caught.

John and Judith Jallall were proprietors of Wards Café and Restaurant in Blackpool, an account which I had opened for Ind Coope. Their catering operation was very successful and they had worked extremely hard to build up the trade. However, they were anxious to move on and build up a larger operation in the Blackpool area. I became very friendly with John and Judith and advised them that I would endeavour to find a suitable operation for them in Blackpool. The Town and Country club was a nightclub directly opposite the North Pier which had also been very successful, however, the proprietor had started to go into arrears with his payments and I had no alternative to put him on cash with order. The club eventually closed and I went straight to John and Judith advising them that in my opinion there was a huge potential to develop a restaurant on the premises. We had long discussions about the potential and a decision was made for them to take over the business. The Town and Country Club became the Town and Country Restaurant and was a huge success. John is Indian and his curries were absolutely superb. Whilst John produced all the food, Judith looked after running the bar. After many successful years running the restaurant operation, sadly, John started drinking excessively, closed the restaurant and left the licensed trade altogether. John became a member of the Blackpool Rotary Club and was very brave when he spoke to the club about his struggle with alcoholism, warning of the dangers of the evil of drink. I can now fully understand the difficulties and temptations relating to alcohol following eighteen years experience in the licensed trade. Fortunately, whilst I do enjoy a drink, over the years I have been able avoid excessive drinking.

The Central Working Men's Cub in Blackpool was without doubt the biggest and most prestigious working men's club in the North West of England. The premises used to belong to Bass Brewery having previously been a bottling plant. This is a huge club with a large concert room providing excellent entertainment for club members. The club operated three fruit machines at the time which contributed a considerable amount of income to their profit and loss account. Working men's clubs were the bread and butter for brewers supplying beers to the free trade in the Blackpool area; they paid their accounts regularly and drank vast amounts of beer. I would call on a regular basis to meet with the club steward and certain committee members. Club committee members liked to meet with brewery reps if only to get a free pint, which would be paid for through the reps expenses. The problem was an agreement with Bass who supplied all draught and bottled beers. I had developed a system of entertaining committee members of clubs by hiring a coach and taking them to Ind Coope's Brewery at Burton on Trent. Later, following a reorganisation with Tetley's; arranging a visit to Tetley's Brewery in Warrington. For more important potential outlets, I would then take the members to the Talk of The North Night Club in Manchester for a night's entertainment, all paid for on my expense account. As a result of taking the committee members of the Central Working Men's Club on one such outing, the decision was made to introduce Tetley's beers to the club. That was a real feather in my cap, having taken some 4 years of cultivating the trust of the committee and the club steward. Tetley's became the main supplier to the club and eventually installed tank beers, such was the volume of trade.

Tank beer was the preferred delivery to working men's clubs where the volume of trade was such that the barrelage warranted such quantities. The Gordon Working Men's Club in Morecambe was one such account dispensing Tetley Bitter via tank. I was stood at the bar of the club one morning chatting with the club steward, when a Tetley Tank driver arrived at the bar having completed his delivery. The irony was that I bought this driver a pint of Tetley's.

Whilst chatting with him over the drink he boasted that as the highest paid tank driver at the brewery, his salary was the third highest in Tetley Walker based at Warrington. The highest paid being the M.D. and the Head Brewer. When I said I didn't believe him he retorted "What can't speak can't lie." He took his wallet out of his back pocket and took out his wage slip, handing it to me. I was flabbergasted to see the amount of income he was earning. He certainly must have been the third highest paid as stated. I told him in a jocular fashion that he should have bought me a pint instead of the other way round.

Certain brewery tanker drivers were on the fiddle; supplementing their already large incomes. This had also been particularly the case with Greenall's Brewery. A Greenall's tanker driver had upset his next door neighbour who rang security at Greenall's, asking the question as to how this neighbour was able to afford a brand new Mercedes car. Their security officer set up surveillance on all their tanker driver's and discovered how the fiddle worked. During the course of a day's deliveries, the driver would short deliver to a number of outlets (mainly managed house pubs) then sell the remainder for cash to certain club stewards of working men's clubs with tank beer. This one telephone call from the angry neighbour high lighted this major fiddle, ending the career of many a tank driver in the Warrington area.

As a Free Trade Rep. I had many requests from Proprietors', Licensee's and club committee's for financial assistance. This would be mainly for the refurbishment of licensed premises or simply supplying furniture. There was a large budget to be used, particularly for working men's clubs where several thousands of pounds would be involved. In return for this assistance; an assurance would be given for stocking draught and bottled beers, very often soft drinks as well and occasionally wines & spirits. I always adopted a policy when approached by advising yes, no or that I would come back with a reply. I always made a note of any such requests in my notebook. My Area Manager Gordon would often promise the earth when accompanying me on visits, but would almost always do nothing about it. This was a constant source of frustration for me and quite embarrassing. I would rather say no than have the humiliation of doing nothing.

# 9

## Deputy Area Manager

Following five successful years in the free trade division of the brewery, I was keen to further my career and applied to transfer to the tied estate. My application was successful and I was promoted to Deputy Area Manager, Managed Houses, to be based at the Duke Street Office of Tetley Walker in Liverpool. I was also to work from the Leigh Office on Brewery Lane covering managed houses in the Leigh and Wigan areas. Having been a policeman on Merseyside for six and a half years had been a really good grounding, enabling me to understand the language and humour, but in particular what made scousers tick. This involved travelling to Liverpool daily from my home in Preston.

Tim Carfoot was my Managed House Director, a truly enthusiastic and dedicated entrepreneur. On my first day I had an encounter with John Smith, also a Managed House Director and Chairman of Liverpool Football Club. John Smith welcomed me to the Liverpool Office and asked me which football team I supported. I could have really wound him up by saying Everton, but did in fact say it was Liverpool. Football was referred to in Liverpool as a religion and probably still does! I found it quite amusing that barbers' in Liverpool prominently displayed the fixtures for both Liverpool and Everton Football teams, obviously to keep well in with all their football fanatic customers. John Smith's loyalties were essentially as Chairman of Liverpool Football Club. It was rumoured that he was quite bitter not to have been promoted beyond brewery director. Monday mornings were reserved for licensee's on John Smith's patch who had been caught fiddling or failing to comply with company policy. The Area Manager would accompany the licensee at these meetings. The bollocking which John Smith gave those licensees was so severe that even the area manager's were quivering in their shoe's!

Stan Percival was a Managed House Area Manager covering the city centre of Liverpool which included the Dock Road. One of my earliest roles as a Deputy Area Manager was to take over the running of Stan's patch for a fortnight whilst he went on holiday. Stan told me there were no problems and all I had to do was call on his pubs and arrange for the collection of any ullage. (Draught beer which has gone off) Famous last words! Stan's desk was the most untidy and disorganised I had ever clapped eyes on! The whole of his desk was a mass of paperwork and yet he claimed he knew where everything was! The first thing I did when Stan left for his holidays was to place a large cardboard box at the end of the desk and shovel all the paperwork into the box. The following morning the office cleaner was amazed. She had never seen the desk top and took great delight in polishing it, spraying copious amounts of beeswax onto the surface.

So much for Stan saying there were no problems on his patch! During the early hours of one morning I was woken by the 'phone ringing. It was Liverpool City Police ringing to say that a Tetley pub in the centre of Liverpool had been on fire, a petrol bomb had been put through the letter box. The fire brigade had attended and put out the fire. I went directly to the pub the following morning where I spoke with Annie, the licensee. She was accompanied by Pete, her boyfriend who was home from sea. Annie told me that Pete and herself were having a late night drink in the upstairs lounge after the pub had closed. They heard a crash from downstairs; Pete grabbed a kettle full of boiling water saying that if anyone was breaking into the pub, he would throw the boiling water over them! When Pete got to the top of the stairwell, the whole of the private entrance to the pub was on fire. This was the only means of entry and exit to the upstairs private accommodation. Fortunately, the fire brigade arrived very quickly and put out the fire.

Investigations by C.I.D. revealed that the cause of the fire was as follows. Unfortunately, Stan Percival had put the Licensee Annie into a Tetley Managed House in the middle of a Catholic stronghold, Annie was a Protestant. Another female Licensee who was a Catholic had unsuccessfully applied for the pub. She was so incensed and bitter about the decision, that a few days prior to the petrol bomb incident, she had gone into Annie's pub one evening accompanied by some local villains who were armed with revolvers, threatening Annie, producing the weapons which punters in the pub saw. This woman actually invited Annie to come from behind the bar to fight her. Annie refused.

After further threats the woman and her cronies left the pub, shouting that they would set fire to the premises.

The C.I.D. arrested the gang and charged them with the petrol bomb attack and possession of weapons. The case went to Crown Court and I was called as a witness, went into the witness box and gave evidence as to the extent of damage caused by the fire. However, the case collapsed when the witnesses failed to attend to give evidence. They had been threatened and intimidated by the gang. Following this incident I was to learn from a conversation with Jim Scragg, security officer for Tetley Walker of the violent nature, protection rackets and the like which went on in Liverpool in the licensed trade. I had never realised as a policeman in Liverpool as to the extent of the corruption and violence which occurred in licensed premises. Perhaps this was because I was in uniform with little or no involvement with the C.I.D.

I was not to spend very long as a deputy in the Managed House Department at Liverpool. During those few short months I came to appreciate the scouse sense of humour and in particular the generosity of the Liverpool Licensee. Whilst I had an expense account, very rarely would a Liverpool licensee allow me to buy a drink. Prior to Christmas the Liverpool area managers, including myself, would be given gifts of bottles of wines and spirits. These were gifts of pure generosity with no suggestion whatever of favouritism or favours being required. I was to discover that there was no other area in Tetley Walker where the generosity and hospitality was as genuine as it was in Liverpool.

The Philharmonic Pub in Liverpool is a large Tetley managed house of great architectural merit, one of many such pubs in the city. However, where the Philharmonic is different is in relation to the gents' toilets! The Victorian urinals are a sight to behold. Apart from visiting the cellars of pubs, I was keen to ensure that the toilets on my area were of a high standard of cleanliness. To this day, when visiting a pub for the first time, I will inspect the toilets before eating or even having a drink. If the toilets are clean, then as a general rule you can bet that the kitchen will also be satisfactory, hence good food.

On arrival at the Philharmonic, dressed in pin stripe business suit and carrying my briefcase, I went straight to the gents' toilets. Imagine my surprise to find a really good looking young lady in the gents, taking photographs of the urinals. She was rather flustered and embarrassed, but I told her that I was from the brewery and gave her my business card. The lass told me that she had the permission of the manager to visit the loo's to take photographs and that she was writing a book about pub toilets throughout the country. When she had taken sufficient photographs, she joined me at the bar and we had a very pleasant chat.

On the subject of toilets! When I transferred as a deputy area manager to tenancy, I was covering the East Lancashire area. The local drunk had staggered into the outside toilet of his local. He held onto the pipe below the header tank on the wall, steadying himself whilst he urinated. He lurched back, pulling the tank off the wall. Fortunately the heavy tank missed his head but crashed onto his foot. The poor man was taken to hospital with a broken foot. The amazing thing was that the man made no complaint whatever to the brewery. This was really a classic case for compensation. However, the injured drunk must have decided that the accident was clearly his own fault.

The first licensee I sacked was running a managed house in Blackpool. I was looking after the area covered by Roy McCurry, the area manager who was away on holiday for a fortnight. The situation reminded me somewhat of the circumstances at the Palatine Hotel, Blackpool where the then licensee Doug Smith was involved with major fiddles.

One of the pub's barmaids 'phoned me at the office in Preston to say that she needed to meet with me urgently, stating that the meeting would need to take place at somewhere other than where she was employed. I met the woman at a pub on the promenade where she told me of all the very serious fiddles which were being carried out by the licensee. The information she gave me tied in with the pathetic and unacceptable results shown on the pub's profit and loss account. i.e. poor gross profit, bad stock results and no bottom line net profit. I had taken my portable typewriter with me and the barmaid was quite happy to give me a statement, detailing all the fiddles which the manager was carrying out. She signed the typewritten statement saying that she would be prepared to go to court to give evidence against the manager.

Armed with this information and the statement, I arranged for a relief manager to meet with me at the pub, together with a joiner, advising them to keep in the background until I had spoken to the manager. I interviewed the manager in the private accommodation, telling him of the allegations of the barmaid, showing him the typewritten and signed statement. He admitted all the allegations. I told the man that his demeanour was tantamount to gross misconduct and sacked him on the spot. The joiner then changed the locks for me, locking the manager off between the domestic accommodation and the pub. I had also arranged for the stock taker to arrive later in the day to check off all the stock and hand over to the relief manager.

This situation occurred before present day employment legislation where even for gross misconduct, unless you go through a very specific procedure, i.e. warning letters etc. you could end up in a tribunal for unfair or constructive dismissal. Therefore, it was far easier to dismiss a licensee than in the present day.

This was to be my first experience with the Managers' Union, the National Association of Licensed House Managers' (NALHM) a branch of the Transport and General Workers' Union. The sacked manger contacted his union to complain about his dismissal, even though in my view he didn't have a leg to stand on. On his return from holiday I told Roy McCurrie that I had sacked this manager, his response was "You can't do this." To which I replied "well I've done it." McCurrie was clearly embarrassed that I had identified a bent manager who needed dismissing, a situation he should have been aware of and had done nothing about.

I moved onto another area and was absolutely furious to learn that this manager had been reinstated. McCurrie and his director, Rod Firth had met with the union representative for the Blackpool area and had been coerced into giving the licensee a warning, putting him back in charge of the pub. Several months after this meeting, the manager had simply carried on with his fiddles and had to be sacked by McCurrie after all.

It was a requirement that all licensee's appointed to run a managed house with the company were to join the union NALHM. This was in a sense a protection racket for those licensee's who were unsatisfactory, lazy, fiddling etc. and was to become the bane of my life during my time with the tied estate. Two or three area managers were under pressure from their directors' for unsatisfactory performance and joined a union which was affiliated to the Transport and General Workers' Union. I had been approached on several occasions by colleague's to join the union, but had refused point blank to get involved, in spite of the fact that many more area managers were joining the union. My view was that I would stand on my own two feet and be answerable for my own performance and results.

The chairman of this union once said to me that I was receiving the benefits of pay increases negotiated by the union without paying subscriptions. I told him in no uncertain terms that I didn't consider there to any benefits whatever in my case. Unknown to the union and because I had refused to join, I was receiving better salary increases than union members because of my personal results. There was a private arrangement with the personnel director who detested the union. He asked me to keep this arrangement with the company confidential.

A vacancy arose for a Deputy Area Manager for the Tenanted Estate to be based at the Liverpool office. This position arose due to the previous holder of that position very foolishly fiddling his petrol receipts for his company car. He stole a blank pad of petrol receipts from a garage, filling them in himself and was claiming back expenses for petrol he had never purchased. Major E I L Mostyn was the Tenancy Director and upon sacking the Deputy Area Manager made a special request for me to transfer to his department. My own director had objected to this wishing to keep me with his team, but Tim Mostyn had pulled rank and overruled his colleague. It would appear that he was keen for me to work for him.

Tim Mostyn was a terrific character, had been a Major in the Parachute Regiment and referred to himself as the black sheep of the family. He was one of the Mostyns' of Wales. He had a reputation as a brilliant communicator, a strict but fair man, a great motivator and his leadership skills were second to none. I considered myself very fortunate to have been singled out to work for him. I was to discover that the attributes referred to regarding E I L M were very true indeed.

I reported to Tim Mostyn on the Monday morning of my first day with the Tenancy Department. His rather grand office at Duke Street, Liverpool was situated next to the boardroom. We chatted about what was expected of me and he gave me two pieces of advice. He told me that it could be very easy to fall into the temptation of becoming involved with a licensee's wife and to be aware of that and never to get involved. He then related a situation to me where one of his tenants had desperately wanted a prestigious pub, signed a blank cheque in his office, handing it to him suggesting he fill in any amount whatsoever, provided he arranged for him to take over the pub. Tim Mostyn had been absolutely furious with the man and thrown him out of the office, telling him in no uncertain terms that he would never be considered for another pub with the company.

Tim Mostyn was a very honest man, so much so that each week his secretary Beryl would advise him of the cost of his personal telephone calls, which he would promptly pay. There were a total of seven Tenanted Area Managers' looking after a total of five hundred pubs in the North West of England and during my time as a deputy, I was to work with all seven.

During my eighteen months as a Deputy Area Manager, I was to discover that Tim Mostyn was probably the finest boss I would ever work for. He was a great encourager and went to great lengths to teach me the intricacies and responsibilities of life as an area manager in the world of tenanted pubs. He was clearly grooming me for promotion to area manager on his patch. His team of area managers' all spoke very highly of him. He was a mans' man and in spite of the fact that he spoke very far back, he could communicate effectively at all levels; from the man in the taproom drinking his pint of Tetley's, to the higher echelons. No doubt this was as a result of his background as a Major in the British Army. He certainly possessed 'The Common Touch.' I've never known a man to swear so politely! One of his favourite swear words was to say "feck orf!" which invariably produced hoots of laughter from the recipient.

EILM had unfortunately lost the sight in his left eye. During the wedding reception of his third marriage, whilst opening a bottle of champagne, the cork had shot out of the bottle striking him in the eye. I'm not particularly fond of champagne, but on the odd occasion when I have removed the cork from a bottle, I've been extremely careful, being mindful of what happened to EILM.

Tim Mostyn once related to his team an experience with the Parachute Regiment. One of his men had made a dreadful landing and he sent him straight back up in the aircraft for 'idle jumping!'

Wednesday mornings were set aside for Tim Mostyn to meet with Tenants who were due to have their rent's reviewed. These discussions took place in the boardroom at the Leigh Office. A tenant from the Wigan area complained that his new rent was far too high. Tim Mostyn pointed through the window at the Tenant's

Rolls Royce parked outside, burst out laughing and said how on earth could he complain when he was able to drive a R.R! The tenant made the mistake of not arriving in an old banger!

On completion of rent reviews, I would accompany Tim Mostyn to the Brewery Inn, together with other Area Managers based at the Leigh Office. This was for a couple of pints and a bite to eat. One lunch time, he dropped a bag of peanuts on the floor and said to Joe Anderson, a tenancy area manager "Pick those peanuts up Anderson." (In a very jocular manner) Joe replied "I don't need the job that bad boss." Tim Mostyn burst out laughing.

Unfortunately, Tim Mostyn had a very bad limp and was unable to walk without the aid of a walking stick. This was as a result of an injury to his hip during his time as a Major in the army. I never once heard him complain about his condition. He once confided with me that he had sought the advice of a fortune teller whilst abroad during the war. After reading his palm, the female fortune teller told EILM that he must never have an operation for the hip problem. Sadly, at the age of fifty three, Tim Mostyn was to die following an operation for a hip replacement. He developed pulmonary embolism, resulting in a heart attack. The irony was that he had been forewarned never to have the operation by the fortune teller.

I needed time off one day to meet with my Barclay's bank manager to ask for a loan to purchase a touring caravan. When I spoke to Tim Mostyn, asking for the following morning off, he asked me the reason. When I told him he said that he was a personal friend of the chairman of Barclay's Bank and to mention it to my bank manager. Furthermore, he went on to tell me that when his friend the Chairman was married, he had been his best man. The wedding was in Venice and following quite a lot to drink, EILM and the chairman had both fallen into the Canal in Venice. Imagine the surprise when I related this story to my bank manager! I was actually offered more money than I needed to purchase the caravan but only accepted the amount I had requested.

# 10

## Tenancy Area Manager

I was very fortunate indeed when Tim Mostyn organised a reshuffle of the tenanted estate. I was promoted to Area Manager and given the biggest and most scenic area in the whole of Allied Breweries i.e. Bolton to Carlisle, inland as far as the Yorkshire border and the Fylde coast which was to include Blackpool. The furthest pub to the north was the Blue Bell at Newbiggin, close to Carlisle. Many of the pubs on the patch were 'Quintessential Olde Worlde Pubs' with beams, open log fires, traditional hand pulled beers providing good food. My sort of pub! I was to have responsibility for seventy two tenanted pubs in the area referred to. Ronnie Walters had been transferred from tenancy to managed houses and was furious that I had been given the plumb area. He had desperately wanted the area given to me and complained bitterly that as the longest serving area manager on tenancy, he had been overlooked for the best area. Ronnie Walters thereafter tried his best to give me a hard time but I took it with a pinch of salt.

It was rather difficult initially taking over such a large geographical area. Journey planning was paramount but the main issue was sorting out many overdue rent increases which the previous area manager had allowed to lapse. The first few months had to be committed to sitting down with tenants' and agreeing rent increases, not an easy task! The tenants' views were that they had worked very hard to increase trade and their thanks from the brewery was to have their rent increased, a view which I could sympathise with.

Whilst Preston was fairly central to my area, Lynn and I had been considering a move from Arnold Close to a detached house in a rural area. Lynn arrived home one day very excited about a house she had seen in Garstang and could we go and see it that evening. We arrived to see the detached farmhouse named 'Tanglewood', situated on Dimples Lane Garstang. The views to the front and rear were stunning. The front was overlooking the grounds of Garstang High School with the school in the distance. To the rear the view was of Beacon Fell and Bleasdale Fell in the distance. Beyond fields at the rear of the house was the canal where barges could be seen moving along, then the main London to Scotland Railway line and finally the M6 motorway. We decided there and then that we simply had to buy the house, even though it was further away from my office in Leigh.

The owners of the house were a Mr and Mrs Platt. He was a solicitor and his wife an artist painting with water colours. At £40,000 this was to really stretch me financially, particularly as at the time I was on the bottom of my salary scale. However, with advice from our good friend Jim Moorby, a local solicitor, we obtained a mortgage and arranged to move to Garstang. Unfortunately, because the move was at my own request and not that of the brewery, all the funding for the move had to come out of my own pocket.

The house move coincided with the business premises of Telehire Limited, situated in Arnold Close being vacated. Their head office was being relocated in Preston town centre. The old convent building was to be demolished and the contract for this had been given to one of my mothers ex pupils. There was a magnificent pitch pine front door on the building which I wanted to acquire for Tanglewood, together with an orchard full of apple trees. I met with the demolition man and negotiated an excellent price to purchase the orchard and front door, for a mere £10, probably because he had been taught by my mother and had a great respect for her

I hired a chain saw and spent a whole weekend sawing the apple trees into logs for the open log fire at Tanglewood. There's nothing quite like the aroma of apple logs burning on an open fire. I stored the logs in the barn at the back of our new house in Garstang and replaced the existing door with the pitch pine one, the door through which many nuns had passed when the building had been a convent.

The reader will recall that the convent building had been reputably haunted. I was determined to discover whether this was the case before the building was destroyed. After all the fixtures and fittings had been removed from the property, I crossed over the road from where we lived armed with my torch, about 12.30am and broke into the rear of the empty building. It was quite scary making my way around the old convent with my torch to guide me. The old training room situated at the top of the building had been the area where the ghost of Rebecca had been most frequently seen. I climbed the stairs with great apprehension not knowing what to expect. On entering the upper room it was quite eerie, the hairs on the back of my neck were standing up. I spent some time just standing there not knowing what to expect. However, I was most disappointed when I didn't see any sign of the ghost. She had probably left the building with all the fixtures and fittings!

The children settled in at local schools very well. Lynn and I integrated into the local community very quickly, worshiping at St Thomas' Church of England. I became a member of the Over Wyre Rotary Club and continued with my Freemasonry in Preston. Lynn's Yoga classes flourished and she built up steadily to a large number of pupils. The position of the house in Garstang proved to be very convenient for my patch, being close to the M6 motorway and I was quite happy travelling the further distance to my office in Leigh.

One of my responsibilities as Tenancy Area Manager, of what was probably the largest geographical patch of Allied Breweries in the U.K. was to attend most, if not all of the L.V.A. (Licensed Victuallers Association) banquets. The purpose was to represent the company at these functions. These social occasions took place at the back end of the year which I called 'the silly season'! It wasn't unusual to attend as many as two or three in one week. Whilst it may have seemed to be a most enjoyable aspect of the job, it could and often would be jolly hard work.

Lynn would attend most of these functions with me. I would forewarn Lynn that certain Tenants may approach her during the evening, having consumed a considerable amount of alcohol to complain about a recent rent increase, or the fact that the kitchen sink was still leaking etc. etc. Fortunately, that didn't happen too often. We had a wonderful arrangement at these banquets. I would drive to the venue and because Lynn doesn't drink alcoholic drinks, she would drive me home often the worse for wear! On more than one occasion when I was in full flight and enjoying myself, possibly as late as 1am or later, Lynn would dangle the car keys in front of me and tell me that she was leaving! I've run after her onto car parks on more than one occasion.

The Morecambe L.V.A. banquet was a memorable event when my M.D. Jack Frost was in the chair and speaker for the evening. I was responsible for ensuring that everything went smoothly, liaising with local dignitaries and L.V.A. officials. We sat down to eat at 7.30pm, followed by dancing. Then at 2am breakfast was provided! Lynn and I arrived home about 4am that morning. We were very fortunate to have an excellent and very reliable baby sister. Sarah Levick, the daughter of our Vicar, Frank Levick. Sarah would baby sit for us enabling us to attend these functions and would stay overnight.

Preston L.V.A. functions took place at the Masonic Hall in Preston. Jack Frost was chairman for the evening at one of these functions. I had arranged for the Tetley Shire Horses to parade around Preston Town Centre, prior to being at the entrance to the Masonic Hall whilst guests were arriving. I had met with Ronnie Booth, the Chief Superintendent to make the necessary arrangements for the shire horses. It was rather odd discussing with Ronnie Booth the fact that the last time we had met were discussions in his office at Seaforth Police station regarding my resignation from the police. Mr Booth had transferred from Seaforth to take charge of the Preston area when Lancashire Constabulary had taken over the Preston Borough Force.

As with most of these banquets, the ladies would arrive in all their finery, displaying jewellery, gold bracelets/necklaces etc. The men dressed in their dinner suits and black tie. On this particular occasion, Jack Tattersall, a real character and chairman of the local L.V.A. association, was so drunk at the end of the night, he was literally crawling out of the Masonic Hall on his hands and knee's! His wife was not very impressed and clearly very embarrassed. Many licensees were serious drinkers and at licensed victuallers banquets they certainly let their hair down. I once saw a table of four consume a forty ounce bottle of Gordon's Gin during the course of an evening and that followed pints consumed at the bar before the function, plus copious amounts of wine at the table during the meal.

The relationship between area manager and tenant was very different to that of the managed house area manager. The tenant is a businessman or women in their own right and it is very difficult indeed to sack an unsatisfactory tenant, whereas a manager is an employee and can be dismissed far more easily than the tenant. When a tenanted pub became available through retirement, or the licensee moved to another pub, personnel department had an extensive number of application forms from prospective tenants. There was no difficulty in finding suitable tenants, particularly on my area.

# 11

## Suicide

I had received an excellent recommendation from one of my tenants for a potential tenant by the name of Jim Hardman. Jim was Detective Chief Inspector at Skelmerdale, a very tough area on the outskirts of Liverpool. I had arranged to interview Jim at the Leigh office, not knowing that on that particular day I was to attend Wigan Magistrates' Court for speeding on the East Lancs Road. Having been fined and my license endorsed, I was not in a particularly good frame of mind on my return to the Leigh Office. Jim Hardman had been waiting for me in reception. I went over and introduced myself to Jim; telling him that he had come for an interview at a not particularly good time, due to the fact that I had been done for speeding at Wigan Magistrates' Court. His response was to simply fall about laughing! That was the best thing he could have done and I saw the funny side of the situation. The interview took place in the boardroom and I had no hesitation in advising Jim that as soon as a suitable tenancy became available, he would be first in line.

Jim Hardman had told me that he was in the process of divorce proceedings, that he was retiring from the force and that his lady friend Sylvia, a very experienced person in the licensed trade, would be joining with him once a suitable pub was available. They were to be married as soon as divorce proceedings were finalised. He also told me that he would not be prepared to take on board a pub fairly close to Skelmersdale, the villains in that area would be only too pleased to make life difficult for him. Jim had sent many a criminal to jail from that part of the world.

The Blue Bell at Newbiggin, close to Carlisle, became available and was in fact the furthest pub to the north of my area. It couldn't be further from Skelmersdale. I arranged for Jim and Sylvia to view the pub, a country public house with plenty of potential. Jim and Sylvia were delighted to accept my offer and arranged to move in within the month.

During Jim's first week, a big strapping farmer who had been barred from the Blue Bell by the previous licensee arrived at lunchtime, parking his tractor at the front of the pub. Having noticed that the name of the licensee over the door was Jim

Hardman, he walked up to the bar to confront Jim saying in a very aggressive manner "So you're the new licensee – are you a hard man?" without any hesitation Jim walked round from behind the bar and replied "Come outside with me and you'll soon find out if I'm a hard man." There was no argument from the farmer, he got on his tractor and was never to be seen again whilst Jim was licensee of the pub. It was no surprise that the farmer didn't take Jim on. Jim was a very well built and muscular guy who could certainly take care of himself.

I came to know Jim very well as an excellent businessman, he also became a friend and not just one of my 72 tenants. My Director, Tim Mostyn spent a day with me visiting my northern based tenancies and met with Jim. He was most impressed with my choice of tenant for the pub and got on with him very well indeed. They had both served as officers in the army. On leaving the Blue Bell Tim Mostyn congratulated me on finding such an admirable tenant for the pub and wanted every detail as to how I had found him. Jim Hardman certainly possessed 'The Common Touch.'

Jim confided with me one day that he had been seconded to Cyprus on a temporary basis from Lancashire Constabulary during all the troubles. He was licensed to kill and had shot and killed Greek Cypriot EOKA terrorists. Whilst the British view was that this was justifiable homicide, the Greek Cypriots view was that this was murder and there was a price on Jim Hardman's head.

I lost touch with Jim when I transferred to the managed house estate, but did receive the occasional report that he was continuing to do an excellent job at the Blue Bell. The last time I saw him was at an annual conference at the Leeds Brewery when Jim told me that he had left the Blue Bell to run a managed house, The Bold at Churchtown, Southport. Over a period of time I heard that Jim was not in good health and was suffering from depression. I very much regret that due to pressure of work that I didn't go to visit Jim in Southport.

On returning to work from holiday, I was absolutely shocked when I received a telephone call from Alan Williams, Head of Security for the brewery, that Jim Hardman had committed suicide by blowing his brains out with a double barrel shotgun. He had gone into the upstairs bathroom of the Bold, placed the shotgun in his mouth and pulled the trigger. I was to learn that a young barman at the pub had without hesitation and without being asked, taken a bucket of hot soapy water into the bathroom after Jim's body had been removed by the undertaker and washed down the ceiling and walls.

On the day of the funeral I went to the Bold arriving before opening time. I entered through the rear entrance and whilst walking round the pub, I was challenged by one of the staff as to who I was. I produced my business card, said I was a friend of Jim's and was there for the funeral and could I speak with Jim's wife Sylvia. Sylvia came down in floods of tears saying she couldn't understand why? Why had Jim felt the need to commit suicide? Sylvia went on to tell me that she had cancer and that this had been playing on Jim's mind, but in spite of this still couldn't understand what drove Jim to such a dreadful and violent end to his life.

The funeral service was held at a church very close to the Bold and was very well attended. I shall never forget the words which the vicar said during his address. He referred to Jim's distinguished service in the army, his dedication as a detective chief inspector in the police, but he posed the question as to why Jim had felt the need to commit suicide. He simply said that it would remain a mystery and that no matter how well you think you know a person, how well do you really know them. I have often pondered on the subject of Jim's death. He had seen a lot of violence in Cyprus and as a policeman in Skelmersdale. He had chosen to end his life in a violent manner. His wife Sylvia didn't think her cancer had too much bearing on his decision. One cannot help but wonder if Jim had received threats which had played on his mind, particularly bearing in mind having killed EOKA terrorists and that there had been a price on his head. It will forever remain a mystery.

A most memorable occasion arose when my boyhood idle, Tom Finney, called at our house Tanglewood in Garstang. The central heating boiler situated in the kitchen was most unreliable. I had contacted Tom Finney's plumbing company for an estimate, never expecting the maestro himself to call. Tom carried out a thorough examination of the existing system, suggesting a brilliant idea i.e. to open up a part of the exterior wall with a door, installing a new solid fuel boiler in that area, thereby avoiding fumes in the kitchen. The new boiler would be fed with anthracite beans via a hopper from the driveway. Tom was an absolute gentleman and left me with an estimate for the work. Before he left, I took the opportunity of telling him how much I had admired him when I was a boy, watching him playing for Preston North End. Unfortunately for Tom Finney and his company, a brewery contractor was able to carry out the same work at a cheaper price. I felt very embarrassed ringing to advise Tom that I had found a cheaper contractor.

The Bay Horse at Thornton Cleveleys, near Blackpool was undoubtedly my biggest tenanted pub in terms of turnover. Overall converted barrelage averaged twenty barrels per week i.e. draught and bottled beers, wines and spirits and soft drinks. The tenant, Bernard Regan was a real character. His wife Vi assisted in the running of the pub but also had other interests. She ran a hairdressers shop in the area.

I always looked forward to visiting Bernard at the Bay Horse. He was undoubtedly one of my best tenants. A regular routine developed on my arrival, I would inspect the cellar, signing the cellar card and establishing that everything was in order maintenance wise. Bernard would then suggest that we went to his house at Skippool Creek, a lovely detached house on the banks of the River Wyre. Bernard would brew up and we would chat about trade and how the past couple of weeks or so had gone. He would often put a Max Bygraves record on whilst we sat there chatting. Bernard loved the licensed trade, he lived, eat and slept his pub and referred to the experience as like having a party every day!

A thing which never ceased to amaze me was the way the carpet in front of the main bar would become matted and shiny with the spillage of beer. The pub was so busy that over a period of time the cleaners would mop the carpet in that area! Once a year the carpet would be steam cleaned and it came up like new. No wonder, it was a quality Wilton body carpet.

The brewery went on strike for a period of three months. Tetley draymen were demanding an unreasonable pay increase and had been supported by their union, the Transport and General Workers' Union. This was a very difficult period when tenants were freed from the tie and were responsible for obtaining their beers from other sources. However, tenancy area managers became very involved, ensuring that their pubs were receiving adequate supplies of beers to continue trading.

Due to the large amount of draught beer consumed at the Bay Horse, I was able to negotiate arrangements for supplies from Theakstons Brewery. I contacted Paul Theakston, Managing

Director, who arranged for stillages to be installed in the cellar of the pub, together with manual beer engines. Whilst Tetley beers had been very popular with the locals, they thoroughly enjoyed Theakstons traditional bitter and surprisingly the sales of bitter actually increased. Once the strike had finished and the Bay Horse returned to Tetley beers, the locals were quite disappointed.

Rent was assessed every three years for Tetley Tenants and the Bay Horse's rent became due to be assessed. I sat down with Bernard at his house in Skippool Creek and went through all the figures with him, informing Bernard that it was inevitable that there would most likely be a hefty increase. When the new rent was assessed by head office, it came out at £10,000 per annum which proved at that time to be the highest rent for any pub in the Tetley region west of the Pennines. I was clearly very concerned as to what Bernard's reaction would be.

I phoned Bernard and arranged a visit to discuss the new rent with him at his house at Skippool Creek. Bernard was horrified at the figure but after a very lengthy discussion agreed to pay the new rent and signed the agreement. I told Bernard very much off the record that I personally thought the rent to be excessive and why didn't he consider buying a free house. Over a period of ten years the rent of £120,000 would have bought him a very nice free house. His response was that if he were ten years younger, he would certainly have considered that as an option. Bernard went on to tell me that the only way he would leave the pub would be in a wooden box.

Bernard did die at the Bay Horse and I attended his funeral. I stood outside the pub with Vi and their son Gary, who had returned from his home in New York to see the coffin being carried out through the front door. I arranged for the transfer of the licence to Vi and she carried on for some time continuing to run the pub very successfully. Vi told me an amusing story of a situation which had occurred the previous week. A stag do had taken place in the public bar when a big strapping local rugby player had climbed up onto a table and started to strip off to the familiar music of the stripper. The locals had gathered around to watch and Vi had tried to get through from the lounge bar to stop the lad stripping, but simply couldn't get through, she just watched from a distance! When the lad had taken all his clothes off to rapturous applaud from the punters, Vi said that she was very disappointed, saying that it was 'only that big' indicating with her finger and thumb!

Paul Theakston referred to himself as the black sheep of the family. He decided to leave the company and form his own brewery in Yorkshire. Undecided as to what name he should give the new company, the story goes that his wife said that as he had often referred to himself as the black sheep of the family, why not call the new brewery 'The Black Sheep Brewery.' The marketing department clearly had a sense of humour when they decided to name one of their bottled beers 'Old Fart!'

Licensees on my patch found it quite amusing when they heard how I relaxed at weekends from the pressure of my job. Apart from walks in the country with the family and our cocker spaniel dog, I would sit in my leather swivel chair with my feet up on the matching footstool by the window of the lounge; with wonderful views of the surrounding countryside and fells in the distance. I enjoyed the occasional cigar, a Henry Winterman's half corona which I would smoke with my headphones on listening to classical music and opera. In addition to this and to set the scene, I would treat myself to a brandy and port in equal measure, which is still my favourite drink. It had to be Courvoisier brandy and a decent port.

I am passionate about music, whether it's classical, opera, cathedral organ, the Wurlitzer or brass bands. Listening to a brass band playing Christmas carols can bring tears to my eyes. However, there is no doubt whatsoever that my favourite music of all time has to be Wagner's Ring Cycle. Many people find it to be very heavy, but to me it is not only emotionally overwhelming, but unbelievably beautiful and moving. This colossal work by Wagner can in parts be deeply troubling but is also the ultimate expression of nineteenth century romanticism.

The following are words from a plaque beside the organ of The Parish Church of St Lawrence in Ludlow, South Shropshire and sums up my passion for music.

> Music can peacefully & wonderfully
> Lift up our hearts & minds.
> It has the power to express
> What cannot be said in words.
> It is truly international & everlasting.
> It transcends all barriers of time
> And culture & gives expression
> To our deepest emotions & feelings.
> Music can bring us into a
> Completely new dimension.
> Please hear and give thanks
> For the gift of music.

During the height of the season in Blackpool, as the Double Diamond Rep. I was able to pop into the Tower Ballroom and listen to the Wurlitzer being played by Reginald Dixon. It's quite a sight watching the organ rise up into the ballroom every alternate hour. I was very amused to hear a story which Noel Rawsthorne, the then cathedral organist at Liverpool Anglican Cathedral told me. Following the Annual Organ Recital, I was chatting with Noel Rawsthorne and happened to mention the Wurlitzer at the Tower Ballroom in Blackpool. He told me that one day he was alone in the cathedral and had played 'I do like to be beside the seaside' and that it had sounded far better on the cathedral organ than the Wurlitzer! The mind boggles.

I became very fond of visiting Liverpool Cathedral and became a patron of the organ. I still attend the annual organ recital to this day, held in October of each year to celebrate the installation of the organ. The present organist, Ian Tracy is internationally acclaimed and gives regular recitals at the cathedral and always plays at the annual organ recital. I love the Gothic architecture of the cathedral. It has the highest and heaviest ringing peal of bells in the World. A trip to the top of the tower via two lifts is awesome. I was once advised by a guide that the best way to view the stain glass windows is through binoculars, the effect is quite stunning.

By the ground floor lift, there is an old red telephone box which is in working order. People ask why it is there. The reason is that Giles Gilbert Scott was the architect for the building of the cathedral, this was his largest ever design and the telephone box his smallest. I was discussing this on one occasion with a Liverpudlian who had never visited the cathedral. I asked him if he knew the significance regarding the telephone box in the cathedral and with a typical Liverpudlian sense of humour he replied "Is it a direct line to God?" I have organised three guided tours to the cathedral, two from Lymm Baptist Church and one from the Rotary Club of Sandbach. They were very successful tours.

Frank was the licensee of The Nelson pub in Bolton, otherwise known as the Flying Ashtray! He was one of my problem licensee's. The pub was filthy and the beer not fit to drink. Unfortunately, I had inherited Frank when I took over the area. At closing time in the evenings, Frank would more often than not be drunk and would hurl small metal ashtrays at his customers to get them to leave, hence the nickname 'The Flying Ashtray.' I invited Frank to resign rather than be sacked, telling him that the Bolton Annual Licensing Magistrates' would be objecting to the renewal of his licence to sell alcohol.

Frank eventually resigned and a decision was made for the managed house division to take over the pub from tenancy. The day of the removal can only be described as hilarious. I arrived at 10am to find the removal van in a side road by the pub. Throughout the day Frank started drinking from a bottle of Gin, getting quite paralytic and making life generally difficult, particularly for the removal men. They saw an opportunity to start taking packing boxes though the rear entrance, bringing the same box back in through the front door, thereby stretching out the time in the hope of gaining more financially from the move. At the end of the day they were never paid!

About 4.30pm with Frank completely paralytic, his long suffering wife had ordered a taxi, I helped her to get Frank into the taxi when he suddenly blurted out that their dog was still in the cellar. He was in no state to go back into the pub for the dog; I didn't want him to get out of the taxi so I told him to stay where he was with his wife and that I would bring the dog. The cellar at the Nelson is below ground and the flap to gain entry behind the bar. I knew that this dog was a nasty Alsatian and would be difficult to get out of the cellar. I lifted the flap to be confronted with this big, nasty Alsatian barking and snarling at me. Fortunately, as the reader will know; I had experience of dealing with police dogs. I reached down, grabbed hold of the dog's collar with both hands, yanked it up as far away from me as I was able, ran out to the taxi, throwing it into the back and slamming the door. I was very fortunate not to be bitten. That was the last I saw of Frank.

The Nelson had to be fumigated and when the upholstery to the fixed seating in the lounge was removed by contractors, hundreds of cockroaches were found crawling around. I knew that the general conditions of the pub were bad, but not that bad. The thought of customers sitting on those seats doesn't bear thinking about.

## 12

### Garstang

Garstang is a very pleasant and popular market town. Whilst we were living there we made many friends and acquaintances. Pat Seed was a resident of Garstang and well known throughout the U.K. for her fundraising activities for cancer. Her husband Geoff was a popular and well known person in the area and reminded me somewhat of George Ekins, my police inspector at Seaforth. Like George Ekins, Geoff had also been a rear gunner in a Lancaster Bomber during the Second World War. We had come to know Geoff quite well, meeting with him after church and at social functions in the area. Whilst it was common knowledge that Pat Seed had cancer, no one was to know that Geoff was to die before his wife Pat.

One of Lancashire's biggest tragedies was to occur on the 23$^{rd}$ May, 1984. Sixteen people were killed and twenty four injured during an explosion at the water pumping station in Abbeystead, near Lancaster. Villagers from St Michaels-on-Wyre and residents of Garstang were being shown round by North West Water officials. Nine people died immediately, while another seven died later of their injuries, including two children. Geoff Seed was one of those killed. The explosion took place in an underground valve house at the plant. An investigation by the Health and Safety Executive found that the pumping station was sited close to coal seams which made it vulnerable to build-ups of methane gas. It was suggested that one of the party had lit up a cigarette which had caused the explosion. A wealthy hotelier and member of the Rotary Club of Over Wyre had also been killed in the explosion.

Alec Dillon was the Tenants Liaison representative for the Preston and surrounding area for Tetley Tenants. He was tenant of The Grapes at Goosnargh and quite a character. I called at the pub early one evening and on entering the pub I saw that there was no one behind the bar. I sat on a bar stool awaiting the arrival of someone looking after the bar and was quite taken aback by an elderly well dressed business man. He walked through from the snug at the back of the pub, went behind the bar, pulled two pints of bitter, helping himself to three drinks from the optics, placing money in the till and taking change.

I continued waiting at the bar without saying a word to the person who had just helped himself to drinks. Alec Dillon arrived on the scene some ten minutes later and I told him of my concern of what I had just witnessed. He found my predicament quite amusing, telling me that the person I had seen go behind the bar was a local Judge and that it was an arrangement he was more than happy with. That particular evening of the week, the judge met with solicitors' and friends for a few drinks before arriving home.

When Alec Dillon retired, I went to his farewell do the evening prior to his departure with flowers for his wife, saying a few words of thanks on behalf of the brewery. I always attended these farewell do's to thank the licensee and his wife for their services to the company. The following morning, both Alec and I arrived at Preston Magistrates' Court, Licensing Division, looking rather bleary eyed from the night before. This was for the transfer of the license to the new tenant. Whilst waiting for the case to be heard, Alec was sat with both hands in his pockets when I noticed that his flies were open. When I pointed this out to him he replied very casually "Bob - a dead bird never fell out of its nest!" It took me all my time not to burst out laughing. That would have gone down like a lead balloon in front of the magistrates'.

'Tales of the Unexpected' was a popular television series and the following circumstances would certainly have qualified for the title of that programme. Our family spent a holiday in Perranporth, Cornwall and during this holiday we visited a retail outlet selling hundreds of second hand books. After browsing for some considerable time, I came across four large and rather dusty books, portraying excellent quality prints of famous paintings hanging in art galleries throughout the U.K. I purchased these books at a very reasonable price with the intention of having a number of them framed. The majority of which were for one of my pubs and the remainder for myself.

There were about twenty two prints which I had selected and took them very carefully out of the books. A Mr Mort specialised in framing pictures for the brewery and was situated a stones throw from York Minster. I took the day off, taking the prints over to York and asked Mr Mort to frame eight of the prints for me, invoicing them separately to me, the remainder to be invoiced to the brewery. Two particular prints were the well known 'And when did you last see your father' and 'One of the family.' I was to discover that both originals hung in the Walker Art Gallery in Liverpool.

On arriving home with my own framed prints, I hung two of them over the fireplace in the lounge at Tanglewood. 'When did you last see your father' on the right and 'One of the family' to the left. I had never been to the Walker Art gallery before and with my growing interest in the Pre-Raphaelite period of paintings, I was particularly keen to see the two originals which hung over my fireplace in Garstang. I took the opportunity of calling in at the Walker Art Gallery en route to the brewery head office in Duke Street, Liverpool. On arrival at the gallery I asked one of the staff where I could find the two particular paintings I was anxious to see. I was directed to a large gallery at first floor level. On entering the gallery, I was absolutely taken aback and totally amazed when I saw the two very large originals in oil, hanging together on the wall, in exactly the same position over my fireplace, 'When did you last see your father' on the right and 'One of the family' to the left. The sheer incredulous odds of that happening are quite staggering. All the way back to Cornwall, with two of the pictures selected from 4 books, hanging in my lounge in the same position as those at the Walker Art Gallery defies logic!

The Walker Art Gallery in Liverpool was founded in 1873 by the local brewer, Sir Andrew Barclay Walker. His company, Peter Walker Limited formed part of what was to become Allied Breweries PLC. This wonderful gallery which displays old master paintings and particularly oil paintings of the pre-Raphaelite period was to become directly responsible for my love of Victorian art and in particular the Pre-Raphaelite period.

The Fenwick at Claughton, Near Lancaster, was a typical quintessential country pub with lots of character and one of the more upmarket pubs on my patch. The licensee, Ernie Nuttall ran a very good public house with excellent hand pulled Tetley beers, providing good home cooked food. Customers would beat a path to the door of the Fenwick from miles around. Ernie was one of life's characters, a true entrepreneur blessed with 'the common touch.' He owned an E-type Jaguar which was in mint condition. Ernie was very proud of his Jag but decided one day to part with it, putting an advert in the press at quite a good price. He was pleasantly surprised at the number of persons wanting to buy the car but decided to withdraw it from sale. He repeated the exercise twice more, increasing the asking price and still, there were persons wishing to purchase the Jag. Finally Ernie decided to keep the car, realising it was such a valuable asset.

About 70,000 of the iconic Jaguar E-type were ever made, between 1961 and 1974 and were to become known as 'the greatest crumpet-catcher known to man!' When Frank Sinatra first saw the car he said "I want one and I want it now!" The 3.8 engine could reach 150 mph. George Best and George Harrison had one. The car was elegant, refined, sexy, aggressive and powerful. No wonder that Ernie Nuttall decided to keep his E-type!

An elderly couple would visit the Fenwick on a weekly basis. They would always sit at the same table towards the back of the pub and close to the car park. Upon finishing his meal one evening, the man suddenly slumped forward onto the table, dead. What a predicament for Ernie! The problem was to avoid taking the body through a pub full of customers. He rang for an ambulance and insisted they came to the rear car park in order to remove the body through the rear entrance. The body was removed without many of the clientele knowing what had happened. Not a very good advert for any pub to have a customer die after a meal! The mind boggles, but what a way to go! I am often heard to say "I'm not afraid of dying; I just don't want to be there when it happens!"

Ernie Nuttall retired from the pub and the Cavalier Steak Bar division of the brewery made a decision to take over the pub from tenancy. I was so concerned that this was the wrong decision. With my local knowledge of the area I knew that it was not a viable proposition. The pub needed another good tenant. I therefore rang Mr Mitchall, Director of the Cavalier Division and arranged to meet with him at his office in Leeds. I told him of my concerns and of my knowledge of the licensed trade in that area. However, Mr Mitchall was adamant that the Fenwick would be viable and that he planned to spend a considerable amount on money on the pub, with a large structural alteration, extending the dining room area.

The Fenwick was closed during very expensive structural alterations. On completion of the work, Graham West, a very successful licensee running a large managed house for the company in Morecambe was transferred to the Fenwick to run this new operation. Sadly, Graham's wife had recently died at his previous pub. The decision to move Graham to the Fenwick by the area manager proved to be a disaster. Graham, full of remorse and suffering from a serious bout of depression due to his wife's death committed suicide in the pub. He took himself up to a front bedroom after closing time late one evening, taking a huge amount of sleeping pills which he washed down with a bottle of Courvoisier Brandy. The Fenwick never recovered from the change from tenancy to the Cavalier Steak Bar division and eventually ended back on tenancy. To the best of my knowledge, the pub struggles to survive to this day.

Tim Mostyn and I attended the Chorley L.V.A. annual banquet together. The guest speaker for the evening was Chief Superintendent Spence who was in charge of the Chorley Division. Mr Spence had risen from the rank of Inspector when he was in charge of the mounted section at H.Q. Hutton and was the Inspector who had asked me to transfer to the mounted section whilst I was a cadet on dog section. Tim Mostyn sat next to Mr Spence on the top table. Towards the end of the evening, Tim Mostyn and I were having a quiet drink together at the bar when he told me that the Chief Super had expressed his concern about the fact that I had given Jim Hardman the Blue Bell at Newbiggin. He based his complaint on the fact that Jim Hardman had divorced his wife and was on his second marriage. Little did Mr Spence realize that Tim Mostyn was on his third marriage! EILM told Mr Spence that Jim Hardman was doing an excellent job and that he had no problem at all with his appointment. Tim Mostyn however didn't tell him that he himself was on his third marriage! Tim Mostyn was very much a man's man, but was also very much a ladies man. His first two marriages had been a disaster, probably due to the fact that he lived, ate and slept his job as a brewery director. He was hardly ever at home.

Competitions within the tenancy department took place periodically. Lowenbrau bottled lager was introduced to the company and a competition was held for the most sales on each individual tenancy area manager's patch. Due to the nature of my area and the fact that I had 72 pubs, it wasn't particularly difficult to win the competition. The prize was a trip to the Munich beer festival in Germany.

Together with colleagues from the managed house division and brewery directors', I flew to Munich where we had lunch in the very prestigious Lowenbrau head office. Their dining room was at the top of a tower, overlooking Munich. Following lunch, excitement and cheering came from a small number of our group who had gathered on the terrace outside. They were waving towards a building opposite. On joining them, there, on a balcony at the top of a block of flats quite close to the brewery tower, was a gorgeous young German girl, topless, lounging on a sun bed. She wasn't the slightest bit embarrassed and started waving back.

We then went to the festival by coach and our guide advised us that the crowds at the entrance would be so vast, we were to link arms keeping together en route to the massive Lowenbrau marquee. It was quite an experience being served with copious amounts of draught Lowenbrau in litre steins. The highlight of the evening was the Bavarian band. They were playing on a raised stage in the middle of the marquee. An American guy had agreed to buy the whole of the band a round of drinks, providing he could conduct them playing a tune of his choice. It was quite a sight watching the American conducting the band with great enthusiasm whilst they played the stars and stripes. On returning to London late at night, the view of St. Pauls Cathedral from the aircraft was awesome. We were all very well oiled! and poured off the plane at Heathrow.

Another competition was held by Grants of St James' the wine and spirit division of Allied Breweries. The winner was to win a trip to the Courvoisier Chateau in France. I was really keen to win this competition. My favourite drink is Courvoisier, which I enjoy with an equal measure of port. However, in spite of the fact that I encouraged all of my licensee's to stock up with wines and spirits, surprisingly, Hector Jones, a Liverpool tenancy area manager won the competition. Many years later whilst on holiday in France; Lynn, my sister Anne and brother-in-law John, had the opportunity of visiting the Courvoisier Chateau when we were taken on a guided tour by a delightful Canadian girl. The tour ended with a visit to the bottling plant where we saw 40oz bottles coming off the bottling line. What an experience that tour was.

Eric and Gladys Biddle were tenant licensee's of The Squirrel at Horwich, Bolton. The pub was quite unique in many ways as a direct result of the manner which it was run by Eric and Gladys. A Matchless motor cycle in immaculate condition was displayed on the end of the lounge bar. Eric was a motor cycle fanatic; he had ridden Norton's on many occasions in the Isle of Man T.T. On land at the rear of the pub were three railway wagons full of various models of motor cycles, mainly Norton's, which Eric had faithfully restored.

Gladys had the reputation of being a bit of a dragon. She didn't suffer fools gladly but for some reason I got on with her very well. Unusually, Gladys always referred to me as boss or Mr Mynett. The relationship which I had with most of my tenants was to use Christian names only. Gladys's food was excellent and I always timed my visits so that I could eat at the pub, combining business with pleasure.

Unfortunately for Eric, he was slowly loosing the sight of his left eye and was particularly concerned that long term he would be unable to carry on his passion of restoring motor cycles to their former glory. Eric rang me one day to complain most bitterly about an injury he had received that morning. A drayman, delivering 36 gallon barrels of bitter had rolled one from the dray wagon down a slight slope towards Eric, a distance of some twelve feet. Eric was standing by the cellar door at ground level and had been quite unprepared. The barrel had struck him on the leg, causing quite a nasty injury. Fortunately, his leg wasn't broken. The nature of the circumstances were such that the drayman was clearly out of order and had totally ignored health and safety procedures.

I went to the Squirrel with my portable typewriter, sitting down with Eric and taking down a statement from him on the typewriter. When I returned to the office I rang George Ware, the distribution manager at the brewery, telling him of the incident at the Squirrel and the fact that I would be forwarding my report to him, with a copy to my director Tim Mostyn. George Ware was in charge of all the Tetley draymen. As far as he was concerned his men could hardly do any wrong. I suspected that was due to the fact that they were members of the very powerful union, the Transport and General Workers' Union. His attitude to the incident at the Squirrel was to totally disbelieve what I had told him, stating that his drayman would simply not be so careless. I was furious at his attitude and told him in no uncertain terms of my disgust and that furthermore, I would be taking the matter further with Tim Mostyn.

The outcome of the incident was that no further action was taken against the drayman. As far as Eric and Gladys were concerned, they were clearly disgusted at the outcome of their complaint. George Ware didn't have the courtesy to call at the Squirrel, particularly bearing in mind that the Biddle's were excellent and highly regarded tenants of the company. Furthermore, they had become personal friends of Tim Mostyn over the years. I have no doubt that no action was taken to avoid further possibilities of industrial action from many militant members of the draymen's union. Tim Mostyn's hands were tied. There was little or nothing he could do considering the sensitive nature of the situation

Rod Firth, a director, had been transferred from an admin job with the company at Burton-on-Trent. He was a bumptious man full of his own importance and not at all popular with his fellow directors' Tim Mostyn called him a whiz kid and had no time for the man whatsoever. His attitude was of a very superior nature and I was to cross swords with the man later on in my career with the brewery. Unfortunately the M.D. Jack Frost had no experience whatsoever with the tied estate. His past had been purely on the free trade side. As Firth had progressed to a more senior position, the M.D. had given him carte blanche with overall responsibility for the tied estate which proved to be a big mistake.

Tim Mostyn had arranged a meeting with his tenancy area managers in the board room at the Duke Street head office in Liverpool. Half way through the meeting, Firth came barging in to the meeting, cutting Tim Mostyn off with no apology, marching across to the top of the table where Tim Mostyn was conducting the meeting, throwing down a number of papers and shouting "What's this Mostyn, these overdue figures are dreadful." He was relating to statistics as to the number of tenants who were late payers. Tim Mostyn was absolutely livid, telling Firth that his attitude was disgraceful and totally unacceptable. You could have cut the atmosphere with a knife. He gave Firth the biggest bollocking he'd probably ever had in his life. We area managers' just sat there transfixed at the scene, lapping up the fact that Tim Mostyn had taken Firth down a peg or two. As an ex major in the army, Tim Mostyn would have no truck with the likes of a jumped up so called whiz kid like Firth.

The Smugglers at Morecambe was run by a lovely elderly couple. Gilbert Norris was the licensee assisted by his wife. During the period I was the area manager for the Smugglers, Mrs Norris died and my director Tim Mostyn and I went to the funeral. We had been invited by Gilbert to go straight to the Smugglers prior to the church service. On arrival before opening time, we found the pub thronging with people who were attending the funeral. Local dignitaries and the chief of police were in attendance. To our surprise, there in front of the lounge bar lay Mrs Norris in an open coffin. Gilbert Norris invited us to go and look at her. Whilst I am far from squeamish, I chose to go and speak with the police chief whilst Tim Mostyn accompanied Gilbert to the coffin. On arrival at the coffin Gilbert said to Tim Mostyn "Doesn't she look lovely?" At the appointed time the undertakers screwed down the lid of the coffin in front of the bar. This was quite surreal; the family were crying and clearly very distraught.

After the church service we went back to the Smugglers for drinks and a buffet. On the way back to the office Tim Mostyn said to me "You have some very strange customs here in the north of England!" Neither he nor I had experienced anything like it before. I am reminded whilst on the subject of strange customs. The Plough at Heaton Moor, Stockport was to become one of my managed houses on transferring from tenancy. An elderly man who drank in the pub had no relatives whatsoever. His friends and locals had been the nearest thing to a family. This man had made a very unusual request that when he died, his coffin was to be taken into the Plough and placed on trestles in front of the bar. The licensee had agreed to this arrangement. The man died and as requested the coffin went into the Plough. The locals were served with a pint of their choice, paid for by the deceased prior to his death. They placed their pints on top of the coffin and drank to the deceased's health!

Apart from licensed victuallers banquets, several other social occasions took place associated with the licensed trade. One very memorable such function was held at a gentleman's bowling club in St. Helens. Tetley brewery area managers' and directors' met with Greenall's brewery opposite numbers for a social evening and bowling match. Whilst I occasionally enjoy the odd game of bowls, unfortunately for me I was drawn against Greenall's champion bowler and was thoroughly thrashed. The most wonderful thing about the evening was that while we were bowling, the St Helens Brass Band was playing at the side of the green. Furthermore, drinks were provided free of charge throughout the evening. Following a couple of pints of bitter I was to spend the rest of the evening drinking my favourite, brandy and port. On completion of the match, Greenall's with their national bowling champion had thoroughly beaten the Tetley team. Probably one of the finest buffets I have ever had completed a most remarkable evening. Fortunately, I was to be driven home by a colleague.

My company car was due to be changed and I ordered an Austin Princess. The vehicle was a front wheel drive and proved to be an excellent towing car for our caravan. Having left one of my tenanted pubs in Morecambe, I was travelling about 45 m.p.h. and heading for the M6 motorway when the steering completely packed up. I lost control of the car but I was lucky that there was little traffic on the road and was fortunate to bring the car to a halt at the side of the road. The steering wheel had become completely disconnected from the ability to steer the car in any direction. I was very fortunate not to have entered the M6 motorway on my way home. Had the steering gone on the motorway, it could well have resulted in a nasty accident.

The car was brand new and under warranty. A dealership in Preston arrived on the scene and hoisted the car onto the back of a transporter, taking it back to their workshop in Preston. The brewery arranged a pool car for me until the Princess had been attended to. After a period of some ten days, Tim Mostyn contacted me to say that the dealership had found the fault to be with the rack and pinion system. It would appear that the manufacturer had assembled the rack and pinion incorrectly! The fault had been attended to and I was to arrange to collect the car.

I told Tim Mostyn that I was most unhappy with the car and refused to drive it until I had been given every assurance that it would be save to drive. Furthermore, I explained that I wanted an independent vehicle examiner to inspect the car, confirming that it would be safe. I arranged for the Institute of Advanced Motorists to examine the car. I had been a member of the institute for many years. In the meantime, the company secretary became involved in the dispute saying to my Director Tim Mostyn "If Bob Mynett isn't prepared to drive that car then he can't do his job." hinting therefore that I could be dismissed. Tim Mostyn was most supportive and told the secretary that he backed me completely and considered my request for a thorough examination of the car to be reasonable.

The report came back in writing from the I.A.M. that the rack and pinion had been inspected. They found the assembly had been incorrectly put back together by the main dealer. The car would have been a death trap and I had fortunately had the good sense not to drive it. Thank goodness I had had the support of my director in that difficult situation. The car was eventually given the all clear and I had no other choice than to accept it back.

Hector Jones left for his annual holidays over the Easter period. One of his tenanted pubs on the Dock Road in Liverpool was holding their annual Easter Bonnet competition and he was unable to attend. Hector asked me to stand in for him. I asked Lynn if she would attend the pub competition with me, saying that she was far more qualified than me to judge such an event. Lynn was a bit unsure about the nature of the pub, but I assured her that it was O.K. We arrived at the dock road pub, a very basic typical Liverpool boozer, to find the pub absolutely packed with ladies wearing the most amazing Easter bonnets. Most of them seemed to be drinking bottles of stout. The atmosphere was very jovial and Lynn and I thoroughly enjoyed ourselves. At the appointed time the ladies paraded around the pub; clearly very proud of their endeavours with their amazing bonnets. Lynn chose the winner and I gave a speech on behalf of the brewery, thanking the ladies for providing such an enjoyable and entertaining evening. Fortunately for me, Lynn drove me home, a little worse for wear!

A further problem arose with my company car immediately prior to taking the family on our annual holiday. We had booked a fortnight's holiday on a caravan site in Cornwall and the pool car loaned to me didn't have a tow bar. Tim Mostyn had recommended the caravan site. A retired colonel from his regiment had set up the site on retirement. Cyril Smith, a Bolton tenant was very friendly with Tim Mostyn and very kindly offered to loan me his Volvo which was a real Godsend. Arrangements were made for Cyril to use the company car and the appropriate insurance was put in place. Towing the caravan down to Cornwall with Cyril's Automatic Volvo was like armchair driving! We had a most enjoyable fortnight with good weather. On our return Lynn took the seat covers off the car and washed them. I thoroughly cleaned the car and the family returned to Bolton to hand the car back to Cyril. He refused to accept any remuneration for the loan of the car.

The pub was closed when we returned Cyril's car. The children were fascinated with the fruit machines and Cyril gave them a good quantity of coins to play on them. They were in their element playing the fruit machines. The children were then taken on a guided tour of the pub, visiting the below ground level cellar. The highlight was Cyril placing a beer crate behind the bar and allowing the children to pull draught traditional beer from the manual beer engines. Our youngest daughter Alison would be about 6 years of age at the time, Mark 8 and Karen 10. The image of the children standing on a beer crate assisted by Cyril and pulling a pint still brings a smile to my face. Whilst Lynn has never drunk alcoholic drinks, the fact that the children's dad worked for a brewery for 18 years, it was therefore never a big deal going into a pub or licensed restaurant. Fortunately, to the best of my knowledge, they have always had a sensible and balanced outlook where drink is concerned.

The Black Horse at Preesall, Near Blackpool was a typical olde worlde pub with beams and very low ceilings. The licensee George Omerod was a lovely man as well as an excellent landlord. The only place in the pub where I could stand upright was between two low beams in front of the bar with my head touching the ceiling. George's son was training to become a solicitor and one day George told me that he had taught him to be a gentleman in drink. I have never forgotten this advice and hopefully my son Mark has taken heed of this. Working for a brewery for eighteen years certainly involves a considerable amount of drinking, if only to check that the quality of the beer is satisfactory! On occasions when I have had a lot to drink, I simply love everybody and ultimately just want to go to sleep. I find it hard to accept the excuse that alcohol is the reason for outrageous and violent behaviour. No matter how much one has had to drink, in the final analysis; surely one is still in touch with one's faculties! This is certainly a mute point which I have debated on many an occasion.

Tetley's Brewery had a number of magnificent shire horses. They were stabled at the Leeds brewery. I was to use the dray horses on several occasions to promote the company, raising money for charity or for the opening of a prestigious pub following structural alterations. The shire horses were used to deliver beer to Leeds city centre pubs whilst I worked for the brewery. A member of the public wrote to a local Leeds newspaper complaining that the shire horses were a nuisance, causing an obstruction and that they should not be allowed to carry on. This proved to be the finest advert possible for the brewery. National newspapers and television carried the story. There was absolute outrage by the population of Leeds, supporting the brewery with deliveries by the shire horses. I have often wondered whether this was some deliberate ploy by a clever marketing person, knowing what the outcome would be! Lots of free advertising.

The chairman of the brewery, Richard Martin, encouraged directors' and area managers' to raise funds for the Licensed Trade Charity, a charity supporting mainly retired licensee's with health problems, trauma or family breakdown and that recognition would be given to those persons raising the most money. I saw this as a challenge and set about to raise a large sum of money in the Bolton area. I held a meeting with Bolton licensee's suggesting a 'crazy carnival' where licensee's, including myself, would dress up in some outrageous costume and walk, ride or drive a distance of five miles through the town. The response and enthusiasm was fantastic. I met with the Chief Superintendent of Bolton Police who was most supportive and between us we established a suitable route.

The number of innovative ideas was simply amazing. I arranged for the Tetley shires to parade around Bolton during the afternoon prior to the event, then to head up the procession during the evening. I rode a white 16 hand horse for the five miles dressed as a Roman Centurian. One licensee borrowed a 40 foot flat wagon and had a Dixieland jazz band playing on the back of the wagon. Some of the costumes and outfits worn by licensees were hilarious. As we all gathered outside a hotel in the centre of Bolton for photographs by the press, my horse started playing up and Tim Mostyn started taking the mickey out of me saying "Come on Bob, can't you ride better than that." The money made from the event raised over £1000 which was donated to the licensee's charity.

I was quite crafty in the way I encouraged directors' and colleague's to sponsor me. I arrived at head office, Duke Street and made a bee line to the M.D.'s office. On telling Jack Frost's secretary the nature of my visit, I went into the M.D.'s office armed with my sponsor form. At that stage there were no signatures on the form. I encouraged Mr. Frost to sponsor me for £20, telling him what I had planned and of course just happened to mention that it was Richard Martin's initiative, the Chairman of the company. Having Jack Frost's signature at the top of the form encouraged other directors', office staff and my own colleague's to be very generous. As I was walking along the main corridor at head office, I was stopped by Rod Firth who asked what I doing. When I told him, he was quite stroppy saying that I should not have been there and surely I had better things to do. Even producing the sponsor form and showing him the M.D.'s signature didn't impress him. The miserable sod refused to sponsor me.

I was to organise a similar event some years later as a managed house area manager. This time it was Wigan licensee's who were determined not to be outdone by the performance of the licensee's in Bolton. The money raised was slightly more than that in Bolton and donated to the same licensee's charity. On this occasion I rode my son's chopper, dressed in a kilt, a Boy Scout hat and funny glasses. My director Tim Hill, joined in with the fun and walked the five miles dressed as a huntsman. Two shires were heading up the parade and unfortunately; as I rode past them getting too close, I received a nasty blow on my right ankle from the huge hoof of one of the shires; my own fault for getting too close.

At the end of the evening I was in a lot of pain with my ankle which had swollen quite considerably. Norman Rae and his wife Chris had attended the event. They were tenants of the Punch Bowl, Churchtown, near Garstang. Norman offered to take me to A & E in Wigan in his Volvo saloon. On arrival at the hospital, I was getting out of the car with some difficulty and holding on to the side of the car, when without warning the car door was slammed shut trapping my fingers in the door. The pain was intense and without those thick rubber seals on the Volvo, I could well have lost some fingers! The sight of me arriving in A & E, supported on either side by Lynn and Norman must have been quite comical, hobbling along with my injured hand giving me grief. I shall never know who slammed the door onto my hand, but Lynn is quite adamant to this day that it wasn't her.

The sight of four shires pulling a dray is in my view absolutely magnificent. These gentle giants were a wonderful promotional tool for the brewery. One event which I organised was the re-opening of a pub alteration in Leigh, near Wigan. I had arranged for the T.V. personality Stuart Hall to open the pub. The Tetley shires were brought over to Leigh the evening prior to the opening. Unfortunately it was raining on the day of the official opening. The man in charge of the shires was a big strapping chap. I was amazed to see him in tears as he was gently bringing the shires out of the huge horse box into the rain. He loved his shires and to see them getting wet; their horse brasses gleaming was simply too much for him and very emotional. He had slept in the horse box with the shires overnight and was so distraught that his beloved horses were getting wet.

I was to attend the Cheshire Show many years later in 2006, when the Tetley shires paraded around the show ring with other brewery shires. It was a sad day. The official announced that it was the last time the Tetley shires would be attending the Cheshire Show. The following article appeared in the Times dated 11th May 2006 headed 'Pulling power given the push.' The Tetley brewery shire horses are to retire, ending a 184-year tradition. The company, established by Joshua Tetley in Leeds, West Yorkshire, says that the animals are too costly and ceremonial events have dropped from 200 a year to 70. The remaining shires, Prince, Charles, John Jo and William, will be harnessed up for the last time in August. A spokesman for Tetley, which was taken over by Carlsberg in 1991, said "They will enjoy a well-earned retirement."

Wally Talbot was the Royal Shire Horse Association official photographer. He took many photographs of the events which I organised using the Tetley shires. I have a wonderful black and white photograph of the Queen taken by Wally. The Queen was attending the Royal Shire Horse Society annual event. As the Queen approached a pair of Whitbread shires, one of the shires bowed to her. She just burst out laughing and Wally was there to capture that very special moment. The photograph was to win the photography award of the year.

Joe Anderson was a colleague and Tenancy Area Manager, also working for Tim Mostyn. Joe was a real character and called a spade a shovel. He was an adopted boy who had been brought up in a very tough area of Liverpool. Prior to joining the brewery, Joe was a purser in the merchant navy. John Prescott, Deputy Prime minister of the Labour Party at the time had worked for Joe on board ship. Whilst in some respects Joe was a bit rough and ready, he was very popular with his colleague's and had a great sense of humour. Tim Mostyn thought the world of him. He was able to control difficult tenants in a pretty tough area of Wigan and surrounding area's. Joe's wife ran a transport café on the A580 East Lancs Road.

Driving home one evening, Joe was pulled up by the police on the East Lancs Road. When the police officer opened the car door, Joe fell out, very much the worse for drink. The police officer breathalysed Joe. He was well over the limit, arrested and bailed to appear in court. When the court case took place, Joe went along with his solicitor and pleaded not guilty. In the witness box he said that whilst visiting one of his tenanted pubs, the lady licensee had been lacing his orange juice with Vodka without his knowledge. The lady licensee had gone to court and went into the witness box, saying on oath that she had in fact laced Joe's orange juice with a considerable amount of Vodka. This was clearly not true, but the case was thrown out by the magistrates' on that basis.

The police were absolutely furious that Joe had committed perjury, together with his lady licensee. On arrival home and during the evening of the court case, Joe's telephone rang. When he picked up the phone a policeman said to Joe "We know you're a lying bastard. You'll need to watch your back from now on because we'll eventually get you." Joe told his solicitor who made an official complaint to the local police chief. The local police were clearly out to get Joe. Unmarked police cars would follow him from the Brewery Inn and other popular drinking outlets including his own pubs, waiting for an opportunity to nail him. About 18 months after the court case, Joe had left one of his pubs after a heavy drinking session. The police stopped him, breathalysing him once more. He was once again well over the limit, was taken to court when the magistrates' had thrown the book at him, disqualifying him from driving for 2 years.

Tim Mostyn was put in the difficult position of having no alternative than to dismiss Joe. Joe was clearly unable to carry out his job without being able to drive. It wouldn't have been viable to employ a chauffer full time to drive Joe around his patch. The outcome was that Tim Mostyn very generously offered Joe a fantastic Tetley tenanted pub, in recognition of the excellent work he had contributed to the brewery. Joe had no hesitation in taking up the offer, made a very good living out of the pub, stopped drinking altogether and became a local councillor. John Prescott would visit Joe at his pub when in the area, reminiscing about the days when they were in the Merchant Navy together.

Tim Mostyn struggled on with his hip problem getting progressively worse. The responsibility of being a director in charge of 500 tenanted pubs was quite considerable. It was said that he was actually doing the job of two men. During his visits with area managers to his tenanted estate, he would be chauffer driven by his driver Frank. Whilst out with me one evening in Bolton, we were entering a pub together when he stumbled and fell quite badly. His chauffer Frank and I assisted him to his feet. He had clearly hurt himself but insisted he was alright and continued with his visit to that particular pub, together with others in the area.

A particular concern on those visits would be in relation to elderly tenants whose whole lives were tied up with the business. Many of them had no hobbies or other interests. Tim Mostyn would regularly ask these elderly tenants what they would do with their lives when they retired. Many of the licensee's hadn't a clue and couldn't see beyond life in the licensed trade, a very sad situation which Tim Mostyn was genuinely concerned about.

A memorable incident occurred on one of my pub visits accompanied by Tim Mostyn. I had been paying for drinks most of the evening and suggested to the boss that it was about time he bought a round! Tim Mostyn was a very generous man but didn't tend to carry much money with him. He therefore asked the licensee for an empty fag packet and wrote an I.O.U. on the back of the packet for a round of drinks. He ensured that his chauffer called in at a later date to settle up.

Bert and Winnie Baverstock were an elderly couple running the Doffcocker in Bolton. This was a large pub and had been earmarked for some time to transfer to management. The couple had resisted retirement and clung on to their pub for grim death. No amount of persuasion would encourage them to retire. Theirs was not a happy marriage. They would have the most dreadful rows behind the bar and in front of their clientele. It was not unusual for Bert to kick his wife behind the bar during these arguments. Fortunately, a rather nice brewery owned cottage adjacent to the Punch Bowl in Churchtown, near Garstang became available. I sat down with Bert and his wife and offered them the cottage on a peppercorn rent. Having viewed the cottage the Baverstock's accepted the offer and moved from the Doffcocker, much to the delight of the managed house division who were to take over the pub. Tim Mostyn and I were glad to be rid of them!

Having spent some 5 years as a tenancy area manager and having gained a thorough insight of the world of tenanted pubs, I was keen to further my knowledge and experience by transferring to the managed house division. I met with Tim Mostyn and told him of my desire to transfer to managed houses. I explained to him that I needed to have experience of every aspect of the licensed trade. It's probably fair to say that I was ruthlessly ambitious to further my career prospects, opening up the way for promotion to director. Tim Mostyn was most understanding and helpful. There was an opportunity to take over the Wigan area which had become vacant due to a re-shuffle and I told Tim Mostyn that I would jump at that opportunity.

Unfortunately, due to the fact that no one suitable had been earmarked to take over my tenanted area, I was unable to organise a hand over and therefore wrote to all my tenants, advising them of my move to managed houses and thanking them most sincerely for all their endeavours during my time in charge of the area.

# 13

## Managed House Area Manager

I have mentioned previously that Rod Firth, a brewery director had overall responsibility for the tied estate of Tetley's. He had been advised by Tim Mostyn of his approval for my transfer to managed houses. However, he insisted on interviewing me for the position and I met with him in his office at the Duke Street office.

One of the first things that he said to me was "You won't be swanning around on managed houses like you were on tenancy." I took great exception to this comment and told him in no uncertain terms that I had worked very hard for Tim Mostyn, that the results of the area spoke for themselves and that E.I.L.M. would vouch for the fact. The discussion developed into a full blown argument, him boasting about the fact that he had worked for Rolls Royce (so what!) and me saying that I wasn't used to being spoken to in such a high handed manner. His lack of leadership, motivation and appreciation for a job well done was pathetic. Firth's superior attitude was probably the furthest thing from 'The Common Touch' that I had the misfortune to experience in the whole of my working life.

The thing that really appalled and upset me in that meeting was when Firth said to me "You'll never get promotion to director in this company, you're far too honest, you've got to be devious." What a disgraceful thing to say. I did wonder as to whether he had taken a dislike to me due to the fact that he was over a barrel with the union when I had sacked the licensee in Blackpool. He had been made to re-instate him by the managers' union. Furthermore, there was no love lost between Firth and E.I.L.M. bearing in mind that I had witnessed the scene in the board room, when Tim Mostyn had taken him to task.

The outcome of this meeting was to ensure that Firth would make sure that I didn't progress further with the company and that is exactly what happened. The M.D. Jack Frost, left promotional matters for the tied estate entirely with Firth and there was little or nothing that other directors' could do about the matter. However, in my case, Tim Mostyn pulled seniority, but not rank, leaving Firth with no option than to allow me to transfer to managed houses. The managed house director, Tim Hill had no problems whatever in accepting me as his area manager for the Wigan area. Tim Hill was to tell me in confidence one day that he had no time at all for Firth. Here was a man who appreciated the fact that I was honest and not devious as Firth had suggested I should be.

My tenancy colleague's thought I was absolutely mad giving up my plumb area on tenancy, especially as I was taking over the Wigan area. No more business trips up to Cumbria or visits to my typically English country pubs. Wigan was a totally different ball game altogether, but for me it was about gaining further experience. The Wigan area consisted of town centre pubs and large estate pubs. Ronnie Walters, who had so desperately wanted my plumb area on tenancy, was to receive a further setback. He had applied to take over my tenancy patch once again but had not succeeded. He was transferred also to the Wigan and surrounding area as tenancy area manager. Whilst he had been very bitter and tried to give me a hard time, I actually felt sorry for him. He was not a happy man.

Taking over 18 managed houses in the Wigan and surrounding area was to open my eyes. Unlike tenanted pubs, the relationship with licensees was totally different. The brewery was the employer and the licensee the employee. The Wigan area had been allowed to go to the dogs as a direct result of the previous area manager. Many of the manager's appointed had been totally unsuitable and should never have been appointed in the first place.

Profit and loss accounts were printed out by computer every month. Some of the Wigan pubs results were quite alarming. Armed with the results I spent a complete weekend identifying the worst and set out a plan of action. Woe betides any licensee who was buying out. This was the ultimate sin for a manager to carry out, other than watering the beer. It became evident that many licensees were buying out keg beers and spirits from the local wholesaler, pocketing the difference from what should have been the correct percentage of sales.

Having visited all the pubs on my patch to introduce myself, I called a meeting of all the managers', including wives and partners, to the Victoria Hotel, a large pub in the centre of Wigan. This was a three line whip; all managers' were required to attend without exception. Word had already gone around the area that I was an ex policeman, that I didn't take prisoners and had already sacked a Blackpool licensee whilst I was a deputy area manager for blatant fiddling. During the meeting, I spelled out to the managers' as to what I expected and that any licensee caught ripping off the company would be sacked for gross misconduct.

The very first licensee I sacked in my new role had very foolishly continued with his blatant fiddle. He was an ex professional rugby player, running a tough estate pub on the outskirts of Wigan. The pub was on tank beer, indicative of the turnover. Licensee's expected visits from the area manager during opening hours, but I would often call first thing in the morning during or before deliveries. I caught this licensee red handed when I insisted on looking in the cellar early one morning. There on the cellar floor were three empty kegs of bitter, together with a clever device for dispensing from keg into the bitter tank. The kegs had been purchased for cash from the local wholesaler. I went through the procedure of getting a local joiner to lock the manager off and arranging for a relief manager to take over the running of the pub. The foolish risk that this licensee had taken, was removing the spiel from the kegs, the pressure within a keg is such that it can blow out with great force and has been known to cause serious injury. In one case a licensee was killed but fortunately not on my area.

I had needed to make an example of a high profile and well known licensee in Wigan. This was a warning to other managers' that I wouldn't tolerate my licensee's ripping off the company. This had been a good start and there was no doubt in managers' minds that I meant business, but there was much more work to be done to improve the profitability of the area.

There is a fine line over making a decision to sack a licensee, particularly with a difficult pub in a tough area. This was generally the estate type of pub. It's all well and good sacking someone, but the difficulty is finding a suitable replacement. Furthermore, there was also the dilemma with a good licensee who you knew darned well was on the fiddle. The yardstick there was as long as the stock results were good, the wage bill satisfactory and in particular the pub was making a healthy bottom line net profit, the sensible area manager simply turned a blind eye to a reasonable amount of takings going into the manager's back pocket.

The Mucky Duck at Skelmersdale was undoubtedly the toughest pub on my patch. It was an estate pub in the middle of an area with a large overspill of Liverpudlians. This sort of pub needed a very special kind of licensee to sort out the villains and Brian Upton was the very man to run this difficult pub. Brian was a solid, very well built man who could certainly look after himself. His appearance alone would have qualified him as a member of the mafia!

The most feared local villain was a man by the name of Andy Shacklady, otherwise known as Andy Shack. This man had convictions for assault on police, had served time in Walton jail and was well known to the local police. He was a huge mountain of a man and ruled the roost in the area. Andy Shack had been barred from the Mucky Duck by the licensee Brian Upton. Prior to being barred, he would threaten barmaids in the pub by saying that unless they gave him a bottle of scotch, he would wait for them at closing time as they left the pub and beat them up.

One Sunday lunchtime, in spite of being barred, Andy Shack walked into the lounge bar of the pub. Brian Upton told him to get out but Andy Shack refused to leave, challenging Brian to a fight. Brian rather foolishly accepted the offer; he felt that he had little or no alternative. He knew that calling the police wouldn't be a good idea and it was his job as licensee to run an orderly house. Furthermore, Andy Shack had been barred from every other pub in the area. He decided therefore to make an example of this local and evil villain, not just for his own satisfaction, but also for the entire licensee's in the area.

The Mucky Duck was very busy this Sunday lunchtime. Brian cleared the furniture in the centre of the lounge and the customers stepped back to watch. Brian Upton and Andy Shack squared up to each other and started a vicious bare knuckle fight in the middle of the lounge. Andy Shack was on a hiding to nothing. Whilst he had been cock of the roost for many years, his ability as a fighter was waning and Brian had the upper hand. Every time Brian Upton knocked Andy Shack to the floor, he stood back, observing Queensberry rules. Andy Shack repeatedly got up several times, but was simply no match for Brian Upton and was beaten fairly and squarely. It goes without saying that the customers who witnessed this fight were delighted that this local criminal had been beaten. As Andy Shack left the Mucky Duck he cursed Brian Upton, threatening that he would get his revenge. He wouldn't accept that he had been beaten and humiliated.

The Marques of Queensberry Rules is a code generally accepted in the sport of boxing. They were so named because the 9th Marques of Queensberry publically endorsed the code. The rules

(4) state that if either man falls through weakness or otherwise, he must get up unassisted, 10 seconds to be allowed to do so.

The following day, I received a telephone call at home from the detective inspector who covered the Skelmersdale area. He was very concerned about the fight which had occurred at the Mucky Duck. An informant had told him that Andy Shack would lie in wait for Brian Upton, most probably when he was going to the bank with the pub takings and intended to kill him, using a knife. The inspector suggested that it would be prudent to move Brian Upton away from the area as soon as possible.

I was naturally very concerned and went straight to the Mucky Duck the following morning. I told Brian Upton and his wife of the threat against him and of the concern of the police. Fortunately, a vacancy for a manager had arisen at the Bold, a pub in the centre of Warrington. I was able to transfer Brian Upton immediately to the Bold, leaving his wife to run the Mucky Duck for 24 hours until I found a suitable relief manager.

Once a suitable licensee had been found for the pub, a decision was made to refurbish and decorate the Mucky Duck and to re-name it The Black Swan! Andy Shack was never to know where Brian Upton and his wife had moved to. The last I heard of him, he had never come to terms with that beating he took from Brian Upton, had gone downhill and died, much to the relief of the local police.

A far more serious situation arose in a pub on the dock road, Liverpool. (Not a Tetley pub) A very dangerous criminal had been barred from the pub by the licensee. The licensee was genuinely worried for his life and had kept a loaded shotgun behind the bar. The man walked into the pub one evening, threatening the licensee who told him to leave but he refused. The man climbed over the bar with a knife to attack the licensee. The licensee took his shotgun from under the bar, pointing it at the man telling him to back off and get out. He refused and charged at the licensee with his knife. The licensee let him have it with both barrels, killing the man instantly.

The whole circumstances were dealt with very quietly. The licensee and his wife were immediately moved from the pub by the brewery to Cumbria. The police were delighted to get rid of the man who had been responsible for many acts of violence on

Merseyside. Whilst clearly it was murder, but justifiable homicide, to the best of my knowledge it was never taken to court.

Whilst the relationship with managers' was totally different to that with tenants, I arranged periodical social evenings for licensee's and their wives. Brewery directors' were always invited. Usually there was at least one director at these functions and Lynn would accompany me on most of these knee's ups. We would have a meal followed by a brief speech from myself plus a few words from the director. Dancing would follow and generally a good time was had by all. The occasional problem arose where a licensee had far too much to drink and had a go at me over some disciplinary issue, but in the main these functions went pretty smoothly.

A licensee on my patch had remembered that one of my favourite dishes for lunch was baked beans on toast, smothered with grated cheese. When the main course arrived at one of these functions, I was served with baked beans on toast, to the laughter of licensee's and guests! My main course proper was to arrive when I had eaten some of the baked beans on toast. As a guest at a licensed victualler's banquet one evening, Lynn and I were sat next to a chap who loved his brussel sprouts; he took a huge portion with his main course. I had a quiet word with the waitress, asking her to prepare a large bowl of Brussels topped with lashings of pouring cream for his sweet. When the dish arrived he was delighted and I couldn't believe that he woofed up the lot without any hesitation!

One of my Wigan town centre licensee's knew Ken Dodd very well. He asked me if it would be in order to invite him to our Christmas social evening. I was delighted to agree, being a fan of Ken Dodd and his hilarious banter. His unique electric shock hairdo, buck teeth and child's sense of humour was just so funny. His lengthy shows would exhaust men half his age. However, the fee was to be £400 for the evening's entertainment. The function was held at a social club on the outskirts of Wigan. Following the meal, Ken Dodd arrived and I was introduced to him, confirming his fee of £400 cash. As anyone who has attended one of Ken Dodd's acts will know, he is just so brilliantly funny and gives more than value for money, far exceeding the allocated time and this function was no exception. At the end of his act, we went behind the bar where I handed over £400 in cash, which went into his back pocket! I had taken the cash from a town centre Wigan pub to pay Ken Dodd, instructing the licensee to enter the amount on his weekly takings sheet under entertainment 'Ken Dodd.' The Managing Director Don Marshall had heard of the arrangement and gave me a rollicking, saying that it was out of order but that off the record, he would have probably done the same himself.

Many years later, Ken Dodd was to be taken to court by the Inland Revenue for tax evasion. This proved to be a very controversial high court action. Following a much publicised court case he was to be found not guilty. The free publicity surrounding the case must have been a wonderfully free advertising campaign for him. Many people were to say that he should have been locked up and the key thrown away!

My touring caravan was stored in the large garage of a Tetley pub in Bolton. I collected the caravan and called in at my office in Brewery Lane, Leigh, prior to going on my annual two weeks holiday with the family. On going into reception, there was a very solemn atmosphere and many of the office girls were in tears. My secretary approached me and told me that Tim Mostyn had died that morning. I was absolutely devastated. The pain in EILM's hip had become so unbearable that he had decided to have an operation for a hip replacement. The operation was at a Harley Street hospital in London. A licensee who had visited Tim Mostyn in hospital following the operation, later related that EILM had boasted that the actress Elizabeth Taylor was in a ward above him, having also had an operation.

The prediction of the fortune teller had therefore proved to be correct. She had told EILM never to have an operation on his hip. The operation had been a success but sadly, pulmonary embolism had set in and had caused his death at the age of 53. The date of the funeral coincided with my holiday with the family in Cornwall and unfortunately I was unable to attend. All of Tim Mostyn's other area managers were to attend the funeral in his home town of Taunton, together with brewery directors'. It was a burial and whilst the coffin was being lowered into the ground, it had started to rain and thunder. Joe Anderson had said at the graveside, words to the effect "You can't keep him quiet even though he's dead!"

Some weeks later, a memorial service was held at Liverpool Anglican Cathedral to celebrate the life of Tim Mostyn. Lynn and I attended the service. About 1,000 people were in the cathedral on the day, not only employee's of Tetley's but many others from the licensed trade who had known and respected EILM. Richard

Pritchard Barrett, the Managing Director of Whitbread's Brewery addressed the congregation from the pulpit. He spoke about the life of Tim Mostyn as a major in the army and brewery director, saying what a marvellous man he was. He went on to say that in spite of his popularity, he was worried about his job, posing the question as to why this should be the case for a man of such standing. Mr. Barrett went on to say that EILM had no time for whiz kids and that this may have had some bearing as to why he should be worried. As far as I was concerned, this was a direct reference to Firth. EILM had no time for him and used to call him a whiz kid. He had been a thorn in his side whilst based at the Duke Street office in Liverpool.

Following the memorial service I decided to remain at the Cathedral. Lynn went home with Norman and Chris Rae from the Punchbowl in Garstang. I went into the Lady Chapel, my favourite part of the cathedral, to reflect on the life of EILM. I was in tears and finding it very hard to come to terms with the death of the man who had been so helpful and supportive of me throughout my career with the brewery. As I sat there reflecting on EILM, I noticed that around the chapel in Old English, were the words from John 3:16, i.e. 'For God so loved the world, that He gave his only begotten Son, that whosoever believeth in Him shall not perish, but have everlasting life.' This had a great impact on me and was to become central to my eventual commitment as a Christian. John 3:16 is a verse in the Bible which has been translated into more than 2,000 languages, telling us of a God who loves us with an everlasting love. The verse, recorded in 28 of the best-known world languages are understood by three-quarters of the earth's population. An awesome statistic!

Lynn and I went to visit Tim Mostyn's grave in Taunton some months following the memorial service. I had spoken with his wife Angela prior to setting off and we had been invited to visit her. Angela Mostyn was a delightful lady who welcomed us with open arms. We reminisced about the life of EILM and looked at many photographs of him throughout the various stages of his life. Angela asked if I would like a beer, to which of course I said yes. It was quite poignant when Angela invited me to choose a tankard from the corner cupboard of the lounge. I chose a pewter tankard with an inscription of EILM's name, presented to him when he was a major in the army.

We were to meet with Angela once more whilst she was visiting Lancashire. She came for lunch to our house in Garstang when we had a very pleasant time. It became very evident that finally, Tim Mostyn had found happiness with his third marriage. Angela had been the widow of a friend of EILM's who had sadly died many years previously.

The Freemasons Arm's in Wigan was an estate pub, one of several such pubs on my patch in Wigan. The pub was to become the bane of my life for what proved to be a very difficult time whilst a managed house area manager. Don Powell, a brewery architect based at the Leigh office had recommended to me a man by the name of Graham Byrne. I interviewed him at the Leigh office together with his wife. I was very concerned that Byrne had tattoo's on the backs of his fingers on both hands, on the right hand was the word 'h a t e' and on the left hand 'l o v e.' I expressed my concern to Don Powell about this but he assured me that in spite of the tattoo's, Byrne was a good man.

I employed Byrne as a trainee manager for the area, also his wife who would assist in the running of public houses; carrying out their training with a senior manager on the patch. I moved the licensee of the Freemason's, a busy estate pub in Wigan, to another pub on the area and offered the pub to Byrne and his wife, having completed what I considered to be a satisfactory period of training. The couple appeared to be quite enthusiastic and keen to acquire their own pub. It proved to be a big mistake moving the Bryn's into the Freemasons.

Initially, the couple settled in well and produced satisfactory figures, but then the warning signs started to surface. The marriage was suffering due to the nature of this difficult estate pub. Byrne had been influenced by a small number of other licensee's to start ripping off the company with various fiddles and was clearly on the downward slope, heading for dismissal. Stock results were totally unsatisfactory, the wage bill was soaring, the pub started to make a net loss and standards of cleanliness were unacceptable.

Without the knowledge of Byrne, I arranged for the company stock taker for my area to meet me at the Freemasons to carry out a stock check early one morning. I had told the stock taker of my suspicions and that I thought Byrne was on the fiddle. On arrival, I had to get Byrne out of bed to let the stock taker and myself into the pub. My suspicions proved to be correct. Whilst the stock taker was examining the spirits on optic, he found a 40 oz bottle of Courvoisier filled to the top with neat black current cordial. Furthermore, the final stock result revealed an abysmal figure, clearly indicating that Byrne was taking company money for his own use.

I sacked Byrne on the spot for gross misconduct, arranging for the licensee of a nearby managed house to take over the pub temporarily, until I made a decision as to whether Byrne's wife was competent to run the pub. On being told of his dismissal Byrne went absolutely berserk, threatened to kill me, also saying that he would kill my wife and children. That was like a red rag to a bull and without hesitation I struck him with my right fist, an uppercut under his jaw, laying him out onto the lounge floor. The relief manager witnessed the incident and had to stop me hitting Byrne further. I shall never know who rang the police, but a young police officer arrived at the pub, by which time I had calmed down and simply told the officer that Byrne had been sacked, denying that I had struck him. No doubt my police inspector, George Ekins' advice of many years ago had influenced my decision to deny hitting the man!

On removing Byrne from the premises, I spoke with his wife who told me that she was very worried for her own safety and that it was probably not a good idea to remain at the Freemasons. She told me that her husband had also threatened her with violence. It became evident that I needed to move her from the pub for her own safety. I told her that I would move her as far as possible from Wigan and would establish as soon as I was able which area would be most suitable.

I received a telephone call late afternoon the next day from Mrs Byrne. She sounded delirious and needed to see me as a matter of urgency, telling me that whilst the pub was closed, I would need to enter the Freemasons through the back door which she would leave unlocked. On arrival at the pub and on entering the lounge bar via the back door, I was shocked to see Mrs Byrne lying prostrate on the lounge floor, practically unconscious with an empty bottle of sleeping tablets beside her. I managed to rouse her with great difficulty, got her to her feet and practically carried her to my car. I wasn't prepared to wait for the arrival of an ambulance and drove straight to A & E at Wigan Infirmary, telling the staff that she had taken an overdose of sleeping tablets, handing over the bottle which I had found beside her in the lounge. Without any delay, a stomach pump was used to remove the contents of her stomach. The woman would probably have died if I hadn't arrived in time, but in an odd sort of way it seemed to me that it was a cry for help and that she needed to be found.

The relief manager continued to run the Freemasons whilst I ensured that Mrs Byrne didn't return to the pub. I visited her in the hospital and told her that I had arranged for her to assist at one of my large managed houses in Bolton. No one, other than me, Mrs Byrne and the Bolton licensee knew of her whereabouts. Graham Byrne had desperately tried to establish where his wife had gone, but for her own protection he never found out where she had moved to.

I submitted a full and detailed report to my director as to the circumstances and in particular, admitted to hitting Byrne. I felt it to be prudent to be totally honest in case of any future repercussions. I said in no uncertain terms in my report that whilst I was angry at Byrne's threat to kill me, what really angered me was the threat to kill my wife and family. Whilst my director Tim Hill could understand my reaction to the situation, he said that in future I mustn't go around hitting licensees!

It was company policy for managers' to bank their pubs takings a minimum of three times a week, the final banking to take place on Monday morning. Managers' foolish enough to be buying out would delay their final banking until Tuesday, using the companies money to buy out from a local wholesaler. The manager of a large pub close to my office in Leigh had started to pay in his final banking on a Tuesday. This was a warning signal that he might be using the company's money for his own use, or buying out.

As I had gained more experience, I was to use a tactic which proved to be very successful in catching out managers' who were at it. It was called a cash check. I would arrive at the particular pub to be checked early on a Tuesday morning to physically count the cash, checking it against the week's takings figures. In many cases there was a satisfactory reason for the late banking, however, in the case of the pub referred to, I caught the licensee red handed with this typical fiddle.

Whilst I was counting the cash at the pub, the body language of this particular manager was such that there was clearly going to be a problem. Half way through the procedure the licensee stopped me and said "I may as well come clean Mr Mynett, you'll find that there's a £1000 short in the cash." On completion of checking the cash, there was in the region of £1000 missing. When asked what he had done with the money, he told me that he had purchased toys for his children and an electrical appliance. I had no alternative than to sack the man on the spot, arranging for him to be locked off by a joiner changing the locks, thereby barring him from the pub and restricting him to the upstairs accommodation. A relief manager took over the running of the premises. Oddly enough, whilst I suspected the licensee to be using the money for buying out, this was a rare situation where this was not the case.

I discussed the circumstances of the dismissal with my director and we jointly agreed that this was a sufficiently serious case whereby the manager should be taken to court. We needed to make an example of him so that other licensee's would think twice before going down that route.

The case was heard at Leigh Magistrates' court, situated just at the top of Brewery Lane where my office was located. Fortunately, I had decided to attend the hearing and what a good job I did. The magistrates' clerk read out the charge to the defendant who pleaded guilty, with mitigating circumstances. His solicitor stood up and told the magistrates' that it was no wonder his client had taken £1000 of the companies money, the brewery were paying the man an appalling salary and that to live to an acceptable standard of living, his client had little or no alternative than to use the companies money. I was stood at the back of the court and saw the local newspaper reporter writing all this down.

When the solicitor had finished speaking, I walked to the front of the court and spoke to the magistrates' clerk, telling him that I would like to give evidence on behalf of the brewery. The clerk announced to the magistrates' that I would like to speak to them. I went into the witness box, took the oath and identified myself, telling the magistrates' that what the solicitor had said was totally untrue. I was armed with the managers' salary, telling the magistrates' what his income was, that on top of that he received bonus payments on results, he received all the profits from food sales, that his accommodation at the pub was free, i.e. no rent to pay and that he had no excuses for taking £1000 of the companies money for his own use. I noticed that the representative for the press was writing furiously whilst I was speaking.

The magistrates' retired and returned with a guilty verdict. The licensee was required to pay back the £1000 over an agreed period of time, plus a fine and costs, bearing in mind also that his solicitor's fee's would also need to be paid.

As I was leaving the court, the solicitor was waiting for me by the exit. He apologised to me, stating that he had a job to do for his client and felt that he had no alternative than to submit the evidence as related to him by his client. I told him in no uncertain terms that I was far from impressed with the tactics which he had used.

That weekend, the local Leigh and Wigan newspaper headline read 'Brewery area manager defends company' with full details of the court case. If I had decided not to attend court for the hearing, the newspaper headlines would have been totally different, claiming that the poor old licensee was in a desperate financial situation because of poor pay etc. etc. The Managing Director and Directors' of the company were very pleased at the outcome and I was congratulated for my intervention at court, particularly bearing in mind that I had preserved the good name of Tetley's in the Leigh and surrounding area's.

There is no doubt that once again, my experience as a policeman on Merseyside had been invaluable. Going into the witness box to challenge the solicitor was not a problem. I had been in far more difficult situations in crown court being cross examined by barristers.

Billy Graham visited Anfield football ground in Liverpool. Lynn and I and the three children were privileged to attend two of his crusade meetings at Anfield. The ground was packed to capacity on both occasions. There is no doubt that Billy Graham was one of the most recognizable figures in the world, who spoke in person to over 100 million people on six different continents, in eighty five countries, and in all of America's fifty states, more than any other man or woman in history. He had ministered to millions around the world, had counselled Presidents and Prime Ministers and was the driving force behind the evangelical movement of the twentieth century. Billy Graham was a man who dedicated his life to the Gospel and became one of the century's most influential figures.

Listening to Billy Graham preaching was a very moving experience, one which I shall never forget. However, I was still sitting firmly on the fence claiming that I was a Christian, quoting the fact that I was baptised into the Anglican Church and had been confirmed at the age of 14 by the Bishop of Blackburn. At that stage in my life I was simply not prepared to take that step forward into committing my life to Christ Jesus. At the end of Billy Graham's preaching, he invited those people forward onto the pitch who had made a commitment to follow Jesus. Hundreds of people went forward but I remained firmly where I stood. It was to be several years before I saw the light and became a committed Christian.

One of Billy Graham's most profound statements was "Someday you will read or hear that Billy Graham is dead. Don't you believe a word of it! I shall be more alive than I am now. I will have just changed my address. I will have gone into the presence of God." Speaking at Richard Nixon's funeral, Billy Graham said these words "There comes a moment when we all must realize that life is short, and in the end the only thing that really counts is not how others see us, but how God sees us. For the believer there is hope beyond the grave, because Jesus Christ had opened the door to heaven for us by His death and resurrection." What an inspiration Billy Graham was for me – a man with 'The Common Touch.'

Celmi in North Wales was an outward bound organisation and managed house area managers' and directors' were to attend a weeks activities in this rugged part of North Wales. The purpose of this residential course was effectively for team building. Competitions between teams involved building a raft from basic materials and sailing across a fast moving river. A night exercise took place using maps, identifying and avoiding 'the enemy' to reach a final destination. At the age of 43 I was one of the eldest on the course but found it very exhilarating. There was a certain amount of choice as to which activities you were interested in. I chose rock climbing and canoeing. I had done neither of these two activities before and it proved to be quite an experience.

Whilst canoeing in deep water, my canoe capsized and I discovered the art of canoeing upside down! I was able to get my canoe upright and ended up like a drowned rat. Then the rock climbing experience. It has to be said that the sheer cliff which volunteers were to climb was quite daunting and scary. The nine participants were roped up to an instructor and we set off for the top. Half way up and immediately in front of me, one of my colleague's froze in terror and I had to shout at him to get a move on. He eventually struggled to the top with me following. None of us knew until we got to the top that we were required to abseil down.

Instructors' explained in detail how to abseil down the cliff whilst harnessed up and astride the cliff top. Half the lads chickened out and couldn't go ahead. They were required to walk back down the other side, quite a considerable walk back to the base of the cliff. The colleague who froze half way up took one look at the height and chose not to abseil down. Fortunately, I went ahead taking one glance down and shouting 'Geronimo', launching off to cheers from my colleague's at the bottom of the cliff.

The most exhausting and difficult part of the course for me was the final exercise, referred to as a river walk. It was a requirement to wear old clothes and I was to soon find out why. We were dropped off by a gently flowing stream and started to walk in the centre of the stream following an instructor. As we progressed, the stream became quite turbulent and we were up to our waist in the water. The first obstacle was arriving at the top of a waterfall with a drop of some 12 feet; the instructor told us to keep our arms close to the body to avoid injury from the rock faces either side. Jumping into this waterfall was quite an exhilarating experience. The next thing was a slope to the right of what had now become a river, a sort of slide at an angle thirty degrees. To avoid hitting rocks it was necessary to put your hands behind your head and slide down. By this time we were soaking wet from head to toe and the water was quite cold. At the end of the 'walk' we arrived at a field some twenty feet or so above the river. There was a low hedge at the edge of the field and we were invited to run to the hedge, jump over it and we would land up in the river some 20 feet below. Only three area managers' were daft enough to do that and I wasn't one of them!

The week at Celmi was an absolutely exhausting, but most enjoyable experience. It took me a couple of days to recover following plenty of sleep. It came to light that on the course previous to ours at Celmi, an office worker who had attended the Celmi experience had returned to work, gone into his office situated at the top of a multi story office building, opened the window and jumped out to his death. It appeared that the poor chap had not coped with the rigours of the Celmi experience and had decided to end it all.

The Clarence Hotel in the centre of Wigan had recently been refurbished and decorated shortly before I took over the area. The licensee Terry Berry and his wife were doing an excellent job and producing good net profits. A problem had occurred in an area of the ceiling in the downstairs lounge bar. A section of ceiling wallpaper was bulging quite badly and instead of having a contractor attend to the problem, I advised Terry that we could sort it out ourselves and save money for the company. I suggested that he borrow a syringe from a nurse who frequented the pub, putting wallpaper adhesive in the syringe, inserting it through the wallpaper, applying the adhesive and sticking the wallpaper back in place.

Before opening time in the morning, I arrived at the Clarence to assist in sorting out the problem. Terry Berry placed a large step ladder under the bulging wallpaper, climbing to the top armed with the syringe. I stood holding the ladder. On inserting the syringe into the wallpaper, without warning the paper ripped apart, showering down stale foul smelling urine all over him. Terry was shouting and cursing and covered with urine! I had stepped back when I saw what had happened and avoided getting covered with urine. That situation went down like a lead balloon. The cause of the problem had been a slow discharge of urine from the gents' toilet in the upstairs lounge bar seeping through the ceiling into the wallpaper below. The urinal was situated over the lounge bar where the problem occurred.

Terry's wife Sheila spoke with a broad Wigan accent. One day on arriving at the pub she said to me "We've got a problem Mr Mynett – Thoovers buggered!" I tried to sort out the problem but ended up advising my building surveyor, Joe Mawdsley that the Hoover needed attending to. Joe had a wicked sense of humour and pinned my report to his office wall. I had printed in large letters 'THOOVERS BUGGERED.' much to the amusement of the building surveyors department.

Everyone loves an 'Olde Worlde' pub with its oak beams, horse brasses and roaring log fires. Nevertheless, no matter how old the pub is itself, the name of the sign outside is probably the most historic thing about the place. The idea of the pub sign came to Britain at the time of the Roman invasion. In the days of a largely illiterate population, pictorial signs were an essential way of advertising the public house or inn. Heraldry has been a recurrent theme on pub signs and often local gentry had pubs on their land named after them.

The swinging pub sign outside the Clarence at Wigan depicted the Duke of Clarence drowning in a vat of Malmsey wine. The Duke had played an important role in the dynastic struggle of the 'War of the Roses' and had made the mistake of plotting against his brother Edward 1V. He was imprisoned in the Tower of London and put on trial for treason. Following his conviction he was 'privately executed' at the tower on 18$^{th}$ February, 1478. Tradition grew up that he had been drowned in a butt of Malmsey wine. The tradition probably originated in a joke based on his reputation as a heavy drinker. Clarence and his wife were buried together at Tewkesbury Abbey in Gloucestershire.

The White Horse pub in the middle of Leigh was one of my managed houses. The licensee, Ken Leddy was a union man and very active in the union N.A.L.H.M. Initially, Ken and I didn't see eye to eye and had many differences of opinion as to how his pub should be run. This situation was to change considerably following his annual holidays. In his absence, the assistant manager had served a young 16 year old school girl one evening. The matter had been reported to the police and the assistant manager was taken to court. I had seen this particular girl one evening in the White Horse with her make up on, wearing high heels and dressed to kill. She looked a good 18 years of age and it was no surprise that the relief manager had served her.

I told Ken Leddy that I would attend court, picking him up at the White Horse together with the relief manager. Other Tetley managers were in attendance at the court wondering what line I would take. The young girl attended court in her school uniform, looking her age of 16 years. The charge was read out by the magistrates' clerk to the relief manager who stood in the witness box. After the relief manager had given his evidence I asked to be called to speak on behalf of the brewery and also the relief manager. I stood in the witness box, pointing to the young girl, telling the magistrates' that I had seen her in the White Horse pub and that there was no doubt whatsoever, that when made up she looked a good 18 years of age. Furthermore, I said that had I been running the pub, I would not have hesitated in serving her myself.

The magistrates' retired to consider their verdict, returned and gave a not guilty verdict.

The decision of the magistrates' and the direct result of my intervention had gained me a lot of brownie points with the union representatives present in court. Ken Leddy became much friendlier and from that point on we got on very well. Word had got round that I had no time for the union, but that situation had certainly helped me to gain some degree of respect for fighting their corner in that particular court case.

A few months after the court case, I arrived at the White Horse to find Ken Leddy looking very pale and exhausted. I told him of my concern and asked why he was not looking at all well. He said that he was passing blood when urinating and that it was like 'peeing broken glass.' I was horrified when he said that he hadn't at that stage been to see his doctor about the problem. I insisted that he took time off sick and to see his doctor. I was very saddened when he later told me that he had been diagnosed as having prostate cancer and that it was terminal. His consultant had given him only a few months to live. Over a period of weeks, I saw Ken Leddy lose weight dramatically. On his death, he had gone from a big strapping fellow down to five and a half stone in weight. So much so, that his wife refused to allow me to see him further towards the end. His body had become so emaciated that his wife wouldn't allow any of his family to see him. The undertaker had been instructed to screw the lid of the coffin down to avoid the trauma of seeing him in that state.

I received a telephone call one day from Alan Skelhorne, free trade area manager based at the Duke Street office covering the Liverpool area. Alan was under a lot of pressure with his very stressful job, looking after free trade area managers' and in particular having great difficulty getting free trade outlets to pay for their deliveries on time. To enable him to get through the day, Alan kept a supply of Gordon's Gin in his cupboard below the desk. It was reputed that Alan used to get through a 40 oz bottle of Gordon's a day. The brewery recognised that he had an alcohol problem and eventually sent him to dry out at a specialist rehab unit.

Alan told me that Tim Hill, managed house director, now looking after a different area than my own had been booked for speeding in Preston, my home town and did I think there was anything I could do to help. He knew that I was an ex policeman and had contacts in the Preston area. I rang Tim Hill and quoted an oft used letter which I had developed over the years. The letter had become a pretty standard type letter, going to the chief superintendent of the particular area where the employee had been booked, on brewery headed paper. I had fortunately been cautioned several times for speeding as a result of this letter! On my advice Tim Hill sent his letter off to Ronnie Booth, Chief Superintendent of the Preston and surrounding area. I rang Mr Booth a couple of days later, explaining that Tim Hill had been booked for speeding, that he was unfamiliar with the particular road he had been booked on and had written to him apologising. Mr Booth said that amazingly, as his phone had rung, he was reading the letter from Tim Hill which was on his desk before him. We had a very pleasant chat, when I reminded him of our last conversation when he had tried to talk me out of resigning from the police. Fortunately for Tim Hill, Mr. Booth told me to advise him that on this occasion he would be sending a letter of caution to him. Clearly, Tim Hill was appreciative of my intervention, which saved having points on his license.

    I was a stickler for cleanliness. Apart from inspecting cellars and toilets, both ladies and gents, I would also on a periodical basis inspect the domestic quarters of pubs on my area. The gents' toilets of a certain managed house on my patch in Cheshire were disgraceful. I had asked the manager to ensure the cleaners brought the toilets up to standard but he had done nothing about it. I had therefore decided to instruct him to bring them up to scratch.

    I arrived one lunchtime at the pub with a quantity of brillo pads in my briefcase. It was possible to enter the pub at the rear and go into the gents' toilets before entering the lounge bar of the pub. In my business suit, I entered the gents' toilets, placing my brief case on the floor taking out two brillo pads. I stood at the urinal cleaning 18" of copper sparge pipe thinking 'If anyone enters the toilets now, it'll look rather odd me stood here with my brillo pad cleaning the pipes dressed as I am.' Sure enough, one of the locals entered the loo, and stood next to me to urinate. I told him I was from the brewery and his response was that he was delighted to see me cleaning the copper pipes. He had also considered them to be disgraceful and as a regular at the pub had not enjoyed visiting the loo. I told him that things were about to change.

The manager of the pub was a lazy individual who I had inherited. I went into the pub and asked him to accompany me into the gents' toilets where I pointed out to him the area I had cleaned on the sparge pipes. The copper which I had cleaned was shining and immaculate, compared to the black imbedded filth of the remainder. I told him firmly and politely that in spite of being asked to clean up the toilets, I was now instructing him to do so, saying that he personally didn't have to do the job, all he had to do was to get the cleaners to do it. I left the pub saying that I would return in one week, to ensure that he had carried out the task, saying that I would confirm this to him in writing.

On returning eventually that day to my office, my secretary informed me that the manager of the pub had rung, and could I return his call immediately as a matter of urgency. I rang the manager; when he told me that he had passed on my comments to his cleaners and that they had refused to clean the gents' toilets. I told him over the phone in no uncertain terms that I was getting in my car to go straight back to the pub and would sack the cleaners on my arrival. Furthermore, I said that I would have no problems whatsoever in replacing the cleaners at his pub with more suitable ones, whom I would personally appoint. This clearly called his bluff and he pleaded with me not to go back to his pub and sack his cleaners; telling me he would sort it out. I sent the letter to the man as promised and returned a week later. The toilets had been cleaned with the whole of the sparge pipes as good as the area I had cleaned.

Another managed house on my area was run by a couple of very slovenly Liverpudlians. Yet another pub I had inherited from the previous area manager. I was simply fed up of telling them to get their act together. The cellar management was appalling with ullage to return and far too many $CO_2$ gas bottles in stock. The draught beer was practically undrinkable. I had sent them warning letter upon warning letter about the disgraceful conditions to no avail. I had decided it was time for a confrontation and arrived unexpectedly out of hours one afternoon, just after closing time.

After inspecting the cellar and the ground floor area's of the pub, I told the licensee's wife that I needed to inspect the domestic accommodation. The entrance was through a doorway in the lounge and up a flight of stairs. The licensee's wife was a big obese woman who told me that there was no way I was going upstairs, folding her arms and blocking the entrance to the private accommodation. I told her very bluntly that whether she liked it or not, I was going up those stairs and would wait there for as long as necessary. It reminded me of the large woman who sat on the Keymatic washing machine in Morecambe, in an effort to stop me repossessing it!

Eventually, the woman realised that I meant business, turned round and went up the stairs as quickly as she could to tidy up. I followed and first of all entered the kitchen. I was horrified at the sheer filth. I have never in my life seen such disgusting conditions, even on Merseyside as a policeman. The licensee and his wife were living like pigs in that domestic accommodation. The kitchen area had clearly not been cleaned for some considerable time, with decayed food lying around and kitchen utensils black with dirt. Worse still, on going into the bathroom and toilet combined, there was human excreta smeared on the walls. The lounge was equally filthy, the carpet had not been cleaned for some considerable time and the seating was in a disgusting state.

I told the licensee and his wife that their standards were totally unacceptable and that I would be sending them a final written warning. The managed house union rep for the area, Jack Fernley, was equally disgusted on receiving my copy letter which I had sent to this couple. Jack supported me 100% in my wish to get rid of them. Not surprisingly, this couple complained to Dennis Smith, the N.A.L.H.M. rep for the North of England. The basis of the complaint was that I should have given the licensee's notice of my intention to inspect the private quarters. Whilst Dennis Smith was also disgusted at the state of the pub, he persuaded me and the directors' of the company to implement a policy whereby licensees would be given adequate notice of intended inspection of their private quarters. I was able to sack this couple shortly after the event for gross misconduct, with no repercussions whatever.

Many months later, I was asked by Alan Williams, head security officer for the brewery, to provide a reference for this couple. They had applied for a Bass pub in Liverpool and the company had insisted on a reference. I refused point blank to give a reference for this disgusting couple of licensee's. It appeared that Tetley's had wanted to continue developing a good rapport with Bass brewery, hence Alan William's further request for a reference from me. I had once again refused, sending a copy of my report to Alan Williams about the disgraceful state the couple had left their pub in. To the best of my knowledge, this couple were turned down by Bass and were to finish once and for all in the licensed trade.

The brewery was to appoint two graduate trainees direct from university. A training programme was devised whereby after a relatively short period of time in all branches of the company, they would be considered for promotion to director. I considered this to be a very odd decision, bringing raw recruits into the company with no experience of the outside world, the licensed trade, notwithstanding that they also had no experience in the business world, particularly in man management, leadership and motivational skills. Mike Sweetland was one such trainee and he was to become a real thorn in my side. He was to spend a period of time with me whilst undergoing his training whilst I was a tenancy area manager and managed house area manager.

Sweetland was given the managed house area of Southport and surrounding area's, an area which had been built up to be very profitable by the previous area manager, Ron Leckie, a man who had been promoted to director. In no time at all Sweetland was boasting to his colleague's as to how successful he was on the area, when all the time he had inherited the previous area manager's success. His attitude didn't go down well at all with his colleague's. I was quite angry when Sweetland was eventually promoted to director, taking over the managed house area covered by myself and my colleague's.

The Leigh brewery offices were to close and new premises were found in Sale, Manchester. My journey from Garstang to the new offices increased my journey time and mileage considerably. Barton Bridge caused considerable delay on my way to the office when structural alterations to add an additional lane to the bridge started. The journey became intolerable. Following lengthy discussions with Lynn, we agreed that it would be good to move closer to my new office. I applied for approval to move house from Garstang to Sale at the company's expense and approval was given. We moved into a very nice detached house on The Avenue, Sale, quite close to my new office. The Avenue was quite a prestigious area of Sale and the chief constable of Manchester, James Anderton was a neighbour, living a short distance away on the Avenue. The upheaval of moving the children's schools proved to be quite difficult, but a tremendous help was the financial assistance from the brewery. I received ten percent of my salary, removal costs were paid for and the cost of new school uniforms for the children were reimbursed. It was most odd when I commented to Lynn that I didn't think we would remain longer than 12 months at the Avenue. It was just instinct which proved to be correct.

The Barley Mow in Warrington had been closed for a period of nine dry years. The pub had been wrapped in cotton wool so to speak whilst the development of the Golden Square took place by Legal and General. On the closure of the pub, Joe Mawdsley my building surveyor and I had made the necessary arrangements for regular checks during those nine dry years; to ensure that it was watertight and in good order. Built in 1561 during the reign of Mary Stuart and the period of the reformation, it is a grade 2 Star Listed Building and the oldest and most famous pub in Warrington. It is the only freehold property within the Golden Square and is of considerable architectural and historical importance.

The pub was re-opened in 1983 following major structural alterations at a cost of £320,000; a considerable expense in 1983. The pub was totally re-furbished, extending and returning the pub to its authentic and original condition. The responsibility of overseeing the development and satisfactory completion of the Barley Mow was very much in my hands, together with directors' of the company. At the official opening the Mayor of Warrington Councillor Bob Taylor pulled the first pint. In his speech the M.D. Don Marshall said "Surely the Barley Mow must be the traditional gem in Warrington's Golden Square." The Barley Mow was to be probably the most prestigious managed house on my patch and took much of my time during its development.

An advertisement for staff prior to the re-opening caused much controversy and hit national newspaper headlines. A decision had been made to require all applicants for bar staff to have 'A' levels, a rather unusual request. The reason behind this was to restrict the number of applicants. We knew that we would be inundated with applications and this tactic did work quite well. The licensee and I interviewed all the suitable applicants. There were some extremely attractive young lady applicants and it was quite an enjoyable experience interviewing them! Probably the most attractive girl had bitten her nails and her hands were quite unsightly. The licensee was most upset when I rejected her. Due to the commitment and time which was necessary to launch the Barley Mow successfully,

Lynn was quite fed up of hearing about the pub and told me in no uncertain terms that she no longer wished to hear any more about it! I was not to know that several years after resigning from the brewery, I would once again become very involved in a national outcry about plans to alter and rename the pub.

Lynn and I started to attend Altrincham Baptist Church for the morning service at 10.30am on Sundays. Paul Beasley Murray was the minister and Glen Marshall the assistant minister. P.B.M. was a brilliant preacher and Glen Marshall a very down to earth Yorkshire man. I was very impressed with both of these men, their sermons were very moving and inspirational; but I still continued to sit firmly on the fence, believing that I was a Christian proper in view of my upbringing in the Anglican Church.

Robin Oake was a member of Altrincham Baptist Church at the time; he was Assistant Chief Constable of Manchester Police when James Anderton was Chief Constable. Robin was to retire from the Manchester force when his appointment was confirmed as Chief Constable of the Isle of Man. Lynn and I came to know Robin very well. He made a great impression on me, particularly his friendly nature and as a committed Christian. Robin was a tall impressive looking man who never referred to his rank, simply saying that he was a policeman. I was challenged by Robin at a social evening held by Altrincham Baptist Church. He said to me "I know where Lynn stands as a Christian, but what about you?" I came out with the usual waffle about considering myself to be a Christian, knowing full well that I hadn't taken that essential step.

A presentation took place at the Square Albert, Manchester, one of my managed houses and Robin Oake attended to receive a cheque on behalf of the Manchester Police Force from the brewery. On arrival at the Square Albert the Tetley press liaison officer greeted my outside saying that Robin Oake was already in the pub. He was clearly in awe of the fact that the assistant chief constable was there. On entering the Square Albert, I saw Robin stood at the bar with a pint of lager, speaking to Bill Bentley, the personnel director. I went straight to Robin calling him by his Christian name, shaking hands with him and him calling me by my Christian name. Bill Bentley was clearly amazed that I knew Robin so well. We had a very pleasant conversation at the bar prior to Bill Bentley presenting the cheque. Robin Oake was one of those rare breed of

*At the wheel of the Double Diamond car, Stanley Park, Blackpool.*

*Lynn and me in our wedding car – 22$^{nd}$ August 1964.*

*Family photograph with our three offspring – Mark, Alison on my knee and Karen.*

*Licensed Victuallers fancy dress party, Tim Mostyn, Lynn (bunny girl) and me (silly glasses).*

*Lynn and me – Yet another Licensed Victuallers fancy dress party in Blackpool.*

*My first beard! It actually came on ginger!*

*My lovely wife Lynn and me shortly after meeting.*

*A matching pair of lovely shire horses.*

*This time the beard came on grey. It didn't stay long. Lynn said it made me look 10 years older!*

*'Actons of Lymm' our reproduction furniture business in Lymm, Cheshire.*

*A small section of the showrooms at our furniture business.*

*My good friend Joe Beetham, probably the finest maritime artist in the world at one of his many exhibitions.*

*Our good friends Jim and Beryl at a dinner dance in Garstang.*

*A stolen car which jumped the traffic lights. Without the ram raid post the bay window would have been demolished.*

*Bob Mynett from Falmouth in Cornwall meets Bob Mynett from Cheshire.*

*In the cockpit of Concorde at Manchester airport. A Rotary visit.*

*Our immediate family celebrating my 70th birthday and Lynn's 65$^{th}$.
Left to right Karen, Mark, Lynn, me and Alison.*

The Rt. Hon. Sir Edward Heath, K.G., M.B.E., M.P.

HOUSE OF COMMONS

18 December 1996

Dear Sir Mynett,

Thank you for your letter of 7 December 1996.

It was good of you to write and I am delighted to read that other people are undertaking similar battles with the breweries as myself.

I very much hope that you will be successful.

Yours sincerely,
Edward Heath

Robert A Mynett Esq
231 Higher Lane
Lymm
Cheshire
WA13 0SD

*Letter from Sir Edward Heath, former Prime Minister re: the Barley Mow.
Allied Domecq Leisure's application was rejected.*

men I had the privilege of knowing who had that essential ingredient of 'The Common Touch.'

A tragic situation was to occur some years later when Robin's son, Stephen Oake, a special branch detective with the Manchester Force was stabbed to death by an illegal immigrant. Stephen was a very popular policeman, a committed Christian who worshiped at Poynton Baptist Church. In response to the murder of his son, Robin appeared on National television saying that he forgave the perpetrator who had killed his son. In my view this was a most courageous thing to do and caused me to question the whole area of forgiveness, an aspect of my faith which I still struggle to understand.

Over a period of time I was becoming quite depressed with the fact that I had been overlooked for promotion to director. I had been shortlisted on four occasions for interview in respect of positions for director for both managed and tenanted houses. The irony was that three of the directors appointed had eventually either been sacked or weren't up to the job and resigned. The fourth had been moved sideways to a different position following allegations of theft. I had tried to console myself that it was a situation that was meant to be and that there were better things in store for my future. I had no doubt whatsoever that Firth had blocked my further advancement with the brewery. He had been instrumental in appointing the four directors previously referred to and it had rebounded on him.

As one of the longest serving members of the team of managed house area managers, and the eldest, I was 43 at the time; I was so frustrated with my director Sweetland, who made it quite obvious that he preferred working with the younger area managers. He had a serious attitude problem considering that he was superior to me and the rest of the team. One of my pet hates is people who think they are better than others simply because of their position, looking down on those who they think to be inferior to them. I had come across many such people during my business career. The most ludicrous situation arose in a meeting when a colleague and I laughed. Sweetland said that we were not allowed to laugh in his meetings! I stood up and almost left that meeting. How pathetic! I would take Sweetland aside quite frequently telling him that in my opinion he simply couldn't treat his area managers in the manner he did. He always apologised but simply continued with his unacceptable behaviour. He was young, inexperienced and couldn't hold a candle to Tim Mostyn. His leadership, motivation and general attitude left a lot to be desired.

Over a number of years I had accumulated 30,000 Allied Breweries shares through a share option scheme, purchasing the maximum allowable on an annual basis. After 18 years I made the decision to resign from the brewery to take up a life long ambition to own my own business. It seemed the most natural thing at the time to purchase a free house. Whilst Lynn was not too happy about this, she did say that if this was my decision, then she would support me and assist in the running of a pub. We viewed several free public houses and eventually found The Sun Inn at Normanby in the Vale of Pickering, North Yorkshire, a country pub with a beer garden, fishing rights on the River Seven which ran at the rear of the pub, a two acre field between the pub and the local church where the current licensee had two ponies. We planned to continue the arrangements with the ponies, purchasing them for the girls to ride. The land was owned by the church who charged a peppercorn rent for the use of the field. The only problem was the living accommodation which was quite small

My brewery shares were an important ingredient to enable me to purchase The Sun Inn, the balance to pay for this free house to come from a business development loan from the bank. The beers stocked at the Sun were from various suppliers and I was in negotiations with Joshua Tetley's free trade division to stock all their beers. I had notified my own company of the decision to purchase the pub. However, everything ground to a halt when I was told by my M.D. Don Marshall that the company would block my purchase of the shares. They had a further 12 months to run before I could exercise my option to purchase. I was therefore unable to raise the required finance being left with no option than to withdraw from the purchase of the Sun.

Continuing employment with Tetley's was the only option left to me at the time. I was becoming quite frustrated and my morale at rock bottom. I went through a period of depression and really struggled to carry out my job effectively. The sensible solution was to wait until I was able to exercise my option and purchase the shares. During my final 12 months with the brewery, Lynn and I spent a lot of time looking at various business opportunities. The businesses being considered were a fruit and veg. retailer, bed and breakfast, general retailing and further licensed premises.

A small advertisement appeared in the Manchester Evening News for a business opportunity to purchase retail premises in Lymm, Cheshire. Acton's specialised in the sale of leather suites, reproduction furniture and gifts. The premises were situated opposite the Jolly Thresher pub at Broomedge on the outskirts of Lymm. Lynn and I met with the owners Frank and Jacqueline Acton at their Farmhouse in Pickmere, where they had been conducting the business for many years. They were one of the first specialists in the sale of leather suites in Cheshire and had started the business from scratch, selling suites from a large barn adjacent to their farmhouse. Frank Acton had transferred the operation to the freehold retail premises in Lymm some 12 months prior to deciding to sell the business due to ill health.

Following negotiations and having arranged for the necessary finance, we made the decision to purchase Acton's, and take over the ownership and running of the business in the December of 1985. The brewery had no option then than to allow me to purchase the shares which I purchased one day and sold the next, making a very healthy profit. The problem with purchasing the shares in one fell swoop meant that the profit was added to my final brewery salary for the year and it was all taxed at 40 %. During negotiations to purchase the business, liaising with the bank and sorting out an accountant, I kept my decision to resign from the brewery confidential.

During mid November of 1985, prior to advising the company that I had purchased a business, I negotiated with the marketing department of Tetley's a final fling before resigning. The annual Beaujolais run to rural France had appealed to me for some time and I was keen to participate, courtesy of the brewery and at their expense using my company car, a Vauxhall Cavalier 1.6sri. The Beaujolais run was the brainchild of Allan Hall, a Sunday Times writer who in 1972 issued a challenge to readers and colleague's to deliver the first bottles of Beaujolais to his desk. The winner would win a case of wine and the admiration of Fleet Street. The challenge was to reach the tiny town of Beaujeu near Macon as quickly as possible, where the first bottles of Beaujolais were uncorked at midnight. (It's an offence in France punishable by a

£675 fine to distribute the wine before the third Thursday in November.)

Brian, a marketing man from a company the brewery outsourced to was to accompany me, together with a mechanic from the vehicle servicing department. (A wise move in case of a vehicle breakdown) We were to share the driving there and back. A second vehicle was to join us on the run, driven by a local from the Barley Mow in Warrington, accompanied by two of his mates. With the approval of the brewery it was decided to promote the Barley Mow by putting stickers at the sides of my car, thereby promoting the pub. Grants of St James', the wine and spirit division of the company heard of my plans and arranged for our team to be wined and dined on arrival at Beaujeu. We left Warrington from the famous Golden Gates where photographs were taken by the Warrington Guardian.

The run is approximately 550 miles each way, but in 1985 the Channel tunnel still hadn't been built, so our arrival in France was to be by Ferry from Dover to Calais. Traditionally, the plan was to get to Beaujeu as quickly as possible and we went like stink en route to Dover. I was driving down the M6 motorway touching 100mph when I overtook a police car which was travelling slowly in the nearside lane. I could hardly slow down and hoped that I was going so fast that the driver of the police car wouldn't be able to see my registration number. Fortunately, we were too far past the police car which wouldn't have been able to catch up with us. My worry then was that a message could be sent to the next section of motorway for us to be stopped, but fortunately that wasn't to be. The only time we had to stop on arrival in France was to refuel and have a cup of coffee.

Whilst I was very keen to complete the Beaujolais run, I wasn't too enamoured with Beaujolais Nouveau itself. Mr favourite full bodied red is of a vintage of France i.e. Chateauneuf-du-Pape. The point of the run was for the experience and to escape the tedious and frustrating nature of the manner in which the job had become.

On arrival early in the evening at Beaujeu, the six of us stormed into the entrance of one of the many venues, full of high spirits and looking forward to an enjoyable evening.

The French doorman wouldn't allow us entry saying he had no knowledge of our booking via Grants of St James. Brian spoke in French to the doorman producing paperwork from Grants of St

James and we blagged our way in; not knowing until later that we had gate crashed the wrong venue. It was an excellent party, we had a superb meal with plenty of liquid refreshment and then the speeches started. We realised then that we were in the wrong venue when various presidents from Rotary clubs in the U.K. stood up and started to speak! However, we remained enjoying ourselves until the early hours of the morning before finally turning in to our hotel accommodation. The following morning we collected several cases of the new vintage of Beaujolais Nouveau and set out on our return journey. I was navigating for part of the journey home and made the error of taking us right through the centre of Paris. We had some very strange looks from locals knowing that the English were here again on their annual jaunt; the Beaujolais run. It was quite an experience getting out of Paris and back onto the correct route.

On returning back to the office there was the most dreadful atmosphere. My colleague's were very despondent in spite of my enthusiasm, relating to them the excitement of my trip to France. I hadn't yet checked my mail in the office when one of my colleagues handed to me a memo from Sweetland which had been sent to all managed house area managers on the area. The nature of the memo was a disgrace. It stated that recent results of sales and net profits were unacceptable and that if things didn't improve, area managers would be sacked. I was absolutely furious and marched into Sweetlands office with my memo, telling Sweetland in no uncertain terms that I was disgusted with the wording of the memo and how morale in the office was rock bottom as a result. His response was "If you don't like it you can resign."

The terms and conditions of my employment with the brewery required me to give three months notice. I had planned to take over the furniture business before Christmas with Lynn running the business with assistance whilst I worked out my three months notice. Sweetland had no idea that I had signed up for the business and was biding my time to leave. Sweetland's suggestion that I resign was like a red rag to a bull! Following 18 years of satisfactory service with the company this was an absolute insult. I called his secretary into the office and dictated to her the following memo to Sweetland, with a copy to Bill Bentley, personnel director and Don Marshall the M.D. 'In accordance with the terms and conditions of my employment, I hereby give the requisite three months notice to terminate my employment.' I stormed out of Sweetland's office telling him that it would be no use screwing up my memo of resignation and that I would personally post off my copies to the personnel director and M.D. myself.

The nature of that memo with the threat of dismissal was tantamount to leaving the company wide open for a tribunal case for constructive dismissal. On reflection, I wonder whether I should have gone down that route. Constructive dismissal is a situation where the employer puts the employee in such a position that they feel they have no other option other than to resign. I suspect that the brewery were aware of this and were no doubt relieved that I didn't take that course of action. My relationship with Sweetland was now such that the company suggested that I take a few days off to cool down. When I returned to the office on a Monday morning, Sweetland walked into my office and an argument ensued about his attitude and unacceptable behaviour. I calmed down and told him that I was no longer prepared to put up with his behaviour and asked him to leave my office. He simply stood there and refused to leave in spite of two further requests from me. I called in a colleague from an adjoining office and asked him to witness my request to once again ask Sweetland to leave my office. He continued to stand there refusing to move. Without hesitation, I grabbed hold of him by the back of his suit collar and threw him bodily out of the office. I was to later learn from Alan Williams, Tetley's head of security, that Sweetland had come into my office to apologise for his demeanour. There is no doubt that he knew he had overstepped the mark and in my mind he had been advised by his superiors to do so.

Bill Bentley had arranged for a farewell do for me with colleagues and staff. I told him that there was no way in which I would allow Sweetland to attend my farewell do. It became clear to the company that things were now so bad between Sweetland and me that it would be prudent to forego my three months notice. The farewell do was cancelled much to my relief. I was advised that my three months notice would be paid in full; in lieu of working the three months and that I could leave immediately. This suited me down to the ground and I was therefore able to leave and launch my new business with Lynn, prior to the busiest trading period leading up to Christmas.

The circumstances leading up to my leaving the brewery after 18 years had left me very depressed. I was concerned about leaving secure employment which provided an excellent pension scheme. However, I was also looking forward to the challenge of taking over the furniture business and the huge potential which it presented. We put our detached house in the Avenue on the market and made all the necessary arrangements to move into the accommodation above the business premises in Lymm.

Immediately prior to leaving the brewery, the most profound thing happened to me on the 22$^{nd}$ November, 1985 which was to completely change my life. My morale was pretty well rock bottom with no sign of my depression lifting and I was becoming quite worried that my normal positive cheerful nature had left me. It may well have helped me at the time if I had been aware of a very poignant saying i.e. 'Are you in control of your thoughts? Or are your thoughts in control of you?' Lynn had given me an N.I.V. Bible for Christmas 1982 with the words 'To my beloved husband Bob, Christmas 1982, Peace and Joy always, Love Lynn.' I randomly opened my Bible to reveal Psalm 16 and read that really powerful piece of scripture:

**Psalm 16**

Keep me safe, O God, for in you I take refuge. I said to the LORD,
'You are my Lord; Apart from you I have no good thing'
As for the saints who are in the land,
They are the glorious ones in whom is all my delight.
The sorrow of those will increase who run after other gods.
I will not pour out their libations of blood
Or take up their names on my lips.
**LORD you have assigned me my portion and my cup
You have made my lot secure.
The boundary lines have fallen for me in pleasant places;
Surely I have a delightful inheritance.**
I will praise the Lord, who counsels me;
Even at night my heart instructs me.
I have set the LORD always before me.

> Because he is at my right hand,
> I shall not be shaken.
> Therefore my heart is glad and my tongue rejoices;
> My body will also rest secure,
> Because you will not abandon me to the grave,
> Nor will you let your Holy One see decay.
> **<u>You have made known to me the path of life;</u>**
> You will fill me with joy in your presence,
> With eternal pleasures at your right hand.

The words in bold jumped out of the page at me, in particular **'You have made known to me the path of life.'** I had reached a crossroads in my life and those words gave me an assurance that all would be well and that I had made the right decision to resign from the brewery. At the age of 45 years I had at last seen the light, committed my life to Christ Jesus, nailing my flag to the mast. I had been sat on the fence for all those years making all sorts of excuses for not making a commitment. It was quite remarkable that my reading of Psalm 16 had totally revealed to me that which I had been seeking for all those years. On reflection, there is no doubt in my mind that it was the fear of my emotional response to such a commitment. I shed many tears on the 22$^{nd}$ November, 1985. How sad that it had taken all those years sitting on the fence. Lynn had been so patient during all those 21 years of marriage in the hope that one day I would become a committed Christian. I am so grateful for her understanding and support, especially through my period of depression and frustrations with the brewery. One of life's greatest gifts is to find a soul mate to share ones hopes and dreams. My lovely wife Lynn was the person who had fulfilled that hope in the here and now.

**If there's hope for the future, there's power in the present.
Hallelujah.**

# 14

## Actons of Lymm

The move into the business premises of Actons proved to be quite arduous. We had sold the house in Sale very quickly and made all the necessary financial arrangements to purchase the business via a business development loan from Nat West, plus the profit from my brewery shares. Our Nat West bank manager required a business development plan. The irony of that very lengthy plan was my comment that irrespective of the economy, there were very wealthy people in Cheshire who would continue to spend, even if there was a downturn in the economy, particularly with an upmarket furniture business which I had planned would be our ultimate aim. Following several years developing the business I was proved to be so wrong with this prediction. The canny wealthy people of Cheshire were the first to stop spending when the recession came.

A lot of work was required to bring the upstairs private accommodation up to scratch. Karen and Alison's bedroom was in the coach house at the rear of the premises, Mark's room was above the front entrance to the showrooms and adjacent to our main bedroom. Whilst familiarising ourselves with the business, joiners were building a split level in the lounge with a balustrade, a new kitchen and complete decorations were also being carried out at the same time.

The business premises had a rather unusual history. Prior to coming into the ownership of Frank Acton there had been three separate businesses on the site. The frontage of the premises on Higher Lane had been a fish and chip shop, to the side and rear on Burford Lane was a butchers shop and a vehicle repair shop with two pits which had been filled in. The well was located in an open yard in the middle of the three businesses. The coach house at the rear; plus the well, were reputed to date back to 1788.

The business specialised in the sale of traditional leather suites, using the best quality British hide. We had our own craftsman based in Bolton making suites to order. Lynn and myself had to quickly familiarise ourselves with all aspects of selling leather suites e.g. posture, colour, choice of hide etc. Whilst I was the one who had had all the sales training, there was no doubt that Lynn was better than me in achieving sales of leather suites. Lynn was more patient than me and was prepared to spend hours discussing the benefits of leather, whereas I was less tolerant. Lynn's background and knowledge of yoga enabled her to speak with more authority than me regarding posture etc.

We decided to take the business more upmarket by introducing quality solid oak furniture, mahogany and yew. I decided to introduce and stock long case clocks (grandfather clocks) a side of the business I came to love. Throughout the six showrooms the walls were covered with pictures and mirrors. We introduced beautiful Italian figurines; lamps and upmarket gifts. Whilst we allocated a realistic budget for advertising, the nature of the business was such that recommendations from existing customers accounted for much of the trade we achieved.

The first structural alteration we carried out was to open up the front showrooms into the rear. The visual impact of this was quite dramatic. This alteration was to reveal a genuine centuries old well located in the middle of the open yard, which was incorporated inside the new showrooms. Rather than fill in the well, we decided to make a feature of it by building sandstone blocks from ground level up to a height of some 4.5 feet. About three feet of mud had to be dug out from the bottom of the well. On completion, the builder Dave Ackerley, Jimmy who dug out the mud and me went down the ladder. Standing at the bottom of the well some 20 feet below ground I had taken a bottle of wine and three glasses and instead of a topping out ceremony, we had a bottoming out ceremony! It was quite amusing down there, there were customers walking around the showrooms who could hear voices below ground, on looking down the well they could see the three of us at the bottom, drinking wine, with Dave smoking a Hamlet cigar. The walls had been thoroughly scrubbed allowing clear water to seep through the sandstone walls, filling the well to a depth of about six feet beneath ground level. The local press arrived to take photographs and wanted me to stand at the top of the ladder holding Suki our cat. The feature to read 'Ding dong bell, pussies in the well' Poor Suki was terrified when she was handed to me by Lynn and put up an almighty struggle to get free. I almost lost my balance trying to hold the cat and received quite a few nasty scratches. So much for the idea of the local press reporter!

Apart from the well making a lovely feature in the middle of the showrooms, customers were fascinated to look down the illuminated interior of the well. The water which came through the sandstone sides was crystal clear. I decided to have the quality of the water tested by the public analyst department at Chester. The result was that the water was remarkably clean but not quite satisfactory for drinking. Bill Brow, a customer who lived locally was the retired head brewer of Tetley's. I had known Bill for many years whilst working for the brewery. Bill and his wife Joyce would occasionally visit our business premises and on one such visit I told Bill about the quality of the water in the well. He told me that it would be quite simple to bring the quality up to a satisfactory standard and would we consider bottling it! We could hardly set up a bottling plant in the middle of a furniture showroom!

Lynn and I started to worship at the small chapel of Lymm Baptist Church on Higher lane, some half a mile from our business premises also on Higher Lane. The fellowship at the time numbered some fifty odd people. This enabled us to integrate into the local community very quickly. The minister, Brian Howden and his wife Chris were to become very firm friends. We were to discover that Brian possessed 'The Common Touch' and over a period of time together with his wife Chris; they increased the congregation of the church to some 200. Surprisingly, I was to visit the church for the first time on my own, Lynn was otherwise engaged.

The second time I met Brian was on Boxing Day outside the Jolly Thresher Pub, directly opposite our business which was to become my local. Traditionally, every Boxing Day a large number of steam traction engines would gather outside the pub. While chatting to Brian, Lynn arrived and I introduced her to him. Lynn clearly didn't quite latch on to the fact that Brian was the Minister at L.B.C. and started to talk about what a wonderful experience it had been for us to visit Jerusalem, emphasising that the wonderful thing was that it wasn't necessary to visit Jerusalem to be a believer. We had travelled there for a day trip whilst on holiday in Cyprus. When I explained to Lynn that Brian was the minister of L.B.C. it proved to be quite amusing. Brian and Chris had also been to Jerusalem.

On parting from Brian and just before the steam engines moved on, I went into the Jolly Thresher for a couple of pints. Lynn was never particularly enthralled that I was to use the pub as my local and returned home. There, stood at the bar was Fred Dibnah! Drinking a pint of bitter. I stood next to him and spoke to him. He was his usual very friendly self and during a pleasant chat I said that I was surprised that he advertised Greenall's beer when he was a Bolton lad where there were plenty of Tetley pubs. He admitted that he preferred Tetley's and frequented Tetley pubs in Bolton more than Greenall's. When he finished his pint I bought him another.

I thoroughly enjoyed watching Fred Dibnah's television programmes. Fred had the knack of making you think during those programmes that he was just talking to you and nobody else. He certainly had 'The Common Touch'. He could communicate effectively on the one hand with a bishop or the man in the street without altering his broad Lancashire accent. He somehow reminded me of the Chairman of Telehire, Arnold Ducket but ARD didn't swear!

Fred Dibnah MBE was a steeplejack and engineer and became a television personality. He was a cult figure and latterly a national institution. As a result of the decline of the cotton industry in Lancashire, hundreds of tall mill chimneys needed to be demolished. Fred devised a system of demolishing tall chimneys without the need for explosives. His enthusiasm and warm earthy manner endeared him to his many admirers in spite of the fact that he couldn't resist the use of the odd swear word here and there. Fred was one of life's characters and would rarely ever be seen without his flat cap. I always felt that Fred had been born before his time because of his love of all things from the Victorian era.

Fred Dibnah died on the 6th November, 2004 at the age of 66 following a three year battle with prostate cancer. Thousands lined the streets of Bolton on the day of the funeral. His coffin was on the back of his favourite traction engine driven by his son with steamroller Betsy following. A life sized bronze statue of Fred was erected in Bolton Town Centre in 2008 on what would have been his 70th birthday, a similar tribute to that of the comedian Eric Morecambe, whose bronze statue graces the promenade at Morecambe.

Lynn and I decided to become members at Lymm Baptist Church and in the Baptist tradition, to have believer's baptism by total immersion. On Easter Sunday of 1986 along with fifteen other members of the church, we gave our testimony to the congregation and were totally submerged in the baptismal pool situated at the front of the little chapel of L.B.C. An elderly lady of 80 odd years was unable to be submerged into the water backwards and simply knelt down. I suggested to Lynn that she went into the pool first to which her response was "Oh no! You can go first; I've waited so long for this moment that I want to see you go first!" Much to the amusement of the fellowship, the Warrington Guardian Newspaper reported on the service stating that 'Seventeen were gathered round the font!' As if total immersion could be achieved in a font!

Having settled into the business, I decided to rename the business from just plain 'Actons' to 'Actons of Lymm' with the wording 'Fine Leather and Reproduction Furniture.' and changing the logo to appear within an oval. Having considerably increased trade enabled us financially to carry out a further major structural alteration, building a large extension to the rear, incorporating at first floor level two additional bedrooms for the girls plus a second bathroom. This enabled the girls to move into the new bedrooms from the coach house. Black and gold leaf swinging signs were fitted to the front and side elevations and the building was painted in a black and white traditional scheme. During the lead up to Christmas, I put coloured lights around the outside of the building with a Christmas tree and lights on the top of the bay to the front. The exterior of the premises looked quite dramatic and we were to be complemented by customers on the visual impact these improvements made. People would say that the building looked like a pub! However, the appearance complemented the nature of the products i.e. Olde Worlde reproduction furniture.

Following a church meeting and much prayer, a unanimous decision was made by the fellowship of Lymm Baptist Church to carry out major structural alterations. This involved extending the side of the church hall to form a new enlarged worship area, building a new baptistery and converting the original chapel into the church hall. The vision for this major step forward had been Brian Howden's, given to him by God as a result of much prayer. It was most importantly to convert the whole of the building into an open centre as well as an enlarged worship centre. A mother and toddlers group would be formed, a water colour workshop and many other activities, particularly as a meeting place for local organisations. I was very concerned that the cost was to be in excess of £400,000 and voiced my opinion that no church in Lymm could afford that sort of expenditure, particularly bearing in mind that the fifty odd members would need to raise the money in conjunction with financial assistance from the Baptist union. The original doubting Thomas! The sum of £40k had been raised from the sale of the previous church premises at Millington; which was a good start for fundraising for the extensions. However, I did eventually vote for the scheme at the church meeting which was convened to make a decision as to whether or not to go ahead. The alterations went ahead during which time we were to worship at the local high school. On completion of the alterations the number of church members increased considerably. Over 200 persons would eventually attend the 10.30am service on Sundays, a testament to Brian Howden's vision for the church.

The business premises were located at a very busy crossroads controlled by traffic lights. Surprisingly, considering this was a residential area with businesses located on all four corners of the junction, including the Jolly Thresher, a very busy pub; there were no speed restrictions other than at that time 60m.p.h. As a direct result of this there were many accidents at the junction. Vehicles would risk going through the lights on red and collide with vehicles crossing the lights from either side of the junction. Unfortunately for us there were many occasions when smashed up cars ended up on our forecourt. There were several situations where the injured driver or passengers were brought into the front showrooms by Lynn or myself and sat down with a cup of tea, awaiting the arrival of the ambulance.

Deliveries were particularly difficult with large furniture vans needing to park on the very small parking area at the front of the premises. Occasionally, it was necessary for the drivers of furniture vans to park on Burford Lane on double yellow lines. They were unable to park on the front due to customers cars parking in that small area. This is where the fun and games started with the residents of No.3 Burford Lane, situated next to our oak room at 1 Burford Lane. A Mr & Mrs Platt were notoriously difficult people who were constantly ringing the police with all sorts of petty complaints. Mrs Platt was the main problem, she was the most bitter and twisted woman I have ever had the misfortune to come across. I nicknamed her 'The Rat Bag' and shall refer to her as R.B.

When a delivery vehicle had to park on Burford Lane, the back end of the wagon would sometimes overhand the driveway of 3 Burford Lane for the short duration of the delivery and R.B. would be on the phone to the police complaining that they couldn't get their car out of the drive. They had no intention of taking their car out; in fact I'd never ever seen them use it on the road. The funniest thing occurred one day when I was in the oak room. A lorry had pulled up at the traffic lights which were on red. R.B. went up to the cab hammering on the door saying "you can't park here." The driver yelled at her "You stupid bitch, the lights are on red and I'm waiting to go."

Bert and Dave were two brothers who used to run the vehicle repair shop which was to become our rear showroom on incorporation of the three separate businesses. The brothers had no end of problems with the R.B. She never stopped complaining to the police about cars coming and going to and from the garage for servicing. R.B. must have spent a fortune on sending solicitors letters to the brothers. It became a joke in the neighbourhood because Bert and Dave pinned the entire solicitor's letters up on the walls of the workshop for the customers to see, causing much amusement.

The licensee of the Jolly Thresher had no end of problems with the R.B. They owned a house also on Burford Lane, close to R.B. A right of way between our premises and the R.B. was necessary for them to gain access to the rear of their property and R.B. tried every trick in the book to stop them using the right of way. The licensee of the pub decided enough was enough and offered the local drunk free beer for the evening if he would go across the road to the R.B.'s house and into the small front garden, knocking on the door and making a general nuisance of himself. Local drunk went over the top and started taking up handfuls of grass and soil from the garden, throwing it at the door and front window. The locals in the taproom were watching from the pub window, falling about laughing. The locals at the Jolly Thresher were convinced that R.B. was a witch!

The right of way to the rear of our business allowed us access for maintenance and repairs to the coach house. I have mentioned that the girls had slept in the coach house prior to the second major structural alteration. One day, the enforcement officer from the local council arrived saying that the council had received a complaint from the R.B. about the girls sleeping in the coach house and that they had no right to do so. I took the officer through the rear showrooms and showed him where the girls were sleeping, Karen downstairs and Alison upstairs, explaining that they only slept there and the remainder of the time they used the main domestic accommodation for meals etc. The officer said that there was no problem with that. I insisted that he then inspected our upstairs domestic accommodation; he was quite reluctant to do so saying that it was unnecessary. He did however eventually agree to look at the upstairs.

I offered the council officer a cup of tea which he readily accepted. During a very pleasant conversation which ensued, he told me that he was a retired police officer who had been based at Widness. My good friend Bob Bateson was a police inspector at Widness and when I told the council officer I was a friend of Bob's, he opened up and told me what had happened when he arrived at the R.B.'s regarding her complaint. He said that during the whole of his experience as a policeman and enforcement officer for the council, he had never come across a weirder and bitter woman than the R.B. He was invited into the house and there, standing against the lounge wall was a coffin. Mr Platt had been in the funeral business making coffins and presumably had made his own coffin for the day when he would finally expire. The council officer went back to the R.B.'s and told them in no uncertain terms that they had no grounds for complaint and that furthermore, he didn't appreciate the fact that the R.B. had wasted his valuable time.

I was decorating the oak room one day when the local police sergeant accompanied by a policewoman came into the showrooms. He told me that his chief superintendent had received a letter of complaint from the R.B. to the effect that I was disturbing them by working in the oak room. I was absolutely furious and told the sergeant that I was fed up with complaints from the R.B. that I knew the Chief Superintendent (which I did from my former days as a policeman) and I would be ringing him immediately they had left the premises. The sergeant looked very uncomfortable and I was to find out why when I rang the Chief Super. I was put straight through to the police chief and told him that the sergeant had stated that he had had a letter of complaint from the R.B. The chief super said that he had received no such letter. The sergeant had obviously been lying. I had a lengthy conversation with the chief super during which time I took the opportunity of telling him of all the years of complaints the police had received, obviously wasting much police time over frivolous complaints. The chief said that he would have the Platt's visit him in his office to put a stop to their outrageous complaints. Shortly after that conversation, I saw the Platt's getting on to a bus into Warrington, something which they never did. I assumed they were on their way to meet with the chief superintendent. Following what must have been a meeting with the chief, the complaints came to an abrupt stop. No doubt the sergeant was also told by the chief super that he didn't appreciate him telling lies and using his name.

The final straw came when R.B. objected to plans which were submitted for major structural alterations. Planning permission and building regulations were required to extend the rear of the property, extending the rear showroom and building two additional bedrooms at first floor level. There were no grounds whatsoever for objecting, it was purely out of spite and bloody mindedness by the R.B. Our local councillor Sheila Woodyatt was a member of the planning committee and was due to be Mayor of Warrington the following year. We were very friendly with Sheila and her husband Neville. Sheila visited the R.B. telling her that there no grounds for objection and that she would be recommending that the application be approved.

Within days of being told that the application would be approved, the R.B. got builders in to erect a substantial post and panel fence 6ft in height, hard up against the adjoining wall of our property. This was clearly with the intent of stopping my builder from erecting a brick wall to the required height. She may not have bothered and could have saved herself a lot of money by not erecting the fencing. My builder took one look at the wall and told me not to worry; he could demolish the existing wall and complete all the bricklaying from our side of the property.

Whilst sitting at my desk in the showrooms one day, a man and his wife were looking round at the furniture when the lady approached me and said "Are you Bob Mynett?" When I answered that yes I was, she told me that they had just moved to Cheadle, Manchester from Falmouth in Cornwall to take over the running of a pub in Cheadle and that their best friends in Falmouth had been a Bob Mynett and his wife. The name Mynett is rather unusual and apparently came from Flemish Weavers who settled in Stroud. I was intrigued to discover that there was another Bob Mynett and decided to contact him.

That evening I obtained Bob Mynett's telephone number through direct enquires and rang the number. Bob was out with a friend at the time and his daughter answered the phone. Following a pleasant conversation with his daughter I arranged to ring back the next day. I rang back the next day and spoke with Bob, noting that he spoke with a slightly Cornish accent. I was delighted that we got on like a house on fire and had many similar interests. Bob asked me if I ever went down to Cornwall and that it would be good to meet. I had arranged to visit my sister Anne and her husband in Jersey and suggested that I could call in to meet Bob en route. The date was confirmed and Bob invited me to stay overnight. Lynn remained to look after the business in my absence.

I arrived at Bob's house in Constantine, located on the outskirts of Falmouth late afternoon. Their charming cottage was close to the area in which Daphne du Maurier had based her book 'Frenchman's Creek.' I didn't quite know what to expect and had wondered what sort of person Bob would be. I was made most welcome by Bob and his wife and it quickly became very evident that Bob and I were singing off the same hymn sheet in so many respects. Bob was nothing like me whatsoever appearance wise, smaller and quite stocky. It was really quite surreal sitting there chatting with another Bob Mynett.

In the evening we went to Bob's local, a real character and typical Cornish country pub where I was introduced to the licensee. Many of the locals were intrigued by the fact that two Bob Mynett's were in their pub. We had walked to the pub through fields and on the way back it was so dark that I had to hold on to Bob to stay on the footpath. On returning to the house Bob's wife had already gone to bed. We sat in the lounge drinking brandy, chatting about the Mynett's and whilst there was no apparent family connection, we were convinced that there must be a link somewhere along the line. Bob was a retired senior probation officer and was working part time at a hotel in Falmouth. We were to discover that we both had a love of classical music, opera, the arts, especially the Pre Raphaelite period of paintings. We both had an interest in the law with me the ex policeman and Bob a retired probation officer. Bob sang with a local male voice choir and said the oddest thing to me. "I've never heard you sing but I can tell that you've got a far better voice than me!" As a direct result of this comment, I was to later join the Warrington Male Voice choir. Lynn had said to me "What makes you think that you're good enough to join such an established and prestigious choir?" However, following an audition I was accepted and joined the baritone section of the choir.

It must have been 2.30am when I finally went to bed. Before retiring, Bob told me that the bedroom I would be sleeping in was haunted. His daughter used the room when home and had often seen the ghost of a young boy who would sit on the bottom of the bed. The boy would be about 14 years of age and wore a rather unusual head gear, suggesting that he had worked in one of the Cornish tin mines. I wasn't the slightest bit nervous to hear this. I had always wanted to experience seeing a ghost if there were such things and spent half the night looking to see if the ghost would appear. Unfortunately he didn't appear and I was quite disappointed! This was the second time that I had hoped to see a ghost. The previous occasion had been several years before when I had hoped to see the ghost of Rebecca in the old Telehire building in Preston. On departing for Jersey the next day, Bob and I said that it would good to meet again.

Twelve months later, Lynn and I were on Holiday in Cornwall when we met up with Bob and his wife at their home in Constantine. Bob's wife had to leave for work and Bob brewed up for us. We were quite shocked and sad when Bob came in from the kitchen carrying a tray with the pot of tea and cups and saucers. His hands were shaking quite badly and he told us that he had just been diagnosed with Parkinson's. Bob is two years older than me and it was so sad to leave with the realisation that Bob had contracted that medical condition.

I couldn't think of a nicer business to run than Actons of Lymm. Living over the business had many advantages. When trade was quiet during the week, Lynn would be able to spend time with the children after school preparing food etc. If I needed assistance, all I had to do would be to ring Lynn on the internal telephone system and she would come downstairs to assist. It was a waste of time opening before 10.30am and we were able to close at 5pm.

Idyllic hours! We closed all day Thursday and usually went to one of the many country pubs scattered throughout Cheshire for lunch. Sunday afternoon was without doubt our busiest trading period. We opened from 1pm to 5pm and would often take as much as £3000 to £5000 in those four hours of trading. However, opening on Sundays did have its problems. A handful of our church members objected quite strongly to us trading on Sunday. This was prior to the relaxation of the Sunday Trading legislation. It was paramount to continue trading on Sunday and we simply had to bear the brunt of those few persons who were far from happy about it.

We found there was quite a demand for yew furniture, in fact sales of yew were proving to be better than mahogany. One day a rather attractive lady was looking at yew furniture with her husband, when she turned to me looking me directly in the eye saying "I love yew." She immediately realised what she had said and blushed, her husband just burst out laughing! That little incident made my day. Unlike our solid range of furniture i.e. oak and a certain amount of mahogany, yew furniture was veneered onto M.D.F. (medium density fibreboard) N.B. not chipboard, the veneer producing those rather special and beautiful markings so typical of the product.

Lynn became a deacon of Lymm Baptist Church responsible for pastoral care. This involved visiting church members at home who had health or emotional problems, but in particular the elderly. May Moss was an elderly widow and Lynn would visit her often. One morning Lynn was a little late in leaving to visit May and set off down Higher Lane like a bat out of hell. I watched as Lynn set off from our forecourt in our Volvo 760GLE estate car, hoping that she would get there in one piece. The de-restricted area ended some half a mile along Higher Lane where it became 30m.p.h. unfortunately for Lynn she didn't reduce her speed to 30m.p.h. and was stopped by a police car and booked for speeding. Lynn told the police officer that she was late visiting an elderly lady taking her home made soup and that whilst he was booking her; it had probably saved someone else being booked!

A rather amusing story relates to a female customer who arrived at our showrooms in a brand new open top Mercedes sports car. This lady purchased a small occasional piece of furniture and when she came to the desk to pay, produced a pink cheque book with bold writing on the front stating 'Rich Bitch!' She certainly looked rather wealthy from the manner in which she was dressed and spoke, so I asked her if she really was a rich bitch, to which her response was rather coy; giving me a demure look! I carried the piece of furniture out to her car but it wouldn't fit into the boot or passenger seat. It was close to closing time so Lynn was able to look after the business. I offered to take the piece of furniture in my Volvo and follow her to her home in Arley, a very pleasant upmarket area a few miles away.

I followed the lady in her Mercedes to her house, a very large impressive property in large grounds. As we approached, huge wrought iron gates opened automatically onto a circular driveway. I carried the piece of furniture through the front door and into the most impressive hall. At the foot of a large curving staircase were almost life sized bronze figures on either side of the stairs. This was a magnificent house with delightful furnishings and original oil paintings adorning the walls. As I was admiring the paintings the lady's husband walked into the hall, introduced himself and shook hands with me. He discussed the paintings with me realising that I had a love of art and then suggested that he would give me a guided tour of the house. We went into every room of the house but the highlight was the main bedroom. A large balcony overlooked the grounds and the view of the gardens was quite stunning.

On returning to the lounge the gentleman asked if I had time for a drink. I readily accepted and sat down with a large brandy, my favourite tipple! I was in my element chatting with the man who told me that he had recently retired as chairman of a large international company. He showed great interest in how my business was going and was very modest about his success in life. When I mentioned his wife's cheque book he roared laughing saying that it was so typical of his better half! Here was a man with whom I had great respect, with no airs or graces, down to earth with not the slightest bit of snobbishness or superiority. What a breath of fresh air! I left the house thinking to myself, 'here's a man with 'The Common Touch.'

The thing which I loved about the business was having the opportunity of following up a sale and getting out into customers homes with the delivery. As often as possible I would accompany the driver to deliver leather suites and large furniture orders. I would deliver the smaller sort of order i.e. corner cabinets and long case clocks in my Volvo estate. Customers appreciated the fact that the owner of the business was prepared to see the end product into their home. My favourite type of delivery was without doubt long case clocks. I would set up the clock in the position of the customer's choice, explaining the mechanism and choice of chimes. An elderly lady in Warrington had ordered the biggest and loudest long case clock. It was rather expensive and I really wondered whether she could afford it. On arrival at the house I asked where it could be located, she pointed to the half landing wall, adjacent to the neighbours adjoining wall. She explained to me that she had bought the clock to annoy her next door neighbour who for years had made the most dreadful noise. It was to get her own back!

Probably the most memorable long case clock delivery was to a lady in Warrington. I carried the clock into the hall where it was to be positioned opposite the stairs. After I had unpacked the clock and was adjusting the mechanism, I looked behind me to see triplets sat on the bottom step of the stairs. They were three little girls of about 18 months old. As I started the Westminster chimes on 12 o'clock their little faces were an absolute delight! They all just broke out into the most delightful smiles you could ever wish to see. I commented to the mother that I was surprised not to have seen a report of the triplet's births in the local newspaper. She told me that she had deliberately kept it quiet as she didn't wish to have all the publicity and all that that entailed.

There are many long case clocks scattered across Cheshire and beyond which I have delivered. Lynn and I delivered one such clock to a wealthy farmer in Warwick on our day off. On completion of all these deliveries I would suggest to the customer that they really must give the clock a name. Because these clocks are also known as grandfather clocks; I would ask what their Grandfather(s) names were. If it was George then invariably the clock would then be named George. It was a bit of fun but generally went down very well.

A farmer had rung me to say that he wished to purchase an oak long case clock but he was only able to call out of business hours one evening. I made a suitable appointment for him and the farmer arrived about 6pm. Farmers seem to think that they qualify for maximum discounts and this particular farmer was no exception! The particular oak LCC which the farmer chose was already on display with a considerable discount. However, that didn't deter him from haggling for more discounts. The bartering continued for some considerable time when by arrangement, Lynn rang down to say that dinner was ready. To get rid of the farmer, I accepted his very low offer, accepted his cheque and arranged a delivery date. Before departing the farmer suggested that we consider ordering our Christmas turkey from him and that his turkeys were the best in Cheshire. I told him that I would consider his offer.

Two weeks before Christmas we ordered a rather large turkey from the farmer. I went to the farm to collect the turkey where I established that all was well with the long case clock. The farmer's wife was dealing with collections on the day in the presence of her husband, so I decided to turn the tables on him re: bartering. When the wife told me the price I responded by saying "What's your best price for cash in return for the huge discount I gave you off your clock?" This was in the hearing of the farmer. His face was an absolute picture and he was completely lost for words; not answering my question. The wife dealt with the situation by knocking a reasonable sum of the price of the turkey and Mr Farmer stood there speechless!

We were very fortunate to have a very skilled and talented upholster to make our leather suites for our customers. Ray Anderton was a Bolton lad and worked from his own workshops producing tailor made suites for our customers. Ray took on board making a suite for one of his own contacts but the customer refused to pay. Ray went round to the house and had difficulty gaining access. Once inside the customer still refused to pay for no valid reason whatever. Ray said to the customer "If you're not prepared to pay, then you're not going to enjoy the use of the suite." Producing a Stanley knife from his pocket, Ray cut through the hide of the settee and two chairs, shredding the upholstery. Whilst he was upset at not being paid, it did give him some satisfaction that he had ruined the suite.

A very scary situation occurred at 1am one morning when a RAM raid took place on our business premises. Lynn and I were in bed when we heard a loud crash from downstairs. The alarm was activated and I jumped out of bed putting on my dressing gown. On going downstairs and unlocking the door from the kitchen into the downstairs showroom, I saw that the front door had been smashed and was lying on the floor. I did the oddest thing! I went straight to the alarm panel and shut off the alarm, probably not wanting to disturb the neighbours! On climbing over the door and going outside, I was confronted by a two door saloon car with two men in the front seats wearing black ski type masks. The engine was running and I saw that the rear of the car was loaded up with figurine lamps taken from the front showroom windows. The drivers' door was open and I was just about to attempt to grab the ignition key when a voice bellowed at me "keep out of it."

A third man, also wearing a black ski mask was running towards me from the Jolly Thresher. He had seen me considering having a go and had yelled at me not to get involved. Fortunately I had the good sense to step back. There was no way in which I would be stupid enough to tackle three of them. The third man jumped into the back of the car and it roared off down Burford Lane.

Peter, the licensee of the Jolly Thresher had been having a late night drink with his wife and son who was chef at the Midland Hotel in Manchester. Paula, the Dutch barmaid was in her bedroom at the time and had witnessed the RAM raid when a stolen car had smashed into the front door of the business. She rang down to the lounge and said to Peter "Quick, ring the police, they're RAM raiding Bob's." Peter's wife rang the police whilst Peter grabbed hold of a heavy bar stool running out of the pub followed by his son. As they crossed over Burford Lane onto our forecourt, the three hooded men were loading up the figurine lamps into the car. Peter threw the barstool at the stolen car windscreen in the hope of smashing it, but the stool just bounced off. One of the men shouted "get the gun." On hearing this Peter and his son ran back to the pub, believing that they were in fact armed.

The most unbelievable thing then happened. One of the men chased after Peter and his son, holding a large heavy figurine stolen from the front showroom window, clearly wasting valuable time. Peter slammed the front door of the Jolly Thresher before the man caught up with them. The man then threw the heavy figurine through the front window of the pub, smashing it. It was when he was running back to the car that he saw me in my dressing gown considering having a go when he had shouted to me not to get involved. The police arrived on the scene by which time the RAM raiders were long gone. The car which was used for the raid had been stolen from Manchester airport.

Fortunately our insurance covered the cost of the value of the stolen Italian figurine lamps. An insurance assessor called to discuss security and recommended that we had a RAM raid post installed in front of the main entrance to the business. The post was installed straight away.

Kevin, a specialist retailer of lighting had a showroom in the centre of Altrincham. He stocked the same range of upmarket Italian figurine lamps that we did, sculpted by the world famous Giuseppe Armani. Kevin was so fed up with his shop windows being broken to steal the figurine lamps that he ceased stocking the range altogether. This increased our sales of the product, being the nearest stockist to Altrincham. Unfortunately, whilst celebrating 21 years in business (since the Actons had formed the business) we had a major promotion with a 20% discount off all figurine lamps. In the first day of the promotion, two beautiful figurines of clowns were stolen. A total value of some £400. On another day whilst I was at the bank paying in takings, Lynn was chatting to a rep. when a couple walked in, the man wearing a baggy coat and the woman carrying a large bag. They had walked out of the showrooms having stolen two very expensive figurines. It wasn't until they had left and Lynn had checked the area where they were displayed that it became evident that they had been stolen. One of the hazards of the retail trade.

Our Cocker Spaniel Blake was very much part and parcel of the showrooms. He had a lovely nature and was very popular with many of our customers who would bring in Polo mints for him, one of his favourite treats. Suki, our cat would often sneak into the showrooms and find a comfortable place to curl up and go to sleep. One day a group of young school children gathered around the bay window of the front showroom, laughing and giggling. Suki had jumped onto the display table and was stretched out between figurines and figurine lamps enjoying the warmth of the sun.

Many of our customers became firm friends and one of these was Joe Beetham. I first met Joe when he ordered a yew cocktail cabinet which I delivered to him and his wife Betty, at his lovely detached home close to the business. Joe is probably the finest living maritime artist and his paintings in oil are quite stunning. Most of his paintings are of Yachts. The detail of the sea is so realistic that you could almost see the sea moving! Joe was an official measurer and member of the Royal Yacht Club. A yachtsman of long standing, he sailed for many years with Peter Brett, internationally known designer of 'Rival' yachts. He is a member of the Royal Ocean Racing Club, an experience which has enabled him to paint ships with great authority.

A collection of fifteen of Joe's paintings depicting the events of the Falklands war belongs to the Royal Marines Museum. This splendid museum is situated in Portsmouth, the very nerve centre of British maritime history. In 1984 the museum was nominated for the museum of the year award, a very prestigious award and was runner up to the winner. Joe was honoured to have a new gallery in the museum named the 'Beetham Gallery.' The paintings were on show in this gallery for three years, after which they were loaned to various commando training units in the south of England. They are now gradually being returned to the museum. A painting of 'HMS Invincible', from the Falklands' collection, was presented to Prince Andrew, Duke of York, who has loaned it to the ship, positioned in the wardroom of which it now hangs.

Joe often commented to me that he was 'a student of Nelson.' He was a great admirer of Admiral Lord Nelson and his oil painting of the 'Battle of Trafalgar' was undoubtedly his finest painting, one which he said he would never part with. The picture hung on the wall of his hall in Lymm and was quite stunning. In my opinion, this painting was far superior to that of the world famous J.M.W. Turner's oil on canvas 'The Battle of Trafalgar' as seen from the mizzen starboard shrouds of the Victory. Joe was rightly proud of such a stunning work of art, admired by his many friends who visited him at his home. In spite of Joe saying that he would never part with his painting of the 'Battle of Trafalgar' it now hangs in a very prominent position aboard HMS Victory.

The Battle of Trafalgar took place on the 21$^{st}$ October, 1805 when 27 British ships of the line led by Admiral Lord Nelson, defeated 33 French and Spanish ships west of Cape Trafalgar. The British victory spectacularly confirmed the navel supremacy that Britain had established when Nelson became and remains Britain's greatest navel war hero. Victory was Nelson's Flagship during the Battle of Trafalgar and is now a tourist attraction in Portsmouth.

Joe's wife Betty would often assist with measuring prior to ocean going races by the Royal Yacht Club. Sadly, Joe's wife was to die of cancer whilst he was half way through painting the sinking of the Titanic. He was unable to continue painting for some considerable time due to depression brought on by the bereavement. I invited Joe in for a coffee and a chat shortly after his wife's death and thereafter it became a regular visit, sometimes twice or three times a week. Joe insisted on bringing in the occasional supply of coffee. Lynn was particularly helpful during this period of Joe's life, as a trained psychotherapeutic counsellor, Lynn had counselled many persons following bereavement.

During Joe's period of depression, Lynn and I took him for lunch to the Sharrow Bay Hotel at Ullswater in the Lake District; our favourite hotel serving exquisite food with magnificent views along the lake. After lunch we went down to the waters edge when Joe said "What I need is a kick up the backside." I said that we could oblige and invited Joe to bend down; when Lynn gave him a gentle kick on his backside. I took the opportunity of recording the event by taking a photograph when Joe bent down. That was a turning point in Joe's life and he started painting once again, completing the awesome and very large painting of the sinking of Titanic. There was something of Joe's bereavement in the painting, depicting the awful nature of that tragedy at sea.

The remarkable thing about Joe's oil painting was that he was self taught. He completed over six hundred paintings in oil, mainly of sailing ships, many of which were purchased by the owners of yachts. His paintings hang in public and private collections in Britain, Europe and America. He also produced limited editions and other prints. Sir Edward Heath, former Prime Minister and leader of the Conservative party, commissioned Joe to paint his yacht 'Morning Cloud', which appears in his book on sailing. During the Falklands war Joe painted non stop, painting the sinking of H.M.S. Sheffield among other sea battles which took place. Chairmen of I.C.I. also commissioned Joe to paint their yachts. Joe had worked for I.C.I before taking early retirement to take up painting full time. I am proud to be the owner of one of Joe's original oil paintings, a sailing ship at dawn, which is positioned in a prominent position in the lounge.

I would assist Joe with many of his art exhibitions, carefully placing several of his oils in the back of my estate car, taking them with Joe to various venue's and assisting in hanging them. The Black Sheep Gallery at Hawarden, Flintshire, was a gallery which Joe and I would visit on a regular basis. We would have lunch at a local pub where Joe referred to the chips as 'proper chips' just like your mother used to make! The owner of the Black Sheep gallery, a retired bank manager had a lot of respect for Joe. He would comment about Joe's enthusiasm and in particular that Joe 'had a twinkle in his eye!' At one such exhibition, a little girl was looking at one of Joe's paintings when she said "Mummy, if a hole was drilled in the sea, would water come out?" Whilst having a coffee at Joe's home one day, I was looking at a painting of a yacht in very rough seas and commented to Joe that I was sure I had seen the sea moving !

Joe Beetham's talent for painting was such that he not only had the incredible ability to paint such realistic paintings of vessels at sea, he could also paint buildings and rural scenes with great skill. A client who was passionate about the paintings of the internationally famous Canaletto, commissioned Joe to reproduce two famous scenes of the canal in Venice. The final result was so stunning that no doubt an expert on Canaletto would find it difficult to distinguish them from the originals. To ensure that everything was above board and legal, Joe signed the two copies as he did with all of his oils 'Joe Beetham.'

Joe had been attending St Mary's church in Lymm, where his wife Betty had been buried. He wasn't particularly happy attending St Mary's and started attending Lymm Baptist Church with Lynn and myself. We were thrilled when Joe made the decision to have believer's baptism and total immersion in the baptismal pool at the church. Not very long after the sale of our business premises, Joe moved to the north east to be close to his son Robert. Whilst Joe is twenty years older than me; we got on so well and I miss seeing him a great deal. His sense of humour, modesty and generosity endeared him to his many friends and acquaintances. Joe is a great friend and possesses that all important gift of 'The Common Touch.'

## 15

## Bereavement – A Service of Hope

Following a period of some three years in a rest home and finally a nursing home in Preston, my Mum died on October 16$^{th}$ 1995 at the age of 87. Whilst I had prepared myself for her inevitable death, I was absolutely devastated when it happened. My sister Linda and I had paid regular visits to see Mum in Preston Private Nursing Home. It was so sad to see her progressive loss of memory through Alzheimer's disease. Her brother, my Uncle Harold Rigby had also suffered from Alzheimer's and had died at the age of 85, two years younger than my Mum.

Mum did not attend church other than high days and holidays. My sisters Anne, Linda and myself chose not to have a church funeral service, it seemed pointless. The funeral service took place at Preston Crematorium on Friday 20$^{th}$ October and I was so grateful when Lynn offered to conduct the service. Lynn had previously conducted a funeral service for a lady who was a member of Lymm Baptist Church. As a Deacon of the church and with considerable experience of counselling; particularly in bereavement, it was so meaningful for my wife to conduct the service. The following is a transcript of the service as prepared by Lynn.

Jesus said "I am the resurrection and the life. Whoever believes in me will live, even though they die; and whoever lives and believes in me will never die." JOHN 11:25-26.
The eternal God is your refuge, and underneath are the everlasting arms DEUTERONOMY 33:27
God so loved the world that he gave his only son, that whoever believes in him should not perish but have eternal life. John 3.16
At every turn life links us to the Lord, and when we die we come face to face with Him. In life or death we are in the Hands of the Lord. Christ lived and died and lives again to establish His Lordship over dead and living. ROMANS 14:7-9.
Things beyond our seeing, things beyond our hearing, things beyond our imagining, all have been prepared by God for those who love him. 1 CORINTHIANS 2:9

We are gathered here to say farewell to Florence Mynett who has died. We are here because in one way or another, this death affects us all. We are here to listen again to some of the great words of the Christian faith; to consider, to remember and in quiet gratitude to give thanks for her life and our own continuing lives. We are here to renew our trust in God who has said "I will never leave you or forsake you."

Let us pray.
Father, your love is stronger than death. We come to you in our need…You have given us birth and now we face the mystery of death. Help us to find You in the Whole of life, its beginnings and its endings. Help us to discover you in our pain as well as our joy, in our doubts as well as our believing that we might find comfort in your word and light for our darkness. In the name of Jesus we ask it. Amen.

ROMANS 8;38-39
I am convinced that there is nothing in death or life, in the realms of spirits or superhuman powers, in the world as it is or the worlds as it shall be, in the forces of the universe, in heights or depths – nothing in all creation that can separate us from the love of God in Christ Jesus our Lord.

> Morning will come…
> Broken hearted…
> How can I bear the pain why?
> Why this?
> Helplessness…hopelessness…
> Life will never be the same again.
> Where are you God?...............
> I'm right here beside you my child.
> Even though you may not feel my presence.
> I'm holding you close under the shadow of my wings,
> I will walk with you through the dark night.
> Do not shrink from weeping.
> I gave you tears to release your emotions.
> Don't try to hide your grief.
> Let it become for you a source of healing,
> A process of restoration

> For I have planned it so.
> Those who mourn shall be blessed. I'll be holding on to you
> Even when you feel you can't hold on to me.
> Seek my face child of mine.
> Receive My promise, impossible as it may seem now,
> That joy will come in the morning.
> It may take some time.
> But I will heal your heartache.
> I know the night seems endless
> But morning will come
> I have promised.

Let us join together in saying the prayer that Jesus taught his disciples: The congregation then said the Lords prayer.

## ADDRESS

We can feel that we have been preparing ourselves for this day and the four days preceding it, for years, a lot of mourning and 'letting go' has already been accomplished, but the final goodbye can only transpire in the fullness of time – Today, and the ones to come. Florence Mynett nee Rigby. Born 16th June 1908, Died 16th October, 1995 at 87 years of age. Daughter of Robert and Mary Rigby. Sister to Harold – now deceased – who was two years younger – she called him in those days 'our kid…..Orchid!'

Florence grew up in Preston, was confirmed at Christ Church on February 15th 1923 and attended school at Christ Church and later at Balshaw Grammar School in Leyland. Florence excelled at school, went on to teachers training college and gained distinction in her exams. She taught in Cheadle, Longridge, Fishwick and Ribbleton Hall Drive Schools.

Florence had a sense of humour, no doubt fostered by the joke telling in teacher's staff rooms! She was a disciplinarian, strict but fair and earned the respect of teachers and pupils alike. The children responded to her discipline which enabled them to learn things they never thought they could. They gained a sense of their own self worth in their accomplishments.

A stylish young woman, proud of her sylph-like figure and athleticism, she loved swimming, sport and excelled in ballroom dancing. Her creative talents were in sewing, crocheting, knitting, tapestry and her love of gardening. She had a passion for poetry and when appropriate would recite lengthy poems word perfect. Hiawatha, Rudyard Kipling's 'If' Tennyson, Shakespeare and particularly Macbeth – she had an amazing memory. 'The Pied Piper of Hamlyn' was her favourite and Granddaughter Sarah spent many an hour in recent times reading this familiar poem to her Grandma – a precious relationship.

Florence met and married Arthur on October $3^{rd}$ 1936. They lived in the early days on Hartington Road. In 1938 Anne was born, two years later Bob and four years on Linda, all at Bairstow Street Nursing Home. Florence's life was a full one – full of relationships. Daughter Sister Friend Wife Mother Aunt Cousin Teacher Mother-in Law Grandmother and eventually four times Great Grandma…and the relationship with all her individual cats.

Daughter Anne, married Johnny and a year later thrilled Florence with her first grandchild – Colin and later Shirley. To Linda, her Mother gave her all her support when another grandson was born into the family. Florence had a share in nurturing and caring for Anthony. There was a special relationship between them! In 1964 son Bob married Lynn, three years on Karen was born, then Mark and Alison, all in the space of four years. Linda met and married John Culshaw in 1973. Six years later blessed Florence with grandchildren 7 & 8 – Michael and Sarah. Yes – a life of special relationships.

I think one of the most important things we can do at a funeral is to be honest. For it helps us all be more real and honest in our own lives and relationships. Family was a priority to Florence. One of her deepest desires was that her three children would have happy marriages. I have it on good authority and would affirm that her three children and spouses clock up collectively a good ninety years between us to prove it! It hasn't been easy, but its character building! Florence was one of life's characters; she enjoyed nothing more than having her family round her, a glass – or two! of sherry in one hand and a cigarette in the other!

Her life was a tapestry of her many threads – it echoed Corrie Ten Booms poem:

My life is but a weaving between my God and me, I do not choose the colours, He worketh steadily. Oft times he weaveth sorrow, and I in foolish pride, forget he sees the upper and I the underside. Not till the loom is silent and the shuttle cease to fly, will God unroll the canvas and explain the reason why, the dark threads are as needful in the skilful weavers hand. As the threads of gold and silver in the pattern he has planned.

The years rolled by – Florence saw grandchildren marrying: Shirley to Russell, Colin to Cindy, Karen to John, Anthony set off to the other wide of the world, finally culminating in his marriage to Jeanette in April earlier this year in New Zealand, but for the past almost two and a half years Florence's home has been in Preston Private Nursing Home where love and care found a tangible expression of the highest calibre and we are so grateful.

For us all, knowing and loving and being loved by Florence has been a tremendous privilege – for as we build relationships, a deeper kind of love is born in our lives and we can praise God for the richness and depth that this loving and sharing brings. We can often feel we can only share that love in the measure it has given to us, humanely speaking, but that's not taking into account 'Divine Love' from God the author and source of Love. For God is Love.

If the infinite and inexhaustible love of God is to flow through us, to touch even a fraction of the need around us, two things are needed: Firstly, we should have assurance that we do have a personal relationship with God through his Son Jesus Christ and that we remain in close touch with that source so that the stream of love does not dry up. Secondly, we must ensure that the stream always finds an outlet, or the spring of divine love within us stagnates and our lives become arid and barren. No – we need to be springs of living water, pervading the love and fragrance of Christ.

Florence was a private person, she liked her own company. She never liked to fuss about anything. Up until the day before she died, she was not confined to her bed. She died quietly, peacefully with no fuss. I am sure that when we leave this service of hope today we will all remember her with great love and affection, as a really genuine person who cannot be replaced. Florence is at peace now. Christ is here amongst us wanting to give us his peace. A peace that the world cannot give. Just relax and feel and receive his peace. Your whole being bathed in the peace of God.

Let us pray. Father God, we praise and thank you for the world in which we live and for the lives you have given us. We thank you for the new life offered to us in Jesus Christ, His death on the cross and your raising Him to life again. Thank you, oh thank you so much for the life of Florence and all that she meant to us and the memories which we can keep, a source of comfort and thankfulness. Thank you that all suffering is now past, that your same love which surrounds us also welcomes Florence! Help us all to be content to release her to you, that our grief may neither be overwhelming, nor unending. Assure us of your love, strengthen our trust in your grace and grant us peace.

We brought nothing into the world and we cannot take anything out of the world. Now that the earthly life of Florence has come to an end, we entrust her into Gods merciful care and compassion. May the peace of God which is beyond our utmost understanding and far more worth than human reasoning – keep guard over our hearts and thoughts now and forever. Amen.

Following the funeral service, family and friends went to Haighton Manor for lunch. Half way through the meal, my brother-in-laws father, Jack Culshaw, otherwise known as 'Jack to Lad' made the most hilarious comment saying out loud for everyone to hear "I'm really enjoying myself; we should do this more often!" That was followed by one or two saying "I wonder who's going to be next?" It's a well known fact of life that more often than not; sadly, the only time distant relatives get together is for a funeral.

# 16

## The Barley Mow

Quite unexpectedly, the Barley Mow pub in Warrington was to once again take up a large proportion of my life. An article appeared in the Warrington Guardian to the effect that Allied Domecq were planning to rename the pub the 'Flail and Firkin' or the 'Furrow and Firkin.' Allied Domecq was the company name following the re-organisation of Allied Breweries and were renaming many of their pubs under the 'Firkin' brand, the length and breadth of the country. I was quite incensed that this traditional pub was to be converted into a 'fun pub' type of operation and became very involved with the Guardians 'Hands off the Barley Mow' campaign, writing to the newspaper strongly objecting to the proposals.

The following is a letter which I sent to Sir Christopher Hogg, Chairman of Allied Domecq which clearly expresses my views about their plans for this historic grade 2 star listed building. I sent copies to the following persons :-

Sir Jocelyn Stevens – Chairman – English Heritage
Sir Christopher Harding – Chairman – Legal & General
Mr David Quarmby – Chairman – British Tourist Authority
Mike Hall – M.P. for Warrington – House of Commons
Doug Hoyle – M.P. for Warrington – House of Commons
Sir Nicholas Winterton M.P. for Macclesfield – House of Commons
Councillor Mary Roblin – Mayor of Warrington
Superintendent Anne Booth – Cheshire Constabulary – Warrington
Mr Richard Morrison – Journalist – The Times
Mr Blatherwick – Magistrates' Clerk, Licensing – Warrington
Golden Square Management Office – Warrington
Mrs Connie Hardy – Warrington Civic Society
Mr Harry Wells – Warrington Civic Society, Listed Buildings Chairman
Mr Dave Roberts – Hands off the Barley Mow Campaign, Warrington Guardian

Dear Sir Christopher,

Re: <u>The Barley Mow – Warrington</u>

I write to express grave concern regarding your company's plans to rename the Barley Mow. It is planned to rename the pub the 'Flail & Firkin' or the 'Furrow & Firkin' under the umbrella of your National 'theme pub' scheme. There are also plans to carry out certain structural alterations which do not on the surface appear to be particularly contentious at this stage. The plans were adjourned but are now being presented before the Licensing Division of Warrington Magistrates' Court on 15 October, 1997.

The Barley Mow was built in 1561 during the reign of Mary Stuart and the period of 'The Reformation.' It is a grade 2 star listed building and the most famous pub in Warrington. The building is situated within the Golden Square development which is owned by Legal & General. It is the only freehold property within the Golden Square and is of considerable architectural and historical importance. The facia of the exterior has beautiful detail in quatrefoil and the pub commands an enviable position in a prime site.

The Barley Mow is a huge tourist attraction and quite recently a party of twenty German tourists were most anxious to be taken to the pub. Warrington's twin town of 'Hilden' in West Germany have named a pub in Hilden the 'Warrington' as a direct result of the town's links with Warrington, but mainly because of their love of the Barley Mow. A retired American General re-visiting the army base of Burtonwood took a party of friends to the Barley Mow and in his own words he was "gobsmacked."

The Barley Mow was closed in 1974 and 'mothballed' for nine dry years whilst Legal and General developed the Golden Square. The pub was re-opened in 1983 following major structural alterations at a cost of £320,000. The pub was totally re-furbished, extending and returning the pub to its authentic and original traditional character. At the official opening the Mayor of Warrington, Councillor Bob Taylor pulled the first pint. In his speech the Managing Director of Tetley Walker, Don Marshall said "Having come through the doors of the Barley Mow today, from the prestigious development of the Golden Square, you will have *seen a totally contrasting world. Surely, the Barley Mow must be the traditional gem in Warrington's Golden Square"*

Since its reopening in 1983, the Barley Mow has been catering for and serving an enormous number of regulars who not only remember the Barley Mow from the past, but new customers who waited nine years for a pub with an abundance of character and tradition to reopen, substantiating the belief the company held i.e. Tetley Walker, that there was a demand for an upmarket traditional pub in the town centre of Warrington, thereby maintaining its reputation for the best in food and drink that the Barley Mow has enjoyed over the centuries, serving the people of Warrington.

It is also relevant to say that the capital and revenue expenditure of £320,000 was an excellent investment. The discounted cash flow basis was used to calculate return on capital invested. Trade exceeded all expectations and the weekly take soon achieved £12,000 with a high gross profit margin. Don Marshall M.D. was delighted and so were the then board of Allied Breweries, proving that the traditional scheme was the correct route to go down. I haven't the inclination to check with my accountant as to what the take in 1983 would convert to at today's prices, but it would be quite considerable.

In view of the foregoing and particularly bearing in mind the historical importance of the Barley Mow, for Allied Domecq to even contemplate a change of name is disgraceful. The Warrington Guardian Newspaper are vigorously opposing the change of name and their 'HANDS OFF THE BARLEY MOW' campaign has resulted in hundreds of petitions being signed by the people of Warrington and other ex-Warringtonians from around the world. People are furious and incensed that a pub of such historical merit should be altered with complete disregard to their views.

Allied Domecq clearly couldn't care less about peoples views and a spokesperson for the company recently stated "It would be doubtful that the hundreds of petitions which have flooded into the Guardian offices will be considered by the bosses as the fate of the pub hangs in the balance." and "It is not the normal practice for this company to consider the petitions which may have been submitted." What a wonderful public relations exercise!

Mike Hall and Doug Hoyle, Warrington M.P.s are opposing the plans and state "The pub would lose its individuality if Allied Domecq enforce a change of name. It's absolute nonsense."

Warrington Civic Society are totally opposed to the plans as are the Cheshire Conservation Officer, Warrington Historical Society, Conservation and Listed Building Associations etc. etc. The fact that the Barley Mow is a listed building apparently does not protect the name by law; mores the pity! However, I believe it will be a totally different matter should the basic nature of the operation at the pub to change considerably.

Most of the hundreds of objectors to the change of name of the Barley Mow are undoubtedly totally unaware of the more insidious agenda which underlies the real nature of what is in store for this unique pub of great character. The 'theme' pubs being developed by your company under the banner of 'Furrow & Firkin', 'Flea & Firkin', 'Finch & Firkin' etc, are destroying the very fabric of pubs like the Barley Mow, but on an even more worrying note, on a national scale.

The British pub is a unique and much envied institution throughout the world and very much a part of Britain's Heritage. Frankly, I am horrified at the way not just Allied Domecq, but other brewers are systematically destroying and carrying out acts of deliberate vandalism to buildings of outstanding historical and architectural merit.

It would appear that the 'Firkin' intention is to rip out everything which is original, putting 'Disneyland' type posters and other ludicrous objects on walls, installing ear piercing sound systems and generally creating a 'Fun Pub' type of atmosphere. Clearly, this policy is to attract the younger drinker. In Warrington in particular the Barley Mow would be targeting the younger drinker and effectively competing with the many night clubs in nearby Bridge Street and other town centre clubs. In my view this is totally unacceptable and I am sure that the many tenants of the Golden Square would be outraged at such a pub operation within their midst, notwithstanding the extra problems the already overstretched police of Warrington would have to cope with.

Obviously, Allied Domecq are required to produce satisfactory results to keep the city and shareholders happy. I can fully understand the reasoning behind promoting 'Firkin' operations. The 'Flea & Firkin' Grosvenor Street, Manchester is a case in point. The targeting of this listed building; formerly a theatre/cinema is clearly a brilliant concept. Its position is ideal being next to Manchester University and it will obviously be a very *cost effective exercise; to spend what I understand to be several hundred thousands of pounds. Upon completion it will undoubtedly be a huge success and I wish your company well with the project. However, the 'Flea & Firkin' is a typical ex theatre/cinema with high ceilings and is crying out to be turned into a theme pub for young drinkers. It bears no resemblance whatsoever to the situation in respect of the Barley Mow.*

*Should your company ignore the genuine plea's of those persons opposed to change at the Barley Mow, then clearly large numbers of customers will vote with their feet and take their trade elsewhere. There is absolutely no way in which Tetley Walker would have even contemplated such a dramatic change of direction, as evidenced by the hugely successful refurbishment and alterations on its reopening in 1983. Surely, this is proof that the 'marketing boys' in those days got it right!*

*The adverse publicity already created by the couldn't care less attitude of Allied Domecq, coupled with the irony of the pending closure of Tetley's Warrington Brewery this year is just too much to stomach and also sadly, we have seen the last of Tetley's famous magnificent shire horses at the Cheshire Show.*

*My ultimate concern is what is happening all over the country, with brewers riding roughshod over the very genuine concerns of ordinary pub goers, the bread and butter of any brewer. Conservationists, Historians, Listed Building associations etc. are given no consideration whatsoever. There is obviously a conflict of interest with the commercial and modern marketing view of the brewer versus conservation and a common sense approach to pub development. The common 'theme' pub which is being developed throughout the country is not necessarily aesthetically pleasing to the majority of pub goers. The adverse impact of these schemes will affect the tourist trade and create irreparable damage to the great wealth of pubs from the past.*

*Unfortunately, young ambitious marketing directors' realize that they can make a name for themselves with such schemes. Old World pubs of great character are being destroyed at an alarming rate and as we approach the millennium, are we going to be looking back on the 20$^{th}$ century saying 'How sad that all those marvellous pubs have gone for ever.'*

*With regards to the Barley Mow, I would consider this to be one of the worst acts of vandalism were the scheme to go ahead.*

Therefore, why not stick with a well proved and winning formula and avoid further very damaging bad press.

I understand that the planned takeover of Carlsberg/Tetley has been referred to the Office of Fair Trading. With the uncertainty which lies ahead, I would conclude by respectfully suggesting that you recommend to the Board of Directors' of Allied Domecq that they do a 'Firkin' U turn and scrap the plans for the Barley Mow.

Yours sincerely

(signed)

Robert A Mynett

P.S. The writer was an employee of Allied Breweries for a period of 18 years. Joining Ind Coope Northern as a free trade salesman. Moving to the tied estate as deputy area manager. Promotion to area manager tenancies and finally transferring to managed houses as area manager. He was involved in the closure of the Barley Mow, supervising building surveyors' during the closure for 9 years. He was actively involved in the plans for the structural alterations, appointed the licensee's on its re-opening and had overall responsibility for ensuring that agreed plans and targets were achieved. He resigned 11 years ago to achieve a lifelong ambition and now runs his own business in Cheshire.

My letter to Sir Christopher Hogg was forwarded on to Mr M J Grant, M.D. with responsibility for the Firkin Chain for his information and attention. In his reply to my letter, he referred to the company's successes redeveloping outlets under the Firkin brand; thanking me for my concern and hoping that his letter had gone some way to allaying my concerns. Grant's letter certainly did not allay my concerns; it was he who said in no uncertain terms that the company did not consider petitions and would go ahead with the scheme irrespective of the general public's opposition. My reply to Grant said that he would appear to be on a different planet in his Ivory tower in Birmingham, furthermore, that he cannot be totally unaware of the tremendous backlash of adverse publicity the Firkinisation of pubs is creating and I quoted 'How dare they desecrate something that has been there since the 16$^{th}$ century in order to turn it into another brash, run-of-the-mill fun pub, which will lose it's sell by date remarkably quickly.' I also pointed out that the anger and resentment their Firkinisation of pubs had created would not go away and in the final analysis, I really did wonder if Allied Domecq really did care about the matter. I concluded by saying that the public response so far was merely the tip of the iceberg, that these were very serious and important issue's which must be addressed and they would simply not go away.

I wrote several letters to the Warrington Guardian which were printed in their weekly publication. One of the first and more lengthy ones was headed 'Don't be fooled by Allied Domecq' The general gist of that letter was that I was appalled and incensed to read in the Warrington Guardian of their plans to Firkinise the Barley Mow; stating 'Don't be fooled by the statement by Allied Domecq that people will approve of the work once completed, that the proposed changes are very minor and that It's basically a refurbishment rather than a structural massacre.' Nothing can have been further than the truth.

Mr A Stephenson was Director of Community Services for Warrington Borough Council. He wrote to me asking me to submit details of my objections regarding Allied Domecq's application for the Barley Mow. I wrote a very lengthy letter to Mr Stephenson, very much along the lines of my letter to Sir Christopher Hogg, Chairman of Allied Domecq, but including the following information.

Sir Nicholas Winterton, M.P. for Macclesfield introduced a Private Members Bill in the House of Commons which had had its first reading. The second reading was to be heard in late November of 1997 to read as follows: 'That this house notes the long standing and ancient historical traditions which lie behind the ancient names of public houses and appreciates the special role which they play in community life. This house deeply regrets the growing trend of theme pubs with contrived names that have no relevance for the local community, which can cause embarrassment, ridicule and a sense of alienation for local people. This house believes landlords should not have the ability to re-name public houses and urges the Secretary of State for the Environment and Home Secretary, without delay that without consultation with the local community, the names of public houses cannot be changed without permission from the local planning authority.

50 M.P.s supported the motion and it is interesting to note that Nicholas Winterton received more correspondence on the subject than any previous campaign he has mounted. Unfortunately the bill didn't go through, mores the pity.

The following comments were made by prominent people regarding the renaming of pubs with ridiculous names :-

Sir Edward Heath M.P. and former Prime Minister was furious that his local 'Guy, the Earl of Warwick' was to be re-named 'The Ferret & Trouser-leg' He said "This particular crass and vulgar proposal has been shelved. The people of Welling will now be spared the indignity of going to the Ferret & Trouser-leg merely because they wish to enjoy an innocent pint."

Sir Nicholas Winterton M.P. for Macclesfield, regarding proposals to rename the Bulls Head, Macclesfield the 'Pig & Truffle.' "The Bulls Head has a long tradition, being in the centre of Macclesfield and was the start of the old coaching service to London. We have no desire whatsoever to have the name changed."

Richard Morrison, Columnist of The Times, "Every week another ancient inn falls victim to what is surely the naffest and smuttiest of all '90s cultural trends. Can nothing be done to deter the smirking Philistines who run our big breweries from their Orwellian mission to erase all traces of local history from the pubs they control?"

Jane Sharman of English Heritage "We find it surprising that Allied Domecq seem bent on offending many in the local communities they purport to serve."

My letter to Mr Stephenson also pointed out that the proposals did not fall into the category of authentic restoration and there was no element of sympathy towards the architectural or historic nature of the building. Pub signs are an index to their past, there is nothing meaningful about the 'Plough or Furrow & Firkin' and the ludicrous renaming of historical pubs is driven largely by commercial and marketing departments, who are seeking to attract teenagers on their seventh pint of lager. These marketing 'whiz kids' are trying to rewrite history and will reap a bitter harvest having pulled the threads from the tapestry of our heritage.

Following my letter to Mr Stephenson, I was invited to attend the planning meeting which was to decide whether or not to approve the application for the change of name for the Barley Mow. About twelve members of the planning committee were present. I was given 10 minutes by Councillor Terry O'Neill, Chairman of the planning committee to explain my objections. I explained my intimate knowledge of the Barley Mow, due to my past as the Area Manager with responsibility for the pub; covering the many points which I had raised in my letter to Mr Stephenson. As a direct result of my intervention, I was delighted that the planning committee turned down the application to rename the Barley Mow. The decision was reported on the front page of the Warrington Guardian which quoted Councillor Terry O'Neill as saying "It's our duty to look after the pub for future generations. We felt that the brewers' proposals would seriously damage its character."

Allied Domecq were not at all happy with the refusal, appealed against the decision and asked for a public inquiry which was held at The Town Hall, Warrington on Thursday 4$^{th}$ December 1997 at 10am. The application was for Listed Building consent for structural alterations at The Barley Mow. An Inspector instructed by the Secretary of State for the environment attended the public enquiry. Following the enquiry the application was refused, thereby saving the Barley Mow from the ridiculous proposals by Allied Domecq.

Allied Domecq had successfully acquired a church building in Brighton and had received planning permission to convert the building into a Firkin Pub. It had been named the 'Font & Firkin' Lynn and I visited the pub. On a marble plaque at the front of the building were the words 'To the glory of God, Henry Varley the great evangelist who for over 50 years in the Lord's vineyard, was the means of winning thousands of precious souls for God's glory.' Next to the plaque on a board were the words 'Come in and sin. Live music every Thursday and Saturday night!' Also at the front of the pub were the words Strictly reserved for the Firkin breweries bike.

On going into the 'Font & Firkin' I was appalled to see the many signs making a mockery of Christianity. I am no prude, but draw the line at the blasphemous nature of what I saw. The following was the wording of signs. The bells of hell. For fonts sake buy me a firkin pint. Firkin brewery – our heavenly tonic. God's grog. Fill that gap with a Firkin Bap. All christenings suspended until further notice due to faulty plumbing. I drink religiously. Sin til ya drop with a Firkin ale brewed on site and the get stuffed we do. Ale Mary. Firkin commandments: thou shalt not abuse the Firkin staff. The upper bar was signed Firkin closed. Firkin commandments – Thou shall not fall over drunk. Confess your sins. Outside the ladies toilet was a sign saying Firkin Female. The gent's sign read Hymns. Any confessions please contact the Firkin management. Please keep your Firkin hands off the plants. In the upstairs bar (which was closed) were the signs Firkin fodder. Pardon me vicar and What's in your Firkin Bap? On the duke box was the sign Music Machine – sounds Firkin amazing.

Biblical pictures depicting the Good Shepherd and photographs of clergy down the years were on display. In a picture frame was the cover of a Holy Bible cover found during refurbishment of the church, plus photographs of the original interior of the church before Allied Domecq's Firkin scheme had taken place. I was so annoyed by what I saw, I wrote to Brighton and Hove Council, complaining most strongly and asking how on earth planning permission had been granted for the conversion of the church, with such appalling signage, making a mockery of religion. I couldn't believe the response. Mr W J Heron, Assistant Director of Environmental Services replied to my letter stating that he had 'Consulted with colleagues and had concluded that there was little the council could do' enclosing a memo from their lawyer saying 'Whether or not a sign is misleading, undesirable or offensive to public morals is irrelevant.' How pathetic! I had also complained to the head of planning in Preston, my home town, regarding a pub which was given approval to be converted into a Firkin outlet; for what was previously the Public Hall in Preston. The council had made no effort whatever to refuse planning permission.

Councillor Mrs Sheila Woodyatt had written to Sir Christopher Hogg expressing her concern regarding Allied Domecq's plans for the Barley Mow. Sheila was an active member of the planning committee and had been most supportive of my input and opposition to the plans. Sir Christopher's letter of reply was as follows:-

Dear Mrs Woodyatt,

**The Barley Mow, Warrington**

Thank you for your letter of 27$^{th}$ September. I note your concern and appreciate your trouble in writing.

We have received several letters concerning our plans for the Barley Mow at a level which is comparable to that relating to similar projects.

Pub names and styles have changed over the centuries to reflect the changing requirements and styles of society. Such changes are not made lightly but, where they are carried out, are vital to the successful re-positioning of the outlet. The proposed conversion of the Barley Mow to the Firkin brand necessitates the re-naming of the pub. This is key to attracting a new customer base, which research and past financial performance shows us is fundamental to the success of the investment.

This approach has proved outstandingly successful, both with customers and with shareholders. Our customers vote with their feet, with increasing numbers using these outlets more frequently. Our shareholders benefit from the extremely attractive returns such investments deliver. We do not make these changes lightly, however, going to great lengths to acknowledge the history of the site. This is frequently achieved by a commemorative plaque on the exterior and by including the original pub signage as part of the original design.

For your information, many of our developments.are part of the successful roll-out of the Firkin brand, have originally encountered some local opposition, but subsequently received accolades and awards. The most recent was the award by the Windsor Council for our development of the Fort & Firkin just outside the castle walls. The Font & Firkin in Brighton is about to receive an accolade in the Sussex business awards for the quality of the development there.

*Clearly, this whole issue will be fully aired at the forthcoming planning committee meeting at Warrington and we will be putting our case fully in that forum.*

*(signed)*

*Yours sincerely*

*Chris Hogg*

I was rather surprised at Sir Christopher's referral to the Font & Firkin at Brighton and was very sceptical as to whether the pub would receive the accolade referred to. His letter didn't impress Sheila or me and of course Allied Domecq's plans to convert the Barley Mow into a Firkin pub had not received the necessary planning approval.

I received two letters of congratulations from the House of Commons for the successful refusal of planning permission to convert the Barley Mow to a Firkin Pub. The first from The Rt. Hon. Sir Edward Heath, K.G.,M.B.E., M.P. and the second from Sir Nicholas R. Winterton, M.P. The letters were typed on House of Commons letter heading and signed by both M.P'.s. I like to think that in some small way, my involvement in assisting to stop Allied Domecq and other brewers from converting historical pubs into ridiculously named theme pubs, did have some impact on future decisions.

My involvement and time required in my objections to the approval of planning for the Barley Mow had taken some considerable time away from the business. Graham Watson, my NatWest Bank Manager had commented that whilst he admired the way I had successfully blocked Allied Domecq's plans, he was concerned that it may well have had an adverse effect on the business. Graham had become a personal friend over the years and it was understandable for him to voice his concern. However, on conclusion of the refusal for planning permission, I chose not to become involved in further correspondence regarding the Barley Mow and was able to concentrate once more on the business.

# 17

## Armed Robbery

An armed robbery took place on the forecourt of our business premises early one evening. The business was closed and Lynn, Mark and I were in the lounge, when we heard a commotion at the front of the building. On looking out of the window, we saw a large Mercedes car reverse from the forecourt, smashing into a medium sized saloon car positioned in the middle of the junction. The saloon car then sped off along High Legh Road in the direction of the motorway.

On going down to the forecourt, the Mercedes car had driven back onto the forecourt. The driver of the car was clearly very angry and badly shaken; his wife was sat in the passenger seat shaking. He told me that they had been the victims of an armed robbery. Lynn, Mark and I invited them into the front showroom of the business where we provided them with a cup of tea. They related to us what had happened while waiting for the police to arrive.

The driver of the Mercedes and his wife were dealers in antique jewellery. They had been to an antique fair at a pub in Warburton on the outskirts of Lymm. Their antique jewellery had been in boxes on the back seat of the car and whilst travelling along Burford Lane, towards the junction where our business was situated, a stolen car with two men tried several times to ram the Mercedes into the side of the road. The Mercedes being the heavier car was not so easy to stop and was able to be driven towards the junction of traffic lights by our business. The antique dealer decided to pull onto our forecourt, believing that by doing so the villains wouldn't dare follow them onto such a busy junction.

The stolen car followed the Mercedes onto the forecourt, the passenger got out with a revolver, pointing it at the antique jewellers head, demanding that he hand over all the antique jewellery. The jewellery was handed over, the passenger jumped back into the stolen car which reversed into the middle of the junction. The antique jeweller reversed back at some speed, smashing into the getaway car, attempting to stop their leaving the scene, but the car was able to be driven off at high speed.

Because of the nature of the armed robbery and high value of the stolen jewellery, the police in conjunction with BBC's programme Crime Watch, had decided to re-enact the robbery and to televise it. We were asked by the BBC for our co-operation by allowing lighting to be installed in our front showrooms which we readily agreed to. It was quite an experience to see how the circumstances were to be re-enacted. The police had persuaded the antique dealer to use the Mercedes and also the owner of the stolen car. The police stopped all traffic on the approach to the junction, stunt men took the wheel of both cars and it was totally amazing how the stolen car was dragged back with chains by a Range Rover. When the Mercedes reversed back, missing the stolen car by inches, it gave the appearance of having struck the stolen car. Broom Edge had never experienced anything like this before with residents and customers at the Jolly Thresher pub totally enthralled watching the action.

Just before the camera man started filming, I walked over to him where he was positioned over the road, on the pavement outside the Jolly Thresher. I asked him if I could look through the lens which he readily agreed to. On looking towards the gable end of the business I said to him, "We've got a problem." I went on to say that the wording 'Actons of Lymm' in old English lettering on the gable end was obliterated by a telegraph pole and would it be possible to move the position of the camera slightly. It was no problem for the cameraman and the camera was moved slightly to show the lettering!

When the program Crime Watch was televised, Jill Dando introduced the fact that an armed robbery had taken place at Broomedge in Lymm, on the forecourt of our business premises. I was delighted to see the lettering Actons of Lymm prominently shown during the very realistic filming. We had many phone calls saying that the business had been seen on Crime Watch, thereby promoting Actons of Lymm.

We received the following letter of thanks from Cheshire Constabulary for our co-operation in the filming of Crime Watch:

*Dear Mr & Mrs Mynett,*

*I am writing to thank you and your family for the assistance that you gave to my officers and the BBC staff, during the recent filming for a forthcoming episode of 'Crimewatch.'*

*I understand that filming went on somewhat longer than expected, and I can only apologise if this caused you undue inconvenience and disruption of your normal domestic routine.*

*I am sure that you appreciate that the exercise was a very necessary one in view of the serious nature of the robbery that occurred outside your premises, and it is to be hoped that the efforts of all concerned will be proved to have been worthwhile at the end of the day.*

*Yours sincerely,*

*(signed M Holland DCI)*

*For Detective Superintendent*

We also received a letter from the BBC which read as follows:

*Dear Mr & Mrs Mynett and Family,*

*Just a quick note to thank you for your help with our Crimewatch reconstruction last week. Your very kind patience and co-operation was very much appreciated and I hope we didn't inconvenience you too much.*
*The film is scheduled to go out on Thursday 18$^{th}$ January on BBC-1 at 10.00 pm*

*Once again, many thanks for all your help.*

*Yours sincerely Jayne Topping,*
*Researcher, "Crimewatch UK"*

To the best of my knowledge, the perpetrators of this robbery were never caught.

We had been able to survive the recession of the early 1990's having trebled turnover in the previous years. This increase in trade had produced a very healthy bottom line net profit, enabling us to purchase a new Volvo 760 GLE Estate Car and also to purchase a house in High Legh, Knutsford as an investment. We were able to afford foreign holidays and to enjoy an excellent standard of living. Graham Watson, our NatWest bank manager was very supportive and delighted at the success of the business. However, sadly, this was to be short lived for a variety of reasons.

Our main supplier of hide was Whittles whose tannery was based in Warrington. The quality of their British hide was second to none. The company got into financial difficulties and ceased production, selling the site to D.F.S. On the opening of the D.F.S. showrooms, our sales of leather suites took a nosedive. The quality of their suites was not comparable to those supplied by ourselves, their main advantage was their four years of interest free credit. As a smaller retailer we simply could not compete.

The next blow was the opening of IKEA in Warrington. In their first year their takings were reputably £9 million. This had an adverse effect on the sales of our furniture. Then the Trafford Centre opened in Manchester. This had a huge impact on trade, not just on us, but many retailers in Altrincham who simply couldn't compete and had to close down. The final straw was when John Lewis's opened in Cheadle, Manchester. This not only affected us, but most other retailers in the area.

The only reason we were able to survive for as long as we did was through a huge overdraft facility, courtesy of Graham Watson. Fortunately, we owned the property freehold, but had to hand the deeds over to NatWest as collateral. The overdraft facility crept up to £85,000. I had already invested the whole of my mother's inheritance to prop up the business. The state of the retail trade was such that many businesses were in financial difficulties and without support from the banks would have gone under. By this time, our turnover had dropped by a third, back to the level when we took over the business in 1985. We made the very difficult decision to put the business on the market, but the state of trade generally was such that no one was interested.

After some 12 months it became obvious that we were not going to sell the business as a going concern. We therefore made the decision to sell the property and to have a closing down sale. Stock was marked down to cost price, in many instances we were selling at below cost but it was vital to move the remaining stock to enable us to clear off the overdraft and pay any outstanding debts to suppliers. 'Actons of Lymm' finally became another statistic of the small family business, with the doors closing for the last time on the 10$^{th}$ May, 1998. Fortunately, we were able to leave with a clean bill of health owing no money whatever to our suppliers.

We had a firm offer to purchase the business premises from a local successful entrepreneur. Barry Green specialised in computer software and planned to move his business from Knutsford to Lymm, close to his home. However, his offer fell short of our asking price and I decided to see if we could secure a better offer. We received a further offer from a Mr Holt, who said he was prepared to offer the full asking price. Thereby hangs the tale! For several weeks he prevaricated by using the oldest trick in the book. Holt had effectively taken the business off the market by offering the full amount, thereby stopping anyone else from making an offer. I became furious at his solicitors constant letters offering considerably less for no valid reason. I became so frustrated that I instructed our solicitor to advise Holt's solicitor that I was no longer prepared to waste more valuable time, saying that I had found another buyer (Barry Green). I had decided that the lower offer was acceptable. Holt's response was to try and contact us (we were ex-directory) but was unable to do so. His solicitor said that his client desperately wanted to have the business and said that he was now prepared to offer the full asking price. After the lies and deceit which we had been subjected to, I wasn't prepared to risk further delays and was more than happy to go along with Barry Green's offer.

It was obvious that we would need planning permission for change of use of the business premises. Barry Green's firm offer was based on planning approval being given for office use. Once again our friend Sheila Woodyatt, our local councillor would prove to be most helpful. As a member of the planning committee, Sheila pointed out that the problem was insufficient parking space for office use. There was only enough room for five or six cars to park on the forecourt.

I had a brainwave! How to overcome the problem of parking. Hyde's Brewery owned the Jolly Thresher car park directly over the road. During lunchtimes there was adequate spare parking for office staff, but clearly it would need the approval of the brewery. David Pepper was the brewery area manager for the Jolly Thresher, he had been catering advisor with Tetley's prior to joining Hyde's, advising and assisting me with my catering pubs. I rang David, asking if he would consider writing to Warrington Planning, stating that the brewery would approve of a certain number of office staff parking at the pub during lunchtime. I said that the benefit to the brewery would be office staff using the pub at lunchtimes for food and drink. He readily agreed, wrote to planning and approval was given for change of use for office premises.

## 18

### High Legh   Knutsford

Fortunately, we were able to move into our house at High Legh, Knutsford, having given the tenant the requisite period of notice. A new chapter in our lives was unfolding, although it was very difficult adjusting to losing what I considered to be the nicest possible business. I couldn't think of a better way of earning a living. We had put our heart and soul into developing a very successful business, only to see it fail through no fault of our own. The three children had already left home by the time we moved to High Legh, Karen was married, Mark had moved into an apartment in Manchester and Alison was a Junior Doctor in Brighton.

Lynn applied for a full time paid employment position with Making Space, a registered mental health charity as a Family Support Worker, specialising in caring for families of people suffering from enduring mental illness, schizophrenia, bi polar etc. Four years before closing the business, Lynn had trained as a Person Centred Psychotherapeutic Counsellor and this clearly stood her in good stead. Head office was based in Warrington and the position which Lynn applied for was to be based in the Vale Royal area of Cheshire. Ben John, a member of Lymm Baptist Church was a consultant psychiatrist for Warrington and surrounding area's and readily provided an excellent reference for Lynn. Ben knew of Lynn's passion for pastoral care and helping the less fortunate in life, particularly members of the church. David Line, the Managing Director of the company had built up the charity from scratch and was delighted to offer Lynn the job following an excellent all day interview.

Meanwhile, I had been chosen by the Directors' of an innovative and exiting new company 'Reverse Guard' to sell their product – the ultimate aid to reversing safely, using submarine technology by bouncing sound waves to identify obstacles. The first person in Lymm to have this new revolutionary reversing aid fitted was Joe Beetham who said in a local press advertisement "I am delighted to have this amazing reversing aid fitted to my BMW. I now have complete peace of mind when reversing in any situation." Whilst this product was excellent, following various technical problems with the product and a disagreement over commission payments, I became disillusioned and moved on to try my hand at network marketing.

I had previous experience in the field of Network Marketing, also known as Multi Level Marketing (MLM) initially with nutritional health products, then venturing into other MLM products. Whilst I have no problem with this system of selling, I was to discover that it simply wasn't for me. There's a lot of hype in the industry and claims of untold wealth, with promotions offering top of the range sports cars and fantastic holidays, cruises etc. Dale Carnegie's well known book 'How to win friends and influence people' for me, did not apply to network marketing. 'How to Lose Friends and alienate People' would be a more apt phrase! Being advised to make lists of all those people you know and then trying to sell them your products, can, and often does ruin a good friendship. The most successful person I know who heads up a nutritional health company refused to approach friends and family, working with his 'cold' market only (those people you don't know) This man is now a millionaire, living in Formby on Merseyside. Very much the exception than the rule!

An advertisement appeared in the Knutsford Guardian series for a marketing manager to be based in Knutsford. The position was to be full time with weekends off and I decided to apply for the position. At the age of 62, I didn't consider that I would be considered for the job. However, following an hour long telephone 'interview' by an agency, I was recommended for the position and attended a further interview at the Knutsford offices. Following that interview I was offered the job and agreed to start work with the company the following week.

The work entailed speaking with Chairmen, Managing Directors' and Directors' of companies regarding their obligations in relation to Employment Law and health and safety issues. I was working in an open plan office with some 23 other staff and by far the eldest in the office. Following an initial period settling in, I was to specialise in arranging appointments with directors' of companies who were being taken to tribunal for alleged unfair or constructive dismissal.

Not long after starting employment with the company, I was struck down with the most dreadful pain in my legs and had great difficulty in walking any distance. My doctors in Lymm were unable to diagnose the problem and simply referred me to

Warrington hospital for an appointment. The pain was such that I was on very strong painkillers. I dreaded going to bed at night when the pain became intolerable. A hospital appointment was not possible for six weeks and I simply couldn't wait that long for a diagnosis.

Our youngest daughter Alison was a junior doctor at the Royal Sussex County Hospital in Brighton at the time, training in anaesthesia and returned to our home one weekend. Alison took one look and me and suggested that I could well be suffering from Polymyalgia Rheumatica, commonly referred to as PMR. This is a debilitating disease of the blood which affects the muscles of the body. I was so fed up waiting for the hospital appointment that I made the decision to transfer to a highly recommended doctors' surgery in Knutsford. Dr Paddy Kearns became my doctor and immediately arranged an x-ray and blood test, something which my doctor in Lymm hadn't initiated. The result established that which Alison had suggested and proved to be PMR. The cause of the illness is not known. Paddy prescribed steroids and the immediate effect was quite miraculous. The pain disappeared overnight but I was still unable to walk very far, assisted by the use of a walking stick. My PMR was to last for seven years during which time it was necessary to take steroids daily. I am just so grateful now that I am completely free of the illness and thankful that Alison and Dr Paddy Kearns had diagnosed the problem.

# 19

## You're never too old

The Knutsford Guardian produced an article about ageism and asked for readers to submit information about their experiences. I wrote to the Guardian and the following full page article appeared on October 9$^{th}$ 2002.

### Company offers answer to an age-old dilemma
### You're never too old

A GROWING obsession with youth coupled with the tendency to view the over 50s as being fit for nothing has led to a shortage of experienced men on the job. This week reporter Shelley Smith asked some of those – viewed by others as 'has-beens' – why the future will be bleak unless British companies change their ways.

It was an age old question that Bob Mynett had asked himself a hundred times. At 62 and out of work, was there any prospect of him getting another job?

"I was only working in the evening but was at home in the day and was fast running out of things to do," he said.

I spent hours and hours going to job centres looking for work and was eventually shortlisted for three jobs but I'm convinced it was my age that meant I did not get them."

But the father of three grown up children was determined to make his mark in the world of work – among a growing sea of youngsters making their way up the ranks.

That determination paid off when the tide turned in his favour and he was offered a job as a business development co-ordinator at a company in Knutsford.

"I felt such a tremendous relief when I got the job," he said. "I had an hour long interview with an agency with quick fire questions which was quite intimidating.

"Then I had a half hour interview at the company and was practically offered the job straight away. Ageism was not an issue."

But had Bob, now 62, not got his big break with one of the fastest growing companies in Europe, his future could have been very different. The granddad would have found himself still seeking work in an ever increasing group of more mature jobseekers.

According to American business consultant Bill Morton, the West will be populated by about 69% more 55 to 70 year-olds over the next 15 years – with two million fewer 25 to 40-year-olds.

"People are living longer," he says.

The problem is compounded by the tendency of many companies to opt for younger employees and ignore a vast resource and wealth of knowledge – the mature worker.

"Many companies would see employing mature people as a risk or even threat," said Mr Mynett, a former policeman and brewery area manager who later became the owner of a reproduction furniture business Actons of Lymm with his wife Lynn.

"But this cannot be the case when you realise the experience and skill that mature people have to offer modern young companies."

"People assume that if you are older you will only work one or two years and then leave a company but that is not necessarily the case; and anyway, how many people work with a company now for over five years? We can help to teach youngsters the right attitude towards the job and many, many skills said Mr. Mynett. Ex-BBC war reporter and Tatton's former Independent MP Martin Bell, who is now in his 60s, recently urged TV bosses not to start culling journalists who are over 40 because of society's growing obsession with youth. He said journalists were already being discarded before their time. There are a lot of gifted reporters who have been pushed out because they are older; which is a shame; because they have skills and abilities that can only be gained by experience," he said.

I had met Martin Bell on three occasions whilst he was the independent M.P. for Knutsford where I saw him at his constituency office. The third meeting was to discuss my objections to a proposed structural alteration to a listed building in Warrington, associated with Oliver Cromwell. Whilst Warrington was not in Martin's jurisdiction, he was happy to meet with me, being an admirer of Oliver Cromwell. I was able to tell Martin that I was also a great admirer of Oliver Cromwell and I was so pleased when he invited me to accompany him to the annual memorial service on Cromwell day, held at the Houses of Parliament on 3$^{rd}$ September, the formal occasion regarding Cromwell's contribution to our history in Britain. Martin is a member of The Cromwell Association, which commemorates Oliver Cromwell (1599-1658) studying Oliver Cromwell and the history during the period of the

Civil War. Unfortunately, I was otherwise engaged on the 3$^{rd}$ September and was unable to attend.

Martin Bell had a distinguished career as a foreign affairs correspondent for over 30 years, making his name reporting from wars and conflicts in Vietnam, the Middle East, Nigeria, Angola and Northern Ireland during the troubles. Whilst covering the war in Bosnia he was seriously wounded by shrapnel. In 1997 he left the BBC to stand as an independent candidate in the Tatton constituency of Cheshire, where the Conservative candidate Neil Hamilton was involved in allegations of sleaze. Martin Bell was elected M.P. for Tatton and hit the national headlines when he met with Neil Hamilton over what was to become known as 'The battle of Knutsford Heath.' Martin Bell is most certainly blessed with 'The Common Touch.'

The Knutsford Guardian was to contact me once again regarding a series of articles called 'Lessons for Life.' The articles ran for several weeks and were essentially about what individuals had learned about life since the age of 18. The following article appeared in the Guardian on October 9$^{th}$ 2002 following an interview with their local reporter. There was a photograph of me at the heading of the article at the age of 18 with my police dog 'Jet.' The dog that had attacked the Deputy Chief Constable.

## Here He tells the Knutsford Guardian what he has learned about since he was 18

Bob Mynett is now 62, has been married to Lynn for 38 years and has three grown-up children. He is still working in Knutsford. At 18 he had just missed out on National Service, but he says that eight years with Lancashire Police provided an excellent grounding in self-discipline. Here he tells the Knutsford Guardian what he has learned about life since he was 18.

That the hardest thing is getting one's priorities right in life and that ruthless ambition for promotion has an adverse effect on family life. When my children were young I lived, ate and slept my job as a brewery area manager and missed out on those formative years as the children were growing up. Hindsight and the 'if only' factor is a wonderful thing. How different things would have been with the gift of hindsight.

That being a Granddad to three wonderful grandchildren, who are encouraged to call me Bob, is really good fun. It is a new chapter in life where you can step back into childhood and be really 'daft.'

That job satisfaction is more important than money and that 'effective' communications and leadership skills are essential for success in the business world.

That attitude in life is paramount. Admit your wrongs and learn from your mistakes.

That time flies. My mother used to say "You will find Bob that the older you get the faster time goes." How very true.

That being the owner of your own business and having financial problems (bank overdraft/cash flow) is one of the most stressful experiences and probably
comparable in an odd sort of way with bereavement/divorce and moving house,
But it is heartening to discover that there is life after the dreadful experience of losing your business through no fault of your own and that life does go on.

That the art of salesmanship is not the gift of the gab, but to be a good listener.

That your happiness depends upon the quality of your thoughts. You are where you are because of what goes into your mind. At 59 I acquired my first computer and discovered the thrilling world of going 'on line' and web sites. It now seems quite bizarre that up until three years ago I was quite nervous at the thought of learning computer skills. I cannot imagine life now without these skills.

That a profound effect in my life occurred on November $22^{nd}$ 1985 when I read Psalm 16. From an Anglican upbringing I became a member of Lymm Baptist Church. I find it very sad that fundamentalism in any religion is the cause of so many problems throughout the world and that Bible thumping Christians do more harm than good.

That I will never again take good health for granted. Having been struck down with PMR this year and having experienced the most dreadful pain, I am now so thankful to my daughter Alison and Dr Kearns, who jointly identified the problem and prescribed the right medication.

That honesty is without doubt the best policy. In spite of being turned down for promotion by being scrupulously honest about the manner in which I would conduct myself as a brewery director, I would prefer to sleep at night in the knowledge that I have been truthful. A good liar has to have a very good memory.

In spite of the fact that my employers were happy to employ older employee's, they had adopted a mandatory retirement age of 65 and I was required to leave on 6$^{th}$ April, 2005, my 65$^{th}$ birthday. I was prepared to continue working for the company and was devastated that my request to continue was not considered. The irony was that the article which the Knutsford Guardian had printed regarding the companies policy towards ageism was no longer applicable to those employee's over the age of 65. However, I was grateful that I had found employment up and till retirement age.

It came as quite a shock that I was unemployed, with little or no possibility of further employment and hence, no further income other than my state pension and a relatively small pension from my 18 years with Allied Breweries. Lynn was still working full time in the field of mental health and after much discussion, we decided that it would be good for Lynn to apply for further promotion to take over a new position based in Derbyshire. Making Space had successfully applied to take over the contract for the whole of Derbyshire. Lynn's application was successful and she was to take over responsibility for 8 Family Support workers for the whole of Derbyshire, including Derby City. Lynn eventually managed to acquire her own office accommodation in the registered office of Willersley Castle, a Christian conference centre and residential hotel in Cromford, Derbyshire.

Lynn was to stay overnight in Sheffield, at the home of our youngest daughter Alison, travelling each morning to her office in Cromford. The journey to her office took her through the spectacular grounds of Chatsworth Park. However, after some 5 months in the position, the pressure and politics of the job became so intolerable that Lynn decided to resign. I had told Lynn that there was no job on the planet worth the stress and anxiety and encouraged her to resign.

We had been quite excited at the prospect of moving to Derbyshire and had put the house on the market, spending much time house hunting. Fortunately, we hadn't found a suitable property in Derbyshire which we could afford and when Lynn resigned, we decided to leave our house in Knutsford on the market and to downsize to a smaller property. Our situation was such that our finances fell far short of being able to maintain the overheads of a large semi; we therefore had little or no option than to downsize. We were keen to remain in Cheshire and eventually moved to Sandbach, having sold our property in Knutsford.

# 20

## Sandbach Cheshire

It's three years now since we moved to Sandbach. The move proved to be most successful and we have integrated into the local community very well, establishing firm friendships through church, Rotary and Inner Wheel. Considering that Knutsford is so relatively close to Sandbach, we have found the residents of Sandbach to be far friendlier than Knutsford. The move proved to be far more stressful than expected. Moving from a large semi into a small bungalow was far from straightforward. We had no less than 90 packing cases which required two furniture vans to complete the removal. Many of the packing cases had to go into the garage until we could accommodate them in the house. Our lovely cocker spaniel Grace, found adjusting to the new house most difficult, she was totally blind by then and was constantly bumping into furniture which she must have found to be quite distressing. I commented to Lynn that I should go on Dragons Den with an invention to produce a crash helmet for blind dogs!

The first Sunday following the move to Sandbach, we went to New Life Church in Congleton and were so impressed by the form of worship. The three very talented music groups were brilliant and I was so impressed by the leader of the church, Steve Hodgkinson. Steve, a retired bank manager took early retirement forming New Life Church from his home 26 years ago (1983) prior to his retirement from the bank and some years later, together with the elders of the church acquired the present church premises where some 200 of the fellowship worship on Sunday mornings. Steve is well known throughout the area as a committed Christian, is very well liked and a brilliant communicator. He has been an inspiration for me through his faith and undoubtedly ranks very highly among those people I have the privilege of knowing who have 'The Common Touch.' I consider Steve to be a personal friend.

Shortly after moving to Sandbach, I became a member of the Rotary Club of Sandbach, taking on the role of Fellowship. This involves organising social trips for members of the club. The first trip was by coach to the Anglican Cathedral in Liverpool (my favourite building) where we had lunch and a guided tour. Many members went via the two lifts to the top of the tower which houses the highest and heaviest peal of bells in the world, followed by lunch in the refectory. Many other successful trips followed i.e. The Beartown Brewery, Congleton, Bridgewater Hall, Manchester, Concorde at Manchester Airport and many others.

Lynn became a member of Inner Wheel, the wives of Rotarians who together with Rotary organise social and fund raising events for local and international charities. As I write, the eradication of polio is the main fundraising activity for Rotary. Bill Gates has donated millions of US$ which has been matched by Rotary International, a most worthy cause. I am looking forward to my year as president of the club in 2010 during which time Lynn will become president of Inner Wheel. A joint venture.

Our eldest daughter Karen is about to gain a second degree qualification. She is a true survivor; having gone through a difficult marriage and then coming out of it to help others in similar circumstances, has raised three children almost single-handedly for the past eight years and is a well respected and loved member of her community with many friends. She is a committed Christian and is an active member of her church in Widnes. Her three children are a delight and blessing to Lynn and I. Sam, her eldest son is nearly 18 and will go to Glasgow University to read medicine in September, her daughter Summer is 15, loves art and animals and has a brilliant sense of humour, Harmony, her youngest is a bungle of energy and has just been diagnosed with special abilities, including a photographic memory like her Mum. The family have recently added a new member to the family, a King Charles Cavalier Spaniel by the name of Muffin. He keeps all the family on their toes, especially the cats!

Son Mark, a talented musician, travelled throughout Europe with his heavy metal rock group and is now a senior lecturer at Huddersfield University, lecturing on the subject of music production and technology. As admissions tutor for his subject he is also able to continue production for bands, using state of the art equipment at his university. Mark has written articles for the magazine 'Sound on Sound' and has presented papers in Austria and most recently Cardiff on the subject of music production. At the age of 41, Mark is still enjoying life as a single man. He is waiting for the right female to tick all the boxes, a pretty impossible task! He has adopted a rescue dog – Lucy, to whom he lavishes his attention in the form of daily 5 mile walks. Time permitting.

Youngest daughter Alison was married to the climber and photographer Ian Parnell in October 2007. They were thrilled to become parents to Suzanna forty weeks later. Following 12 years of hard work as a junior doctor and registrar, Alison has recently gained the position of consultant anaesthetist in Sheffield at the age of 38, specialising in cardiac surgery. Son-in-law Ian (Parnell) has summited Everest. He refers to this achievement as 'a walk in the park'! In March of 2007 he took Ranulph Fiennes 'the World's greatest living explorer' up the north face of the Eiger to the summit, no mean feat!

We are justifiably proud of our three children and their achievements. Fortunately, all three are living reasonably close i.e. Karen in Appleton, Warrington, Mark in Stockport and Alison Sheffield. Unlike my youngest sister Linda, whose eldest son Tony lives in New Zealand, daughter Sarah, Newcastle and youngest son Mike living in Dublin. My eldest sister Anne, husband Johnny and their two offspring, Colin and Shirley all live in Jersey. A delightful island some 14 miles off the coast of France.

Christmas of 2009 was a most enjoyable occasion with the family. However, Mark had gone to New Zealand to spend a month over the Christmas period staying for 5 days with my nephew Tony and family in Wanaka, South island. We had agreed to look after Mark's dog Lucy during his time away.

I find the following hilarious story to be most amusing! Lynn and I were walking our dog Grace, along a country lane near to our home in Sandbach. I was dressed in army khaki combat gear and I commented to Lynn "Wouldn't it be funny if we met up with someone who thought I had been in the army!" I went on to say "If we do I'll say I was in the S.A.S." (As if!) Lynn just collapsed laughing at the thought of me being in the S.A.S! Without hesitation; Lynn then said "More likely the silly arseholes society!" We stopped to speak to neighbours also walking their dog and related the story to them and they couldn't stop laughing!

On 30th December, our lovely Cocker Spaniel Grace had become so ill. She had been unable to eat or drink over the previous two days and the inevitable became obvious. In spite of being so very poorly, she was still able to wag her tail when stroked and spoken to! Lynn and I were absolutely devastated that Grace could no longer survive. I rang the vet in tears, saying that Grace would have to be put to sleep. Arrangements were made to take Grace to the vet at 11am the next day, New Years Eve. Lynn had always left it to me with our previous 6 Cocker Spaniels to take them to the vet's to be put down, but on this occasion said she would like to come with me. I was very appreciative of her support. Our vet, Cameron Muir of Cheshire Pet Medical was very compassionate, confirming that Grace would have to be put to sleep. What an emotional experience that was, Lynn was sobbing, I was in tears as the vet injected Grace in her leg as I was supporting Grace's head, fondling her ears and talking to her all the time and within 30 seconds she gently slumped down to die peacefully.

Grace was 12 years old (84 in human terms) and without doubt the loveliest dog we had ever owned. Sadly, she had become progressively blind over the past 3 years and towards the end of her life very confused, but was surprisingly still able to go for reasonably long walks, but Mother Nature knew that it was time for her to go. Grace gave us 12 years of happiness, bringing such joy into our lives and will be sadly missed. I think it is fair to say that only doggy people can fully understand the emotional impact of the death of ones dog. They are without doubt one of the most faithful members of the family. Our grandchildren were particularly upset at the news. Grace had been such a part of their lives as they had grown up. Even little Suzanna, our youngest granddaughter at the age of 18 months had found Grace to be so gentle and loving.

On the $2^{nd}$ January, 2010 we received a lovely bouquet of flowers from the vet, expressing their condolences. Attached to the flowers was a card with the following words 'Grieve not, nor speak of me with tears. But laugh and talk of me as if I were beside you...I loved you so- 'twas Heaven here with you. *Isla Paschal Richardson.* Signed...*from Cheshire Pet Medical.*

As I reach the conclusion of my book, I find it quite unreal that I actually started to write it on the $5^{th}$ October, 2002. Over those past 7 years there were periods of several months where I was simply unable to devote any time to writing; particularly as a result of the house move; preparing the house in Knutsford for sale and a considerable amount of work which was necessary to bringing our bungalow in Sandbach up to scratch. It's been a lovely journey recording my experiences, often recorded on pieces of scrap paper as an aid for inclusion in the book. It is my hope that our family and in particular 4 grandchildren (at present!) will enjoy reading of my experiences.

I started the book by referring to Rudyard Kipling's 'IF' and would like to conclude by referring to a piece which is so similarly poignant – The Paradox of our time and 'Common Sense.'

## 21

## The Paradox of our Time

Some thoughts based on an e-mail from a Columbian High School student and delivered in an address at Coventry Cathedral by David Alton, Lord Alton of Liverpool, on Sunday November 19$^{th}$, 2000

The greatest paradox of our time is that we have taller buildings but shorter tempers; wider freeways, but narrower viewpoints; we spend more, but have less; we buy more, but enjoy it less.

We have bigger houses, and smaller families; more conveniences, but less time; we have more degrees, but less sense; more universities, but less learning; more knowledge, but less judgement; more experts, but fewer solutions.

The paradox of our time is that we have multiplied our possessions, but reduced our values. We talk too much, love too little, and hate too often. We've learned how to make a living, but not life; we've added years to life, but not life to years; we engineer new life, and then destroy it on an unparalleled scale.

We've been to the moon and back, but won't cross the street to meet the new neighbour; we've conquered outer space, but not inner space, we've cleaned up the air, but polluted the soul; we've split the atom, but not our prejudice; we have higher incomes, but lower ethics; we're long on quantity but short on quality.

These are times of men with short character; steep profits, and shallow relationships. These are times of world peace but domestic warfare; more leisure, but less fun; endless kinds of food for some, and starvation for others.

The paradox of our time is that these are the days of two incomes, but more divorce; of grander houses, but broken homes; of drugs that save, and drugs that kill; of endless acquaintances, but fewer friends; of frenzied activity but isolated loneliness; of greater freedom, but strangled liberty.

This is the time when technology can bring a letter to you through Cyber-space, and a time when you can choose either to read it and start making a difference, or just hit delete. This is a time when you can view anything you like; but see nothing at all; say what you want, but hear nothing that matters. This is the age of more rights and more choice than ever before; but a time when we fail to make the only choice that brings true liberty, true happiness and true freedom.

Finally, I would like to quote from an email I received regarding an article headed 'Common Sense' an obituary printed in the London Times. It is in my view sadly, very much a sign of the times.

## Common Sense

Today we mourn the passing of a beloved old friend, Common Sense, who has been with us for many years. No one knows for sure how old he was, since his birth records were lost long ago in bureaucratic red tape. He will be remembered as having cultivated such valuable lessons as:

Knowing when to come in out of the rain;
Why the early bird gets the worm;
Life isn't always fair;
And maybe it was my fault;

Common sense lived by simple, sound financial policies (don't spend more than you can earn) and reliable strategies (adults, not children, are in charge).

His health began to deteriorate rapidly when well intentioned but overbearing regulations were set in place. Reports of a 6-year old boy charged with sexual harassment for kissing a classmate; teens suspended from school for using mouthwash after lunch; and a teacher fired for reprimanding an unruly student, only worsened his condition.

Common Sense lost ground when parents attacked teachers for doing the job that they themselves had failed to do in disciplining their unruly children. It declined even further when schools were required to get parental consent to administer sun lotion or an aspirin to a student; but could not inform parents when a student became pregnant and wanted to have an abortion.

Common sense lost the will to live as the churches became businesses; and criminals received better treatment than their victims.

Common sense took a beating when you couldn't defend yourself from a burglar in your own home and the burglar could sue you for assault.

Common sense finally gave up the will to live, after a woman failed to realize that a steaming cup of coffee was hot. She spilled a little on her lap, and was promptly awarded a huge settlement.

Common Sense was preceded in death, by his parents, Truth and Trust, by his wife, Discretion, by his daughter, Responsibility, and by his son, Reason.

He is survived by his 4 stepbrothers;
I Know My Rights
I Want It Now
Someone Else Is To Blame
I'm A Victim

Not many attended his funeral because so few realized he was gone. If you still remember him, pass this on. If not, join the majority and do nothing.